DRUG-CRIME CONNECTIONS

Drug-Crime Connections challenges the assumption that there is a widespread association between drug use and crime. Instead, it argues that there are many highly specific connections. Trevor Bennett and Katy Holloway draw together in a single volume a wide range of findings from a study of nearly 5,000 arrestees interviewed as part of the New English and Welsh Arrestee Drug Abuse Monitoring (NEW-ADAM) program. It provides an in-depth study of the nature of drug-crime connections, as well as an investigation into drug use generally among criminals and the kinds of crimes that they commit. They also explore topics that previously have fallen outside the drug-crime debate, such as gender and drugs, ethnicity and drugs, gangs, guns, drug markets, and treatment needs. The book aims to provide both an up-to-date review of the literature and a concise summary of a major study on the connection between drug use and crime.

Dr. Trevor Bennett is professor of criminology and director of the Centre for Criminology at the University of Glamorgan. He has published widely in the area of drug use and crime, most recently as coauthor of *Understanding Drugs, Alcohol and Crime* (2005) with Katy Holloway and as a contributor to *Substance Use and Misuse*, the *British Journal of Criminology*, and the *Journal of Psychoactive Drugs*.

Dr. Katy Holloway is a research fellow at the Centre for Criminology, University of Glamorgan. She is also a lecturer on the M.Sc. in Criminology and Criminal Justice program. She has published widely in the area of drug use and crime, most recently as coauthor of *Understanding Drugs, Alcohol and Crime* (2005) with Trevor Bennett, and as a contributor to *Substance Use and Misuse*, the *British Journal of Criminology*, and the *Journal of Psychoactive Drugs*.

CAMBRIDGE STUDIES IN CRIMINOLOGY

Editors

Alfred Blumstein, *H. John Heinz School of Public Policy and Management, Carnegie Mellon University*

David Farrington, *Institute of Criminology, University of Cambridge*

Recent books in the series:

Drug-Crime Connections

Trevor Bennett

University of Glamorgan, Pontypridd

Katy Holloway

University of Glamorgan, Pontypridd

CAMBRIDGE UNIVERSITY PRESS
Cambridge, New York, Melbourne, Madrid, Cape Town, Singapore, São Paulo, Delhi

Cambridge University Press
32 Avenue of the Americas, New York, NY 10013-2473, USA

www.cambridge.org
Information on this title: www.cambridge.org/9780521867573

First published 2007

Printed in the United States of America

A catalog record for this publication is available from the British Library.

Library of Congress Cataloging in Publication Data

Bennett, Trevor.
Drug-crime connections / Trevor Bennett, Katy Holloway.
  p. cm. – (Cambridge studies in criminology)
Includes bibliographical references and index.
ISBN 978-0-521-86757-3 (hardback) – ISBN 978-0-521-68714-0 (pbk.)
1. Drug abuse and crime–Great Britain. 2. Prisoners–Drug testing–Great Britain.
3. Interviewing in law enforcement–Great Britain. I. Holloway, Katy. II. Title.
III. Series.
HV5840.G7B385 2007
364.2′4–dc22   2007007241

ISBN   978-0-521-86757-3 hardback
ISBN   978-0-521-68714-0 paperback

Contents

Preface

In July 1999, after two developmental stages, the UK government established a program of arrestee monitoring, similar to the ADAM program in the United States, titled the New English and Welsh Arrestee Drug Abuse Monitoring (NEW-ADAM) program. The program was designed primarily to collect urine specimens and to conduct personal interviews with recently arrested offenders to understand better the nature of the drug-crime connection. The surveys also provided information on related issues, such as use of weapons and guns in crime, gang membership, and drug markets.

The main aim of this book is to bring together the results of the NEW-ADAM program in a single volume. Some of the findings of the program have already been published in government reports and in articles in peer-reviewed journals. However, other findings have not been published. This book provides an opportunity to combine both published and unpublished material from the NEW-ADAM program in a single source.

The main research issue covered by the book is to investigate the nature of the association between drug use and crime. It is widely believed that there is a connection. Nevertheless, the findings of research on the topic are mixed. There have been many studies that have shown that there is a connection. However, there have been others that have shown that there is none. There have been some studies that have shown that drug use is associated with more crime and others that drug use is associated with less crime.

The title of the book refers to the title of one of the earliest and most influential volumes on the topic by Inciardi (1981) called *The*

Drugs-Crime Connection. Although the editor did not argue that there was only one drug-crime connection in the book, the title could be interpreted to mean that there is. The current book is called *Drug-Crime Connections* to make the link with one of the earliest books in the field and to emphasize the possibility of multiple connections. As a result, it seeks to investigate both themes and variations in these connections to discover not only whether drugs and crime are linked but also the ways in which they are linked.

Trevor Bennett and Katy Holloway
June 2007

Acknowledgments

We are indebted to the many authors who have generated the knowledge base on drug misuse and crime from which the study builds. We are also indebted to the many people who have worked on the project who have affected our thinking in various ways. These include the staff at the Home Office who worked with us at various stages of the NEW-ADAM program. Special thanks are due to Malcolm Ramsay, who worked closely with us in designing and implementing the program. We are also grateful to the Home Office for funding research. We are particularly indebted to the large number of researchers (more than 30 in total) who have worked with us on the project at various times. In particular, we thank Stuart Lockhart who worked on the project from the very beginning as a researcher and toward the end as Deputy Director of the program. We also thank the staff at the Institute of Criminology and the Forensic Science Service who helped in various ways in developing the research. We acknowledge the cooperation of the 13 forces that took part in the research and the many thousands of arrestees who agreed to be interviewed. Finally, we thank the many other people who have given us ideas, influenced our thinking, or assisted in the implementation of the program.

PART ONE

INTRODUCTION

CHAPTER ONE

Background

INTRODUCTION

In 1999, the UK government allocated £6 million of new money for research and information gathering in support of the government's strategy to reduce drug-related crime. Part of the £6 million was used to set up a national program of research to investigate drug use and crime among arrestees. In July 1999, after two developmental stages, a program of arrestee monitoring was established in the United Kingdom under the title of the New English and Welsh Arrestee Drug Abuse Monitoring (NEW-ADAM) program.

The program was designed primarily to collect urine specimens and to conduct personal interviews with recently arrested offenders to understand better the nature of the drug-crime connection. The surveys were also to provide information on related issues, such as use of weapons and guns in crime, gang membership, and drug markets. The program was initially funded to run for three years with the view of continuing funding subject to review.

The broad aim of this book is to present the findings of the NEW-ADAM surveys. Some of the results of the NEW-ADAM program have already been published in government reports and in articles in peer-reviewed journals. However, other findings have not yet been published. As a result, the findings of the NEW-ADAM program have not been fully documented in a single source. This book brings together the results of the NEW-ADAM program in a single volume by summarizing the findings of previously published papers and presenting new findings.

To provide a context for the study, this first chapter summarizes the development of the NEW-ADAM program.

UK GOVERNMENT POLICY

The NEW-ADAM program and the earlier developmental stages of the research were closely linked to government policy on drugs. In 1994, the Conservative government issued a white paper called 'Tackling Drugs Together: A Strategy for England 1995–1998' (Cabinet Office, 1995). The paper noted that there was no reliable statistical measure of the amount of drug-related crime. It identified a need to reduce drug-related crime as one of the key aims of the strategy and proposed the development of new ways to measure the impact of drug misuse on crime to evaluate its progress.

In April 1998, the new Labour government published a parliamentary paper called 'Tackling Drugs to Build a Better Britain: The Government's 10-Year Strategy for Tackling Drug Misuse', based on a review conducted by the UK Anti-Drugs Coordinator (Cabinet Office, 1998). The publication identified four main elements of the strategy: (1) to help young people resist drug misuse; (2) to protect communities from drug-related, antisocial, and criminal behavior; (3) to enable people with drug problems to overcome them; and (4) to stifle the availability of illegal drugs on the streets.

The 'First Annual Report and National Plan' of the UK Anti-Drugs Coordinator (UKADCU), published in 1999, elaborated on the main objectives of the policy and presented key targets relating to them.

Key Objective 1 aimed to reduce drug use generally and drug use among young people in particular. The key performance target relating to this objective was to reduce the proportion of young people using the drugs which cause the greatest harm (heroin and cocaine) by 50 percent by 2008. Other targets included delaying the age of onset of use of Class A drugs by six months and reducing by 20 percent the numbers of 11 to 16 year olds who use Class A drugs (as defined in the Misuse of Drugs Act 1971 as the most harmful drug types).

Key Objective 2 aimed to break the links between drugs and crime and reduce the levels of repeat offending among drug-misusing offenders. In particular, it aimed to reduce levels of repeat offending among drug-misusing offenders by 50 percent by 2008. Other targets included reducing the proportion of arrestees who tested positive for Class A drugs.

Key Objective 3 aimed to increase the participation of problem drug misusers, including prisoners, in drug treatment programs that have a positive impact on health and crime by 100 percent by 2008. A further aim was to reduce the number of users in treatment who report injecting drugs and to reduce the number of those injecting who report sharing their equipment.

Key Objective 4 aimed to reduce the availability of illegal drugs on the streets. In particular, it aimed to reduce access to drugs which cause the greatest harm, particularly heroin and cocaine, by 50 percent by 2008. Other aims included increasing the percentage of heroin and cocaine seized that was destined for Europe and the United Kingdom.

In this document, the NEW-ADAM program was specifically mentioned as a tool that would be used to measure the progress of the government's drug strategy (UKADCU, 1999). Specifically, it stated that the government would "set up a large-scale program of urinalysis and interviewing of arrestees, NEW-ADAM, and run it in eight sites in England and Wales" (p. 15). Two of the targets it claimed were measurable by NEW-ADAM:

- To reduce the levels of repeat offending among drug-misusing offenders by 50 percent by 2008 and 25 percent by 2005
- To reduce the proportion of arrestees testing positive for Class A drugs from 18 percent (1998–9 baseline) to 15 percent by 2002

During the next three years, NEW-ADAM data were used to monitor progress in achieving these targets.

PRECURSORS TO THE NEW-ADAM PROGRAM IN THE UNITED STATES

The Drug Use Forecasting Program (DUF)
The NEW-ADAM program was strongly influenced by the procedures and general approach of the DUF Program in the United States. The

DUF Program began in New York City in 1984 with a feasibility study based at the Manhattan Central Booking Facility. The research was funded by the National Institute of Justice (NIJ) and was conducted by staff from Narcotic and Drug Research Incorporated (NDRI). As part of this research, NDRI staff interviewed and obtained voluntary urine specimens from recent arrestees. The authors concluded that the project was successful in achieving its objectives and in generating high response rates. Ninety-five percent of arrestees approached consented to be interviewed, and eighty-four percent of these provided a urine specimen (Wish and Gropper, 1990).

In September 1986, the researchers returned to the Manhattan Central Booking Facility to obtain specimens and conduct interviews with a second sample of male arrestees. The second survey was also successful in achieving similarly high response rates from among the arrestees. However, the study was also successful in another unexpected way. The timing of the study was in a sense fortuitous because between 1984 and 1986, New York City experienced a substantial increase in the use of cocaine, especially crack cocaine. The study detected this and showed that the prevalence of cocaine use among arrestees almost doubled over the two-year period from the first to the second survey (42% in 1984 to 83% in 1986). The results of the comparison were striking and identified a trend in cocaine use over a year before it was detected by any of the other indicators of drug misuse (e.g., new treatment admissions, overdose deaths, and emergency room admissions; Wish and Gropper, 1990).

In 1987, the NIJ established the DUF Program in 12 large cities across the United States. This was soon expanded to 23 adult and 12 juvenile sites. Over the next decade, DUF staff conducted quarterly surveys of arrestees held in the booking facilities covering the research sites. The data were collected and analyzed centrally by DUF staff at NIJ who published quarterly and annual reports of the results. The reports contained prevalence trends of the percentage of positive tests for arrestees for each DUF site for 3 of the 10 main drug types analyzed (cocaine, opiates, and marijuana), along with 'any drug' and 'multiple drugs'. The early reports included breakdowns of the urinalysis results in terms of age, sex, and race of the arrestee, and later reports included additional breakdowns based on the type of charged offense.

The ADAM Program

The ADAM program was launched in 1997 by the NIJ as a successor to the DUF program. The main aim of the ADAM program was to maintain and eventually improve the DUF system of interviewing and drug testing arrestees. In particular, it was intended that the new program would expand in size to cover up to 75 urban areas and would include more detailed data collection (NIJ, 1997). A revised program was launched in 2000 which increased the number of sites covered by the scheme from 23 to 38. This included a revised sampling and data-collection method. In the past, sites and arrestees were selected using a form of convenience or nonprobability sampling. In 2000, a new method of probability sampling was introduced.

In practice, the larger version of the ADAM program, envisaged in the 1997 report, never happened. In 2004, the ADAM program was disbanded, and arrestee data collection ceased (see Chapter 16 for a discussion). Nevertheless, it achieved its broader aims of geographic expansion and improvement in the sophistication of data collection and analysis. It also achieved its aim of setting up the I-ADAM program as the first stage in the process of generating a global surveillance system that could monitor drug trends worldwide.

The I-ADAM Program

The I-ADAM program (International Arrestee Drug Abuse Monitoring program) was based on a partnership of countries involved in conducting research based on interviewing and drug testing arrestees. The program was modeled on the US ADAM program. I-ADAM was launched in 1998 at an international conference in Miami attended by representatives of eight countries including Australia, Chile, England, The Netherlands, Panama, Scotland, South Africa, and Uruguay. The main aim of I-ADAM was to generate standardized data on drug use among arrestees to compare patterns and trends in drug use over time. It also aimed to provide an international research base for coordinating drug research and drug control policies. NIJ provided technical assistance to I-ADAM countries in initiating and operating the program. ADAM-type programs were eventually set up in nine countries: Australia, Chile, England, Malaysia, The Netherlands, Scotland, South Africa, Taiwan, and the United States. However, I-ADAM was by default disbanded in 2004 at the same time as the ADAM program. Although I-ADAM researchers still keep in contact with one another, the system of annual international conferences funded and organized by NIJ has ceased.

PRECURSORS TO THE NEW-ADAM PROGRAM IN THE UNITED KINGDOM

In 1995, the Home Office (the government department responsible for national policy) funded a small feasibility study to determine whether it would be possible and useful to interview and collect voluntary urine specimens from arrestees. The aim of the research was to examine methods of determining drug use prevalence among offenders and to understand more fully the links between drug misuse and crime. The report of the study reviewed the research on interviewing and drug testing in the United States and concluded that it was feasible to develop such a study; furthermore, it urged implementation of a similar program in England and Wales (Bennett, 1998). In the same year, the Home Office commissioned the first stage of developmental research. The research was conducted in five police areas in England and Wales over 18 months during 1996 and 1997. The results of the research were published in 1998 (Bennett, 1998).

In 1998, a second developmental stage of research was commissioned by the Home Office with the aim of building on the earlier developmental research and moving closer toward a research design that might be used as a basis for a national program. The research was based in three police force areas and included two new sites and one repeat site surveyed previously in the first developmental stage. The aim of including a repeat site was to test some of the principles involved in measuring trends in drug misuse among arrestees over time. The results of the second developmental stage were published in 2000 (Bennett, 2000).

THE NEW-ADAM PROGRAM

The NEW-ADAM program was launched in July 1999 and was funded to run for three years in the first instance. The program was based on financial years, with the first year (a shorter year) running from July 1999 to March 2000. The second year ran from April 2000 to March 2001 and the third year from April 2001 to March 2002. In each financial year, eight surveys were conducted in police force areas in England and Wales. In Year 1, eight sites were surveyed and in Year 2, eight additional sites were surveyed. In Year 3, the first eight sites were revisited for the first round of repeat surveys. It was originally planned, subject to funding, that in Year 4, the second eight sites would be revisited for the second round of repeat surveys. Hence, the core NEW-ADAM program was designed as a rolling program of research based on 16 locations, surveyed at two-year intervals. In practice, however, the funding for a fourth year was not available, and the NEW-ADAM program ended in March 2002 after three years of data collection (see Chapter 16 for a discussion).

There have been a number of outputs from the NEW-ADAM program. A force report was produced for each survey at each location and was made available to the local police in the months following the survey. It was originally intended that annual reports containing the findings of the previous year, plus trend analyses relating to earlier years, would be published each year. In practice, the Home Office published only summary results from the first year of the program (Bennett et al., 2001). In 2004, however, three further publications were released. Two of these presented findings relating to the first two years of the program (Bennett and Holloway, 2004a; Holloway and Bennett 2004), and one presented summary trend results comparing the first and third years of the program (Holloway et al., 2004). A more thorough trend report comparing the results collected in the first eight sites over time was written but never published. In addition to these government publications, several academic articles drawing on NEW-ADAM data have also been published (Bennett and Holloway, 2004b, 2004c, 2005a, 2005b, 2006; Holloway and Bennett, in press).

Other researchers have also used the results from the NEW-ADAM. Bramley-Harker (2001), for example, used data from the program to help size the UK drug market. In this case, 'sizing the market' meant estimating the total expenditure on drugs by all drug users over a set period of time. The study concluded that the best estimate of the total value of the UK market in 1998 was £6.6 billion.

OTHER MEASURES OF DRUG USE AND CRIME IN THE UNITED KINGDOM

A key element in determining the effectiveness of government antidrug strategies is to monitor patterns and trends in drug use over time. A number of other sources of information, in addition to the NEW-ADAM program, have been used to monitor the prevalence of drug use in the United Kingdom. The major sources of information on prevalence of drug use are general population surveys, surveys of young people, school surveys, and offender surveys. In addition, surveys of users in treatment provide information about the prevalence of problematic drug use. Official data relating to the number of drug seizures and the number of convictions for drug offenses also provide some indication of the extent of drug use in the United Kingdom.

General Population Surveys

The major national self-report survey of drug misuse is the drugs component of the British Crime Survey (BCS). This component was first included in the 1996 sweep of the BCS and continues annually. In the 2002–3 sweep, additional drug questions were added to monitor changes in the frequency of drug use. The latest published figures are for the 2004–5 sweep (Roe, 2005). The survey focuses on people aged 16 years or older living in private households and provides information on drug misuse among the general population.

The 2004–5 BCS estimated that 35 percent of people aged 16 to 59 had used illicit drugs at least once in their lifetime (Roe, 2005). Eleven percent reported that they had used an illicit drug in the last year, and seven percent said they had done so in the last month. The published figures provide useful information on the spread of drug misuse across England and Wales. The 2004–5 survey results show that about half (46%) of young people aged 16 to 24 had used at least one illegal drug at some time in their lives, and 26 percent had done so in the last year. Cannabis is the most widely used illegal drug, reported by 26 percent of young people aged 16 to 24. Consumption of heroin was rare (reported by less than 1 percent of respondents). However, 5 percent of young people aged 16 to 24 said that they had tried cocaine at some time in their lives.

One of the most important sets of findings of the last survey concerns trends in illegal drug use over the last few years. Over the period from 1996 to 2003–4, the surveys showed a significant increase in recent use (in the last 12 months) of cannabis from 24 percent to 31 percent and of cocaine from 3 percent to 7 percent. More recently, however, there has been a reduction in the prevalence of cannabis use from 31 percent in 2003–4 to 30 percent in 2004–5, and of cocaine from 7 percent to 6 percent.

Surveys of Young People

One source of information on drug misuse among young people in the general population is the Youth Lifestyles Survey (YLS; Goulden and Sondhi, 2001). The 1998–9 YLS was a self-report study based on 4,848 young people aged 12 to 30 living in England and Wales. The results of the survey showed a higher prevalence of drug use among young people than shown in the two surveys reviewed in the previous section. In total, 43 percent of all young people interviewed reported having used an illegal drug in their lifetime, and 27 percent said that they had used a drug in the last year (Pudney, 2002).

A second source of information on the prevalence of drug use among young people is the Offending, Crime and Justice Survey (OCJS; Budd et al., 2005b). The OCJS is a national, longitudinal, self-report offending survey for England and Wales. The survey covers people living in private households and was first conducted in 2003. Its main aim is to examine the extent of offending, antisocial behavior and drug use among the household population, particularly among young people aged from 10 to 25.

The results of the 2004 sweep of the survey showed that 22 percent of people aged 10 to 25 reported having used an illicit drug in the last 12 months (Budd et al., 2005b). Cannabis was the most frequently used drug, reported by one-fifth of respondents. Just under 5 percent of people reported having used cocaine in the last year, and less than 1 percent reported having used crack or heroin. These figures closely match the results of the British Crime Survey in relation to the 16 to 24 age group.

School Surveys

The National Center for Social Research (NCSR) and the National Foundation for Education Research (NFER) carry out a regular series of surveys of schoolchildren for the Department of Health. The most recent figures for 2005 cover interviews with more than 9,000 children aged 11 to 15 in 305 schools in England (NCSR/NFER, 2006). In 2005, 39 percent of pupils reported that they had been offered illicit drugs at least once in their lifetime, and 19 percent reported that they had used an illicit drug in the last year. Boys were no more likely than girls to report having used drugs during the 12-month period, but the prevalence of drug use was higher among older pupils than younger ones (34% among 15 year olds compared with 6% among 11 year olds). Cannabis was the drug used by the most pupils (11%). Cocaine powder was reported to have been used by 2 percent of pupils, and heroin and crack had been used by 1 percent. No pupils reported use of methadone, tranquilizers, or anabolic steroids.

One of the longest-running surveys of school children is organized by the Schools Health Education Unit in Exeter. These surveys have been conducted annually since 1986. The most recent report of these surveys conducted in 2004 was based on interviews with 40,439 schoolchildren aged 10 to 15. The research comprises a number of independent surveys conducted within 452 schools across England and Wales. Although they do not constitute a nationally representative sample, they nevertheless cover a large number of schools and a large number of schoolchildren (685,000 since 1986).

The 2004 survey showed that approximately one in five pupils in Year 10 (aged 14–15 years) had reported trying at least one illicit drug in their lifetime (Balding, 2005). This was four times as many pupils as in Year 8 (aged 12–13 years). Cannabis was by far the most likely drug that pupils had tried, with more than one-quarter (27%) of 14 to 15 year olds and 7 percent of 12 to 13 year olds reporting use.

Offender Surveys

It is widely believed that there is an association between drug use and offending, and offenders might be viewed as generally a more deviant subset of the general population and more willing to try illegal substances (Bennett and Holloway, 2005c). The results of surveys among various samples of offenders tend to support this assumption.

There are two main sources of information on drug use among offenders in the United Kingdom: the Community Penalties Criminality Survey (CPCS) and the Prisoner Criminality Survey (PCS). The CPCS was conducted in 2002 with 1,578 men and women serving one of four community orders. Sixty-one percent of respondents in the CPCS reported that they had used at least one illicit drug in the previous 12 months (Budd et al., 2005a). Cannabis was the most popular drug, with 54 percent reporting use in the last 12 months. In contrast to the general population, use of Class A drugs was fairly common among the CPCS respondents. More than one-fifth (22%) reported having used heroin in the last 12 months, 21 percent reported having used ecstasy, 19 percent reported crack use, and 18 percent reported cocaine use. Overall, nearly one-third of respondents said that they had used heroin, crack, or cocaine in the last year.

The Prisoner Criminality Survey was carried out in prisons in England and Wales during April and May 2000 (Budd et al., 2005a). The results of this survey show a higher prevalence of drug use among offenders than was found in the CPCS. Indeed, 73 percent of inmates reported having taken an illegal drug in the 12 months before imprisonment. Almost half (47%) had used heroin, crack, or cocaine in the same 12-month period.

Treatment Population

Another source of official data on drug misuse is drug treatment databases. Up until the end of March 2001, data on the number of people presenting to services with problem drug misuse in England were collected by the Regional Drug Misuse Databases (RDMDs). After a strategic review of the RDMDs, a new National Drug Treatment Monitoring System was introduced in England and Wales in April 2001. Recent figures show that 160,450 individuals were recorded as having been in contact with structured drug treatment services in England in 2004–5. This is a 27 percent increase on figures for 2003–4 (125,545; National Treatment Agency, 2006).

TABLE 1.1. *Prevalence estimates of use of drugs in the last 12 months reported in selected surveys*

Survey	Population	Age group (years)	Drug type	Prevalence (%)
BCS 2004/2005	General	16–59	Any illegal drug	11
NCSR/NFER 2005	General	11–15	Any illegal drug	19
OCJS 2004	General	10–25	Any illegal drug	22
YLS 1998/1999	General	12–30	Any illegal drug	27
Community Penalties 2002	Offender	16+	Any illegal drug	61
Prisoner Criminality 2000	Offender	17–59	Any illegal drug	73
BCS 2004/2005	General	16–59	Cannabis	10
NCSR/NFER 2005	General	11–15	Cannabis	12
OCJS 2004	General	10–25	Cannabis	20
YLS 1998/1999	General	12–30	Cannabis	22
Community Penalties 2002	Offender	16+	Cannabis	54
Prisoner Criminality 2000	Offender	17–59	Cannabis	64
BCS 2004/2005	General	16–59	Heroin	<1
NCSR/NFER 2005	General	11–15	Heroin	1
OCJS 2004	General	10–25	Heroin	<1
YLS 1998/1999	General	12–30	Heroin	<1
Community Penalties 2002	Offender	16+	Heroin	22
Prisoner Criminality 2000	Offender	17–59	Heroin	31

Sources: British Crime Survey (BCS) 2004/2005 (Roe, 2005); National Center for Social Research (NCSR)/National Foundation for Education Research (NFER, 2005); National Center for Social Research and National Foundation for Educational Research (NCSR/NFER, 2006); Youth Lifestyles Survey 1998/1999 (Goulden and Sondhi, 2001); Community Penalties Survey 2002 and Prisoner Criminality Survey 2000 (Budd et al., 2005a). OCJS = Offending, Crime and Justice Survey; YLS = Youth Lifestyles Survey.

Until recently, more detailed information on the individual characteristics of users seeking treatment and information about the type of drug misused were provided by the Department of Health in its regular bulletins presenting results from the RDMDs. The last of these bulletins presented statistics for the six months ending March 2001 (Department of Health, 2002b). During the period March 1993 to March 2001, the number of persons in each six-month period presenting to agencies in Great Britain increased by nearly 100 percent (from 20,221 to 40,181). During the last full-year period of published data (March 2000 to March 2001), the number of persons presenting to health agencies increased by approximately 3 percent (from 39,055 to 40,181). In 1993, the peak age for presenting to treatment was in the 25 to 29 age band. In 2001 to 2002, the peak age was in the 20 to 24 age band.

In the six-month period ending 31 March 2001, the most commonly recorded drug of misuse in England was heroin (67% of all users), compared with 64 percent of all users in the previous six-month period and 46 percent in the six-month period ending September 1993. The second most commonly recorded drug of misuse was cannabis (9%), followed by methadone (8%) and cocaine (7%). Three percent of users presenting for treatment were recorded as having amphetamines as their main drug of misuse compared with 11 percent of users in the six months ending September 1993.

Drug Seizures

The Home Office publishes data on drug seizures and offenders processed through the criminal justice system for drug offenses in its statistical bulletins. Data on drug seizures cover the operations of both the police and Her Majesty's Customs and Excise and reflect in part organizational activity. The reports show that over the previous ten years, the number of seizures tended to increase (Mwenda et al., 2005). In 2003, however, the number of seizures dropped from 114,550 in 2002 to 109,410, a decrease of nearly 5 percent. Most of this decrease was a result of a decrease in seizures of Class B drugs (as defined in the Misuse of Drugs Act 1971 as moderately harmful). Between 2002 and 2003, the number of heroin seizures decreased by 16 percent and ecstasy seizures by 8 percent. Cocaine seizures, however, increased by two-fifths, and crack seizures increased by 15 percent.

Official Convictions for Drug Offenses

Data on offenders processed for drug offenses show a similarly increasing trend (Mwenda and Kumari, 2005). Over the previous ten years, prosecutions for all supply (trafficking) offenses tended to increase. In relation to the three main drug supply offenses (production, supply, and possession with intent to supply), the increase peaked in 1998 and then dropped back slightly. However, there is some variation in this trend by type of drug. The trend in the number of prosecutions for cocaine, crack, and heroin has shown a steady increase over the last few years. Prosecutions for offenses relating to ecstasy have remained stable or increased slightly. Hence, trends in prosecutions for drug supply offenses more or less reflect other indicators of demand and supply of drugs, showing a steady increase in drug misuse.

STRUCTURE OF THE BOOK

The book comprises 16 chapters. This introductory chapter is intended to provide background information on the NEW-ADAM program and information about the extent of drug use in the United Kingdom. Chapter 2 discusses the research methods used in the NEW-ADAM program and summarizes the main features of the research design and the procedures adopted. The third chapter investigates the extent and frequency of drug misuse among arrestees and compares the findings of arrestee surveys in other countries. The 13 remaining chapters each focus on a specific drug-related issue. Chapter 4 explores drug-related health issues, and Chapter 5 examines the relation between drug use and crime. Chapter 6 disaggregates the relation between drug use and crime, focusing on specific drug types and specific crime types. Chapter 7 investigates multiple or polydrug drug use, and Chapter 8 looks at the perceived connection between drug use and offending behavior reported by arrestees. Chapters 9 and 10 examine gender and ethnic group differences, respectively, in drug use and associated problem behaviors. Chapter 11 explores drug use among gangs and gang members, and Chapter 12 examines the use of weapons and guns among drug-using arrestees. Chapter 13 investigates drug markets and the methods by which users purchase heroin, crack, and cocaine. Chapter 14 considers treatment issues and explores the treatment needs and experiences of arrestees. The penultimate chapter compares findings from the NEW-ADAM program with findings from arrestee surveys conducted in other countries. The concluding chapter summarizes and discusses the contribution of the findings from NEW-ADAM to the research on drugs and crime and the debate about drugs policy.

CHAPTER TWO

Research Methods

INTRODUCTION

The New English and Welsh Arrestee Drug Abuse Monitoring (NEW-ADAM) program was based on surveys of arrestees currently held for official processing, typically in relation to a suspected offense, in police custody suites in England and Wales. The research methods were similar to those used in the early version of the Arrestee Drug Abuse Monitoring (ADAM) program in the United States and in other International Arrestee Drug Abuse Monitoring (I-ADAM) programs. The main methods of data collection were structured face-to-face interviews and collection of urine specimens suitable for urinalysis.

It should be noted that the main features of the research design were outlined in the specifications for the research prepared by the Home Office. Some of these criteria emerged from the experience gained during the two developmental stages of the research. Other criteria, such as the overall budget and scale of the research, were determined from the outset by the Home Office based on financial and policy considerations. Hence, the final research design comprised a combination of elements generated by the Home Office and the research team.

SAMPLES

Sampling Method

The NEW-ADAM surveys used two-stage sampling. In the first stage, 16 sites were selected using a method of 'purposive' sampling of custody

suites. In the second stage, approximately 210 arrestees were interviewed in each site. The decision to include 16 first-stage sampling
points and 210 second-stage cases was influenced in part by practical
aspects of conducting the research. These are discussed in more detail
later in the chapter.

The first stage involved the Home Office contacting all police
forces in England and Wales by letter. This requested information
on the willingness of the force to take part in the research and their
annual throughput of arrestees. Information was requested on the
throughput of arrestees because it was necessary to include sites that
had sufficient number of arrestees to generate a useable sample during the data collection period. Forty-two of the forty-three forces in
England and Wales were contacted, excluding the City of London
Police on the grounds that the area was unusual in terms of its low
residential population. It was determined from the developmental
stage research that a practicable throughput of arrestees to achieve
the target sample size of 210 cases was approximately 600 arrestees per
month. Seventeen forces had throughputs of 600 or more arrestees
per month. Hence, this decision set a limit to the maximum number of forces that could be included in the research. Thirteen of
the seventeen forces were selected on the grounds that they provided a good geographic spread across the country (for example,
two distant forces would be selected in preference to two adjacent
forces) and that they were willing to participate in the research. In
total, the 13 forces covered 16 suitable custody suites. One force (the
Metropolitan Police in London) had four suitable sites, and 12 forces
had one suitable site. Each of the custody suites was visited prior to
the research to confirm its suitability. All 16 sites visited were found
to be suitable for the research and were selected to be part of the
NEW-ADAM program.

The second stage involved selecting arrestees for interview. The aim
of this stage of the research was to interview all eligible arrestees.
Hence, the initial aim of the research was to conduct a census of
the population of eligible arrestees. However, in practice, there were
limits to what could be achieved and it was not possible to contact every
arrestee during the research period. During busy periods, for example,
it was not possible for the single researcher on duty to interview all

arrestees currently held. Interviewers staffed the custody suites for 24-hours a day and seven days a week over the survey period. Each survey period lasted approximately 30 days.

Survey Sites

Table 2.1 shows the 16 sites surveyed in the NEW-ADAM program and gives the dates that each survey was started and completed. The first survey was conducted in Sunderland in July 1999. The last survey was conducted in Hammersmith in March 2002. The NEW-ADAM program was designed to be a rolling program of surveys in which each of the 16 sites would be resurveyed every other year. In practice, because funding was terminated after three years, it was only the first eight sites that were surveyed twice (in Year 1 and Year 3).

Sample Size

The target sample size for the program was set within the range of 200 to 225 arrestees. The decision to use this particular target range was based on the fact that it was the recommended target sample size of the early version of the ADAM program in the United States; it was found during the developmental stages of the research to be feasible to interview about this number of arrestees during a one-month survey period; and it was a sufficient number of cases to conduct significance tests.

It also has been argued that using this number of cases produces a fairly representative sample. Attempts to compare the characteristics of arrestees selected for interview and drug testing and the character-istics of all arrestees processed in the same site have tended to show a close correlation between the two (Decker, 1992). In practice, the target sample size for all surveys was set at 210, which was an approxi-mate midpoint of the range discussed earlier. No separate targets were set for particular subgroups.

Eligibility

The main grounds for exclusion were that the arrestees had to be fit for interview, they had to be able to understand what was said during

TABLE 2.1. *Locations of NEW-ADAM survey sites*

Year	Location	Description	Date started	Date completed
Year 1				
1	Sunderland	City center custody suite	09/07/99	06/08/99
2	Norwich	City center custody suite	13/08/99	11/09/99
3	Newport	City center custody suite	22/09/99	24/10/99
4	Southampton	City center custody suite	06/11 /99	09/12/99
5	W. Wolverhampton	City center custody suite	08/01/00	03/02/00
6	Bournemouth	City center custody suite	11/02/00	11/03/00
7	London (Bethnal Green)	Borough custody suite	15/03/00	11/04/00
8	London (Hammersmith)	Borough custody suite	16/03/00	15/04/00
Year 2				
1	Middlesbrough	City center custody suite	15/05/00	10/06/00
2	Leeds	City center bridewell	23/06/00	18/07/00
3	Liverpool	Force custody unit	25/08/00	24/09/00
4	Plymouth	City center custody suite	04/10/00	25/10/00
5	Bolton	City center custody suite	16/11/00	13/12/00
6	Nottingham	City center bridewell	09/01 /01	29/01 /01
7	London (Colindale)	Borough custody suite	12/02/01	14/03/01
8	London (Brixton)	Borough custody suite	13/03/01	11/04/01
Year 3				
1	Sunderland	City center custody suite	18/05/01	13/06/01
2	Norwich	City center custody suite	28/06/01	23/07/01
3	Newport	City center custody suite	29/08/01	26/09/01

(continued)

TABLE 2.1 *(continued)*

Year	Location	Description	Date started	Date completed
4	Southampton	City center custody suite	09/10/01	10/11/01
5	W. Wolverhampton	City center custody suite	23/11/01	17/12/01
6	Bournemouth	City center custody suite	07/01/02	03/02/02
7	London (Bethnal Green)	Borough custody suite	20/02/02	22/03/02
8	London (Hammersmith)	Borough custody suite	20/02/02	21/03/02

the interview, they had to be considered suitably safe to be interviewed, and they had to meet various drug-testing requirements. The details of the main criteria of ineligibility used in the program are shown in Table 2.2.

TABLE 2.2. *Ineligibility criteria*

General category	Specific criteria
Fit for interview	Arrestees who were persistently unfit due to alcohol intoxication
	Arrestees who were persistently unfit due to drug intoxication
	Arrestees who were persistently unfit due to ill health or physical condition
Comprehension of interview and informed consent	Arrestees who were mentally disordered
	Arrestees who would require an interpreter
Potential danger to interviewer	Arrestees who could be potentially violent
	Arrestees who were deemed ineligible at the discretion of the custody sergeant
Drug-testing requirements	Arrestees who had been in custody in excess of 48 hours
	Prison transfers and arrestees not at liberty prior to entering the custody suite
Other research selection criteria	Children and juveniles
	Arrestees held only for 'breath-test' or 'drunkenness' offenses
	Arrestees previously interviewed

METHOD OF CONTACT

After being booked into the police custody suite, arrestees were approached by NEW-ADAM researchers and asked if they would be willing to be interviewed about their past drug use and offending behavior. Arrestees were informed that the interview was part of an independent study conducted by the University of Cambridge and funded by the Home Office. The researchers reassured the arrestees that their responses would be treated in strict confidence and would not be shown to the police nor discussed with them. The researchers also informed the arrestees that at the end of the interview, they would be asked to provide a urine specimen. Arrestees were under no obligation to provide a specimen and were interviewed regardless of their willingness to provide a sample. Those arrestees who agreed to be interviewed were asked to sign a form indicating their consent to be interviewed. Those arrestees who agreed to provide a specimen were asked to sign a second form indicating their consent to provide a specimen.

DATA COLLECTION

Questionnaires

The NEW-ADAM questionnaire was divided into two main parts: (1) a core questionnaire, which included questions comparable to those used in ADAM surveys in the United States and (2) two follow-up questionnaires (versions A and B) containing additional questions on weapons and gun ownership (version A) and drug purchasing and drug markets (version B). All interviewees completed the core questionnaire. The interviewees were then randomly allocated to complete either version A or version B of the follow-up questionnaire.

The main schedule was divided into sections covering the principal topic areas of the research, including self-reported drug use (ever, in the last 12 months, in the last 30 days, and in the last 3 days), injecting drugs and sharing needles, dependency on drugs and alcohol, drugs and crime, legal and illegal sources of income, amount spent on drugs, and treatment needs. The questions were mainly structured with preset response categories, although some were open-ended. The questionnaire comprised more than 200 questions and was designed to be completed in about 30 minutes.

The first follow-up questionnaire (version A) on weapons and guns contained questions on recent and lifetime gun possession, whether they mixed with people who had access to guns, and use of guns and weapons in crime. The second follow-up questionnaire (version B) on drug markets contained questions on recent purchases of heroin, crack, and cocaine. These included how far the user traveled to purchase drugs, whether the sources were open or closed markets, and the amounts purchased.

Urinalysis

The urinalysis was based on procedures for specimen collection and drug testing recommended by the Forensic Science Service (FSS) in the United Kingdom. The Drug Use Forecasting (DUF) and ADAM programs used a 'chain of custody' procedure to ensure that urine samples were unadulterated and that test results were accurately matched to the people providing the samples (Wish and Gropper, 1990). A similar 'chain of custody' procedure was recommended by the FSS and was followed in the NEW-ADAM research.

Arrestees were required to collect the urine sample in a specimen collection container and to hand this container to the researcher. The collection container had a heat-sensitive strip on its side that registered (by the changes in the color of indicator spots) whether the sample was close to body temperature (specifically, whether it was in the range of 90–100 degrees Fahrenheit). The contents of the collection container were then transferred to two sample vials in equal volumes. The lid of each vial was sealed, and a security strip was placed across the lid and the base of the vial. Prenumbered, bar-coded labels were then placed on the vials, and both vials were placed in a sealed security bag.

The remainder of the chain of custody procedure was based on carefully completed documentation provided by the FSS, which monitored the movements of the specimens and their conditions during transport. In most survey sites, the specimens were held in a refrigerator in a medical room in the custody block and later collected and transported through the local police carrier system for body samples directly to the FSS. The specimens were then stored in a cold store until they were ready to be tested.

Drug-Testing Methods. There are two main types of technology for drug testing. The first is collectively referred to as immunoassays and is used primarily for drug screening. The second is collectively referred to as gas chromatography and is used primarily for drug confirmation following screening. The former tests are less expensive and less reliable, the latter tests more expensive and more reliable.

The main method used in the DUF and ADAM programs in the United States were the immunoassay Enzymes Multiplied Immune Testing (EMIT) tests. However, all positive results for amphetamines were confirmed by gas chromatography to eliminate positive results caused by over-the-counter drugs such as some allergy and cold medicines. The main method used in the NEW-ADAM research was an immunoassay screening test, similar to the EMIT test, called the 'On-Line' Kinetic Interaction of Micro-Particles (KIMS) test. The choice of a screening test was based on a balance of its cheapness and accuracy.

Various factors affect the accuracy of screening tests. The two main issues that have been discussed in the literature are (1) specificity (the ability of the assay to identify a single-chemical component in a mixture of chemicals and biological materials and (2) cross-reactivity (the ability of a substance other than the drugs in question to produce a positive result). Screening tests are less powerful than gas chromatography in their ability to differentiate between drug types. It cannot differentiate between cocaine powder and crack cocaine, between amphetamine and methamphetamine, or among the various kinds of opiates (e.g., heroin, morphine, opium, and codeine). Screening tests are also less powerful than gas chromatography in guarding against other drugs, unrelated to (or chemically similar to) the drug under test, producing a positive result. Some over-the-counter allergy and cold medicines can produce a positive result for amphetamines, and some codeine-based painkillers can produce a positive result for opiates.

The issue of specificity could not be avoided, and the research had to be based on what the KIMS screening test was able to deliver. This was a particular problem for the current study in relation to differentiating heroin and other opiates and between crack cocaine

TABLE 2.3. *Drug types included in the urinalysis tests*

Drug type	Drug details
Cannabinoid metabolite	This test identifies all forms of cannabis including its herbal and resin forms.
Opiates	The test covers all forms of opium-based products including the pure compounds such as codeine and morphine and the semisynthetic compounds such as heroin.
Methadone	This detects methadone which is a wholly synthetic opiate usually classified as an opioid.
Cocaine metabolite	The includes cocaine hydrochloride and is unable to distinguish the powder form, which is sniffed or injected, and the nugget form (crack), which is typically burnt and inhaled.
Amphetamines	This includes amphetamine sulphate, methamphetamines, and similar amphetamine-like drugs such as ecstasy.
Benzodiazepines	This test includes all the minor tranquilizers such as diazepam and temazepam.
LSD	This identifies lysergic acid diethylamide, which is a powerful hallucinogen.
Alcohol	This covers all ethyl alcohol or ethanol-based products.

and cocaine powder. The issue of cross-reactivity was guarded against by asking all arrestees whether in the last three days they had used prescription or over-the-counter drugs, and estimates were calculated of the likely error in prevalence figures resulting from this.

Drug Types Tested. In the NEW-ADAM program, urine specimens were tested for the presence of eight drug types: cannabinoid metabolite, opiates, methadone, cocaine metabolite, amphetamines, benzodiazepines, LSD, and alcohol. The details of the test are shown in Table 2.3.

The approximate duration over which these drugs can be detected in urine varies. It has been estimated that amphetamines are detectable up to two days after use; opiates, methadone, cocaine metabolites, and benzodiazepines are detectable up to three days; and cannabinoid metabolites are detectable up to three days from single use, up to 10 days with daily use, and up to 27 days from chronic use (Wish and Gropper, 1990).

TABLE 2.4. *Cutoff levels used to determine whether a urine specimen tested positive or negative for selected drug types*

Drug type	Cutoff levels (ng/ml or mg/100 ml)
Alcohol	10
Amphetamines	500
Benzodiazepines	100
Cannabis	50
Cocaine	150
Methadone	300
Opiates	300

Note: Cutoff levels are expressed in nanograms per milliliter, with the exception of alcohol, which is expressed as milligrams per 100 milliliters.

Cutoff Levels. The cutoff levels used in the current research were generated in collaboration with the FSS to provide the best balance between oversensitivity and undersensitivity. The reason for doing this was to balance the levels of both Type I errors (saying that a test was positive when it was not, i.e., false positives) and Type II errors (saying that the test was negative when it was not, i.e., false negatives). Details of these cutoff levels are shown in Table 2.4.

ACHIEVED SAMPLES

During the course of the research, 15,393 arrestees passed through the custody suites, and more than half of these (57%) were deemed eligible for interview on the basis of the criteria outlined in Table 2.2. Of the 8,768 eligible arrestees, 62 percent were approached for interview. The main reason arrestees were not approached for interview was because there was not a long enough time gap within which to conduct the interview. Of the 5,450 arrestees who were approached, 85 percent were interviewed. The majority (92%) of the 4,645 interviewed arrestees agreed to provide urine specimens. Only 3 percent refused to give a specimen. The remainder were either unable to do so (3%) or had other reasons (sometimes on religious grounds) for not doing so (1%).

The characteristics of interviewed arrestees and noninterviewed arrestees are compared in Table 2.5. The figures show that there

TABLE 2.5. *Characteristics of arrestees interviewed and not interviewed (years 1, 2, and 3)*

Site	No. eligible, n (%)	No. ineligible, n (%)	No. approached,[a] n (%)	No. not approached, n (%)	No. interviewed,[b] n (%)	No. not interviewed, n (%)
Sex						
Male	7,272 (83)	5,566 (84)	4,646 (85)	2,626 (79)	3,990 (86)	656 (82)
Female	1,495 (17)	1,046 (16)	804 (15)	691 (21)	655 (14)	149 (19)
Sig. of difference	*		***		**	
Age group						
Under 17	0 (0)	2,052 (32)	0 (0)	0 (0)	0 (0)	0 (0)
17–19	1,943 (22)	621 (10)	1,255 (23)	688 (21)	1,102 (24)	153 (19)
20–24	2,205 (25)	937 (15)	1,382 (25)	823 (25)	1,212 (26)	170 (21)
25–29	1,583 (18)	754 (12)	986 (18)	597 (18)	824 (18)	162 (20)
30+	3,029 (35)	2,098 (33)	1,826 (34)	1,203 (36)	1,507 (32)	319 (40)
Sig. of difference	***		*		***	
Ethnic group						
White	7,025 (81)	5,465 (83)	4,343 (80)	2,682 (82)	3,718 (80)	625 (78)
Nonwhite	1,705 (20)	1,087 (17)	1,102 (20)	603 (18)	926 (20)	176 (22)
Sig. of difference	***		*		ns	
Offense arrested for						
Property (theft) offense	3,233 (37)	1,760 (27)	2,139 (39)	1,094 (33)	1,830 (40)	309 (39)
Not property offense	5,497 (63)	4,829 (73)	3,299 (61)	2,198 (67)	2,808 (61)	491 (61)
Sig. of difference	***		***		ns	
TOTAL	8,768	6,625	5,450	3,318	4,645	805

[a]No. approached refers to the number of 'eligible' arrestees ($n = 8,768$) who were approached for interview.
[b]No. interviewed refers to the number of approached arrestees who were interviewed ($n = 5,450$). Some missing cases.
*** $p < .001$, ** $p < .01$, * $p < .05$, ns = not significant.

was no significant difference between the two groups in terms of race (approximately one-fifth of each group was nonwhite) or in terms of the offense for which they had been arrested (approximately two-fifths of each group had been arrested for a property or theft offense). However, the groups differed significantly in terms of sex and age. Interviewed arrestees were significantly more likely than noninterviewed arrestees to be male and aged under 25. The differences between the sample and the population in terms of sex and age may have implications for the results obtained. Attitudes and behavior (such as drug use and criminal behavior and the perceived connection between the two) associated with these characteristics are likely to be overrepresented in the results.

VALIDITY

There are advantages and disadvantages to both urinalysis and self-report measures of drug use. The main advantage of drug testing based on urinalysis is that it provides a scientifically valid measure of drug use within the known limitations of the test. The main disadvantages of urinalysis (based on screening tests) concern specificity and cross-reactivity. The tests are also limited by the period of detectability of the test.

The main advantage of self-report measures is the ability of the researcher to collect information over a variety of time periods and to cover a wide range of related issues. The main disadvantage of self-report methods is the memory of the respondent and his or her ability to recall drug use over defined time periods. The results are also dependent on the veracity of the respondent and his or her willingness to share this information with the researcher. The NEW-ADAM program was based on both urine specimen collection and structured interviews. This was done to obtain the advantages of both methods of data collection and to cross-check (when appropriate) the results of each.

The results of research on the validity of urinalysis and self-report measures of drug misuse are fairly mixed. Some writers have argued that self-report measures underestimate drug use when compared with the results of urinalysis (Fendrich and Yanchun, 1994), whereas other writers have argued that urinalysis measures underestimate drug use when compared with the results of self report (Edgar and O'Donnell, 1998). The results of the urinalysis were therefore compared with the results of the self-report drug inventory. There was generally good correspondence between self-reported drug use over the last three days and the urinalysis results in relation to the negative test results. In other words, there was little evidence of overreporting drug use (i.e., reporting use of a drug in the last three days but testing negative for the drug). In relation to most drug types, the proportion of arrestees overreporting their drug use was no more than one or two percentage points. Indeed, less than 1 percent of arrestees overreported opiate use and only 2 percent overreported cocaine use. The greatest disparities were found in relation to alcohol use. This is almost certainly a result of the fact that alcohol is metabolized rapidly in the body (approximately at a rate of one unit of alcohol per hour) and only very recent or heavy use of this drug is likely to be detected by urinalysis.

The correspondence between self-reported drug use and the urinalysis results was less strong in relation to the positive test results. For most drug types, the proportion of arrestees underreporting their drug use (i.e., reporting 'no' use of a drug in the last three days but testing positive for that drug) was higher than the proportion of arrestees overreporting their drug use. For example, 6 percent of arrestees underreported heroin use (compared with 1% overreporting), 8 percent underreported cocaine use (compared with 2% overreporting), and 10 percent underreported cannabis use (compared with 8% overreporting).

LIMITATIONS

There are several limitations to the current research design which should be made explicit.

Arrestee Population

It should first be acknowledged that the samples of arrestees were not drawn from a naturally occurring population. Instead, they comprise a created population generated out of a combination of factors including offender behavior and police arrest decisions. Hence, the population of arrestees might vary from area to area and over time.

Selection of Sites

The selection of 16 sites in the first stage was based on purposive rather than random sampling. Hence, it is unlikely that the sites would be representative of custody suites in the United Kingdom as a whole. Instead, they were selected not to be representative because it was important that they had high throughputs of arrestees. It is possible that high-throughput custody suites are unusual in some way. They might be more likely to be located in city center or urban areas and might include only those kinds of arrestees found in these areas.

Interview Response Rates

Overall, 62 percent of eligible arrestees were approached for interview. Hence, 38 percent of eligible arrestees were not approached. The main reason for not approaching an eligible arrestee was the lack of a time period long enough during the police process to conduct the interview. This problem could have been reduced in cases in which the arrestee was missed because the researcher on duty was already interviewing another eligible arrestee. This could have been achieved by doubling or trebling the number of researchers available. However, this was not feasible within the budget for the research and would not have helped those cases in which the arrestee was in custody for only a short period of time in total.

The majority of arrestees (85%) who were approached for interview were interviewed. This means that 15 percent of arrestees who were approached were not interviewed. The main reason for not conducting an interview was because the arrestee refused. It is possible that those who agreed to be interviewed were different to those who agreed. An analysis of the sociodemographic characteristics of refusers and nonrefusers showed that arrestees who were interviewed were significantly more likely than noninterviewed arrestees to be male and aged under 25. These differences in terms of sex and age may have implications for the results obtained.

Urinalysis Response Rates

The majority of interviewed arrestees provided urine specimens, but a small proportion did not. The use of alternative methods such as saliva or hair testing might have yielded a higher response rate. It should be noted, however, that at the time the research was conducted (1999–2002) these alternative methods were not fully developed and were not recommended by the FSS.

It is possible that there are differences between arrestees who provided specimens and arrestees who did not. Analyses of sociodemographic factors showed that arrestees who provided specimens were significantly more likely than arrestees who did not provide specimens to be white. There was no difference, however, in terms of sex or age. The racial difference may have implications for the results obtained.

Questionnaire Design and Implementation

The questionnaire was designed to be completed in a 30- to 45-minute period. As a result, the questionnaire had to be restricted in length, and not all questions that could have been asked were asked. To try and maximize the number of issues covered, two follow-up questionnaires were developed: one covered questions on drug markets and one on weapons and guns; arrestees were randomly allocated to complete just one of these. Limiting the questions on these issues to one-half of the sample meant that the number of responses was reduced. The sample size was further limited by the fact that some of the issues under investigation (e.g., gun ownership) were relatively rare, and only a small proportion of the arrestees interviewed could answer them. The small sample size reduced the statistical power of the results, which, on some occasions, made it difficult to conduct useful statistical tests.

DISCUSSION

This chapter has provided details about the research methods used in the NEW-ADAM program. Issues regarding the validity of the methods used have been discussed and the limitations of the research have been noted. It is important to acknowledge, however, the considerable difficulties of interviewing arrestees in custody suites. These are fairly chaotic places with arrestees being brought in on a frequent and regular basis. These are people who are often highly agitated and sometimes violent who shortly before had been free on the streets and, in some cases, had only recently committed the offenses for which they were held. The processing of arrestees by the police is a particularly sensitive area and is tightly controlled by the Police and Criminal Evidence Act 1984. Any processing errors by the police can lead to complaints against them or can be used by the defense lawyers to win their case. It is also difficult to interview arrestees who until a short time earlier were free on the streets. It is necessary to calm them down and win their trust while making it clear that they cannot disclose anything relevant to their current case. At the same time, it was necessary to ask them to disclose in some detail past criminal behavior and drug use. Nevertheless, it was found to be possible to overcome these difficulties, and the research team succeeded in interviewing more than 4,500 arrestees during the research period and collected urine samples from almost all of them.

PART TWO

DRUG MISUSE AMONG CRIMINALS

CHAPTER THREE

Drug Misuse Among Arrestees

INTRODUCTION

Several methods of monitoring drug misuse already exist, including surveys of the general population, medical records of users entering treatment, and official statistics on prosecutions for drug offenses. However, each of these measures has problems in providing an accurate estimation of drug misuse. General population surveys do not cover the entire population and tend to omit difficult-to-reach groups, such as homeless people and those currently living in institutions. They also exclude those who are criminally active who might decline to be interviewed and those in custody (either in prison or in police cells) at the time of the survey. Similarly, medical records and official statistics do not cover the entire population as they exclude drug users who do not present for treatment and those not convicted of a drug offense. On each occasion, the omitted groups are likely to include the most problematic drug users. It is important in assessing drug-use patterns that monitoring covers a broad spectrum of the population and, therefore, that information is available on the more difficult-to-reach groups and more problematic drug users.

This chapter aims to shed light on drug misuse among one of these difficult-to-reach groups. The following sections examine what is known about drug misuse among arrestees from the results of the New English and Welsh Arrestee Drug Abuse Monitoring (NEW-ADAM) surveys. In particular, it looks at the proportion of arrestees that use various types of drugs, the rates of drug use among drug users, and weekly expenditure on drugs.

PREVIOUS RESEARCH

The main body of research on arrestee drug misuse monitoring derives from those countries associated with the I-ADAM (International Arrestee Drug Abuse Monitoring) program. I-ADAM was launched by the National Institute of Justice in the United States in 1998 and was closely linked to the US Arrestee Drug Abuse Monitoring (ADAM) program. A number of countries have been involved in collecting ADAM-type data since the inception of the program. However, some of these ceased collection for one reason or another, and others failed to publish their results. In practice, the most substantial findings come from just three countries: the United States, Australia, and South Africa. Hence, the following review focuses mainly on the results obtained from these three countries.

The most recent published findings from the US ADAM program are for 2003 (Zhang, undated) and cover the urinalysis results of 39 sites. Overall, the median proportion of adult male arrestees testing positive for cannabis was 44 percent with a high of 55 percent (Oklahoma City, Oklahoma) and a low of 30 percent (Honolulu, Hawaii). The median value of positive tests for opiates (including heroin) was 6 percent, with a high of 28 percent (Rio Arriba, New Mexico) and a low of 2 percent (Woodbury, Iowa). The average proportion of arrestees testing positive for cocaine (including crack and powder cocaine) was 30 percent (median), ranging from a high of 51 percent (Chicago, Illinois) to a low of 3 percent (Woodbury, Iowa).

The latest findings of the DUMA (Drug Use Monitoring in Australia) program cover 2004 (Schulte, Mouzos, and Makkai, 2005). The DUMA program is based on monitoring arrestee drug misuse in seven sites. The results for adult male arrestees showed that the median proportion of arrestees testing positive for cannabis was 62 percent. The highest rate was 72 percent in Elizabeth, South Australia, and the lowest rate was 39 percent in Bankstown. The median proportion of arrestees testing positive for opiates was 12 percent, with a high of 25 percent (Bankstown) and a low of 8 percent (East Perth and Elizabeth). The median value of positive tests for cocaine was 2 percent, with a high of 6 percent (Bankstown) and a low of 0 percent (Southport).

TABLE 3.1. *Median percentage of positive tests among adult male arrestees in various countries*

	ADAM program, United States	DUMA program, Australia	3-Metros program, South Africa
Cannabis	44	62	43
Opiates	6	12	3
Cocaine	30	2	5

Sources: ADAM (Arrestee Drug Abuse Monitoring), Zhang (undated); DUMA (Drug Use Monitoring in Australia), Schulte et al. (2005); 3-Metros, Parry et al. (2004).

The most recent publication on the 3-Metros study in South Africa covers 2000 (Parry et al., 2004). The program was based as its name suggests on three sites (Cape Town, Durban, and Johannesburg). The urinalysis results showed that the median percentage of arrestees testing positive for cannabis was 43 percent. This ranged from 24 percent (Johannesburg) to 50 percent (Cape Town). The median proportion of arrestees testing positive for opiates was 3 percent, with a high of 3 percent (Johannesburg) and a low of 2 percent (Durban). The urinalysis results for cocaine were a median value of 5 percent, ranging from a high of 6 percent (Durban) to a low of 3 (Cape Town).

The results in Table 3.1 show some variation across countries and across types in terms of the proportion of arrestees testing positive for these drugs. The highest median proportion of positive tests for cannabis and opiates was in Australia, whereas the highest median proportion of positive tests for cocaine was in the United States. When the NEW-ADAM program was piloted in the UK in the mid-1990s, it was unknown how Britain would compare with the drug use prevalence rates of arrestees in other countries. The findings that follow help provide some answers to this question and summarize the extent and nature of drug misuse among arrestees in the United Kingdom.

PREVALENCE OF DRUG MISUSE AMONG ARRESTEES

It is important to know the proportion of arrestees who used drugs for a number of reasons. It provides a measure of drug use among a high-risk population. On the basis of the findings of research on risk factors for offending (Budd et al., 2005a), it would be expected that arrestees would be more likely than nonarrestees to be involved in drug use. In estimating drug misuse generally, it is useful to know the scale of the difference between these two populations. Information on the prevalence of drug misuse among arrestees also provides useful evidence that can be used in estimating the drug-crime connection. Although an association between drug use and crime is not a sufficient condition of causality, it is a necessary condition. In other words, if drug use were connected with crime, it would be expected that arrestees would be more likely than nonarrestees to be drug users. This section presents the main findings of the research on the prevalence of drug use among arrestees.

Urinalysis

In the current research, urinalysis tests were conducted on seven drug groups: cannabis, opiates (including heroin), cocaine (including crack), benzodiazepines, amphetamines, methadone, and alcohol. In most cases, a positive urinalysis test identifies drugs consumed in the last three days. However, there is some variation between drugs. Marijuana can be detected in a urine specimen up to a month after consumption, depending on the level of drug use. Alcohol can only be detected in urine samples a few hours after consumption because it is metabolized very rapidly in the body (estimated at a rate of roughly one unit per hour).

Prevalence of Recent Drug Use

The proportion of arrestees testing positive for seven drug types and for various combinations of these drugs is shown in Table 3.2. Overall, 69 percent of arrestees tested positive for one or more of the six illicit drug types tested. More than one-third of arrestees tested positive for multiple drugs (two or more illicit substances).

The way in which this prevalence varies by drug type is shown in the middle rows of the table. The first three drugs comprise what might be called recreational drugs. The most common of these detected was cannabis, evidence of which was found in the urine of almost half of the arrestees (48%). By comparison, benzodiazepines (minor tranquilizers) were detected in less than one-seventh (15%) of cases

TABLE 3.2. *Proportion of arrestees testing positive for selected drug types*

Drug type	%	n
Any drug	69	1,958
Multiple drugs (two or more)[a]	39	1,116
Cannabis	48	1,352
Amphetamines	6	169
Benzodiazepines	15	432
Opiates (including heroin)	33	921
Cocaine (including crack)	26	732
Opiates or cocaine	41	1,154
Methadone	7	187
Alcohol	23	647

Note: Among arrestees who provided urine specimens ($n = 2,833$).
[a]Excluding alcohol.

and amphetamines in less than one-tenth (6%). The data show that cannabis is by far the most common of the recreational drugs used among arrestees.

The next three drugs might be referred to as the addictive or more serious drugs. A positive test for opiates identifies recent use of heroin or other opium-based substances. A positive test for cocaine identifies recent use of either cocaine powder or crack. The most commonly found serious drug was opiates identified in the urine specimens of almost one-third of arrestees. About one-quarter (26%) of arrestees tested positive for cocaine, whereas the percentage of arrestees testing positive for methadone was seven percent. Forty-one percent of arrestees tested positive for opiates and/or cocaine.

The mean percentage of positive tests for alcohol is shown in a group on its own to reflect the differences between alcohol and other drugs. First, alcohol is not an illegal drug. Second, because alcohol is metabolized rapidly by the body, the test can only detect recent use. Nevertheless, the results are of interest in that alcohol can be relevant in relation to multiple drug misuse and in relation to some of the problems associated with drug misuse including crime. The table shows that nearly one-quarter (23%) of arrestees had consumed alcohol close to the time of their arrest.

TABLE 3.3. *Proportion of arrestees testing positive for opiates and/or cocaine*

Drug type	%	n
Opiates only	37	422
Cocaine only	20	233
Opiates and cocaine	43	499
Opiates alone or in combination with cocaine	80	921
Cocaine alone or in combination with heroin	63	732
Opiates or cocaine	100	1,154

Notes: Among arrestees who tested positive for opiates and/or cocaine ($n = 1,154$).

The results of the urinalysis for specific drug types can be compared with the urinalysis results from the United States, Australia, and South Africa discussed in the previous section. In relation to cannabis, the highest rate was in Australia at 62 percent and the UK was second with 48 percent. The United States and South Africa had fairly similar rates of just over 40 percent. The results for opiates showed that the NEW-ADAM findings at 33 percent were the highest of the four countries. In comparison, the US rate was 6 percent, and the rate for South Africa as lowest at 3 percent. However, the US rate for positive tests for cocaine was highest at 30 percent, with the UK result close behind at 26 percent. The lowest rates were Australia with 2 percent of arrestees testing positive for cocaine. Hence, the results show some variation across countries in terms of the drug involvement of arrestees in relation to specific drug types. Opiates were more likely to be consumed among arrestees in the United Kingdom and cocaine was more likely to be consumed among arrestees in the United States. Arrestees in South Africa rarely used either of these drugs.

Opiates and Cocaine Combinations

Table 3.3 examines the way in which opiates and cocaine are combined among arrestees who tested positive for these drugs. Because both drugs might be associated with problem behaviors, it is important to know whether they tend to be used in combination or separately. Among those who tested positive for opiates ($n = 921$), approximately half of them (54%, $n = 499$) used opiates in combination with cocaine and half (46%, $n = 422$) used opiates without cocaine. In contrast, those who tested positive for cocaine ($n = 732$) were more likely to use them in combination with opiates (68%, $n = 499$) rather than alone (32%, $n = 233$).

Variations by Location

The results presented so far represent mean percentages across all 16 locations. In fact, there was some variation across sites in relation to recent drug involvement. The median percentage (the midpoint of the range) of arrestees testing positive for cannabis was 47.3 percent (mean 48%). Because there is an even number of sites, the midpoint has been defined as the eighth highest position. This ranged from 35 percent (Middlesbrough) to 62 percent (Brixton). The proportion of arrestees testing positive for amphetamines and amphetamine-like drugs including 'ecstasy' ranged from 1 percent (Colindale) to 7 percent (Sunderland), with a median value of 5 percent (mean 6%). The urinalysis showed that between 9 percent (Wolverhampton) and 25 percent (Sunderland and Newport) of arrestees tested positive for benzodiazepines, with a median value of 13 percent (mean 15 percent). The proportion of arrestees testing positive for opiates ranged from 13 percent (Southampton) to 57 percent (Middlesbrough) with a median value of 30 percent (mean 33%). The proportion of arrestees testing positive for cocaine (including crack) ranged from five percent (Plymouth) to 49 percent (Liverpool). The median proportion of positive tests was 28 percent (mean 27%). The proportion of arrestees testing positive for methadone ranged from 2 percent (Southampton, Wolverhampton, Plymouth) to 19 percent (Bolton), with a median value of 5 percent (mean 7%).

It is possible that there is an association between type of drug identified in the urinalysis and type of area. One hypothesis is that the more serious drug types will be found in greater frequency in the large metropolitan areas. Four survey sites were located in London and one in Liverpool (two of the largest urban conurbations in the United Kingdom). The highest four prevalence rates of positive tests for cocaine were found in three of the four London sites and the Liverpool site as hypothesized. However, this pattern was not found for opiates with the metropolitan areas spread more evenly within the distribution. This might be a result of the fact that heroin is a well-established drug in the United Kingdom and has had time to permeate to most cities. However, cocaine is relatively new and has had less time to permeate beyond the larger cities. Nevertheless, some cocaine use was evident among arrestees in all locations.

Characteristics of Drug-Using Arrestees

It is possible that there is some variation in drug misuse among arrestees by demographic characteristics. Table 3.4 provides a breakdown of the urinalysis results by sex, age, and ethnic group.

The table shows that male arrestees were significantly more likely than female arrestees to test positive for cannabis and alcohol. Female arrestees, in contrast, were significantly more likely than males to test positive for opiates, methadone, cocaine, and benzodiazepines. Female arrestees were also significantly more likely than males to test positive for multiple drug types. Possible explanations of gender differences in drug misuse among arrestees are discussed in more detail in Chapter 9.

The table also shows some differences among arrestees in terms of age. There were significant differences in the proportion testing positive for various drugs among the four age groups. Younger arrestees (17–24) were more likely than older arrestees (25+) to test positive for cannabis. However, for most other drug types, older arrestees were more likely than younger arrestees to test positive. Those aged 25–29 were more likely than the other age groups to test positive for opiates and cocaine. They were also more likely to test positive for amphetamines, benzodiazepines, and methadone. The oldest group (30+) was more likely than the other groups to test positive for alcohol.

There were also significant ethnic group differences in the likelihood of testing positive for certain drug types. A significantly higher proportion of white arrestees compared with nonwhite tested positive for opiates, methadone, amphetamines, benzodiazepines, alcohol, multiple drugs, and opiates and/or cocaine. In contrast, nonwhite arrestees were significantly more likely than white arrestees to test positive for cocaine. Further information on ethnicity and drug use is provided in Chapter 10.

TABLE 3.4. *Proportion of arrestees testing positive for various drug types by sex, age, and ethnicity*

	n	Cannabis	Amphet-amines	Benzo-diazepines	Alcohol	Opiates	Cocaine	Methadone	Any drug (excl. alcohol)	Multiple drugs (excl. alcohol)	Opiates and/or cocaine
Sex											
Male	2,432	50	6	14	25	30	24	6	69	38	39
Female	401	34	7	21	12	46	35	9	68	47	53
Sig. of difference		***	ns	**	***	***	***	*	ns	**	***
Age											
17–19	633	55	4	5	21	15	15	1	65	24	23
20–24	735	55	7	14	23	38	26	7	78	44	46
25–29	530	46	8	22	19	48	35	10	76	55	56
30+	915	38	5	20	26	32	28	8	61	38	40
Sig. of difference		***	ns	***	*	***	***	***	***	***	***
Ethnic group											
White	2,269	47	7	17	25	36	25	7	70	42	43
Nonwhite	563	51	1	7	13	19	29	3	67	29	34
Sig. of difference		ns	***	***	***	***	**	**	ns	***	***
TOTAL (n)	2,833	1,352	169	432	647	921	732	187	1,958	1,116	1,154

Notes: Among arrestees who provided a urine specimen (*n* = 2,833).
Chi-square test: *** *p* < .001; ** *p* < .01; * *p* < .05; ns = not significant.

TABLE 3.5. *Self-reported drug use over various periods by drug types*

Drug type	Ever	Last 12 months	Last 30 days	Last 3 days
Cannabis	82	67	59	44
Amphetamines	56	19	9	4
Ecstasy	51	27	13	5
Heroin	38	32	28	26
Crack cocaine	38	31	23	16
Cocaine powder	43	26	13	5
Methadone	23	15	9	6
Alcohol	95	87	76	56
Any illicit drug (19 types)	87	78	72	62
Multiple drugs (2 or more)	74	59	48	33
Heroin and/or crack and/or cocaine	57	48	39	31

Notes: Among all arrestees ($n = 3,135$).

Demographic variations in the prevalence of drug misuse are important because they can help identify prevention strategies. Drug strategies aimed at demand reduction might be more effective if they target specific drug-using groups. The importance of disaggregating findings and targeting drug strategies is discussed in more detail in Chapter 5.

Self-Reported Drug Use

In addition to the urine specimen collection and analysis, arrestees were asked about their drug use. There are a number of advantages in asking arrestees to provide self-reports on their drug consumption. It is possible to examine use over longer periods of time than can be measured using urinalysis. It enables more information to be collected about a wider range of drug types. It is also possible to ask arrestees supplementary questions concerning rate of drug use and expenditure on drugs. All arrestees were asked about their illegal drug use in their lifetime, in the last 12 months, in the last month, and in the last three days. The respondents were asked about the use of 19 types of drugs and alcohol and tobacco. The results of the most relevant eight drug types are reported in Table 3.5.

The proportions of arrestees reporting use of each of the drug types during four specific time periods (ever, last 12 months, last 30 days, and last three days) are shown in Table 3.5. The most commonly consumed drug was alcohol, used by almost all (95%) arrestees at some time in their lives and by more than 80 percent in the last 12 months. The most commonly consumed illegal drug was cannabis, used by 82 percent of arrestees at some time in their lives and by two-thirds (67%) in the last 12 months. The remaining recreational drugs were used less frequently. Ecstasy was consumed by more than one-quarter (27%) of arrestees in the last 12 months and amphetamines were used by approximately one-fifth of the sample (19%). Heroin was used by just under one-third (32%) of arrestees in the last 12 months and crack was used by a similar proportion (31%). Use of cocaine powder was slightly less prevalent than crack at 26 percent, and methadone was used by just 15 percent of the sample.

The differences in use of crack and cocaine powder are interesting considering that their pharmacological properties are almost identical and metabolize to the same compounds in the body. In the longer term (ever and in the last 12 months) there was little difference in the proportion of arrestees who used these two drugs. In the last three days, the prevalence of crack use was almost three times the prevalence of cocaine powder. This switch from cocaine powder being the most prevalent over the lifetime to crack being the most prevalent in the last three days could be explained by a number of factors. It could reflect the fact that crack users are more likely than cocaine users to be dependent, and therefore more frequent, drug users (see Chapter 4 for details). It could also be explained by a change in preference for the two drugs over time or by external factors such as changes in availability or price.

It is also possible to compare the prevalence rates for arrestees for some of the drugs discussed with the rates of the general population in the 1999 British Crime Survey (BCS), which was conducted about the same time as the NEW-ADAM surveys. In relation to cannabis, the BCS results showed that 9 percent of the general population reported consuming cannabis in the last year compared with 67 percent among arrestees (a ratio of almost 1:7). Even greater differences occurred in relation to other recreational drugs. The prevalence ratio of amphetamine use in the general population and among arrestees was 1:11, and the ratio for ecstasy was 1:17. However, the largest differences could be seen in relation to the more serious drug types. The proportion reporting use of cocaine powder in the last 12 months was 1 percent compared with 26 percent among arrestees (a ratio of 1:26). The proportion of the general population that reported consuming heroin in the last 12 months was less than 1 percent (the precise rate was not reported) compared with 32 percent among arrestees.

The findings of the self-report survey support the results of the urinalysis in showing high levels of drug misuse among arrestees. They also provide additional insights into drug misuse over longer periods of time including in the last 12 months, which in some ways is more useful than urinalysis findings over the last three days. There is some suggestion that the prevalence of drug misuse among arrestees is many times greater than among the general population. However, it has to be borne in mind that the two populations are not the same, and the losses resulting from incomplete sampling in relation to the general population surveys might enhance these differences. Nevertheless, the evidence points in the direction that arrestees are more likely than nonarrestees to be involved in drug misuse and more likely to consume the more harmful drugs.

Validity

The availability of urinalysis and self-report measures of recent drug misuse provides an opportunity to test the validity of the self-report responses. The issue of validity testing using these measures is complex because urinalysis is not a wholly valid measure as the test can produce false positives and false negatives. It should also be noted that the comparisons for some drug types are only approximate. The urinalysis test for opiates will detect heroin use. However, it will also detect use of other opium derivatives such as those included in codeine. The urinalysis test for cocaine will detect both crack and powder cocaine. Nevertheless, the test provides a reasonably scientific measure of drug use and can provide some insight into the validity of self-report responses.

In conducting the comparison, it is useful to make a distinction between Type I and Type II errors. In this comparison, a Type I error is defined as occurring when the urinalysis shows a positive result, but use of the drug is denied. Hence, this type of error represents what might be referred to as underreporting of drug use. A Type II error is defined as occurring when the urinalysis shows a negative result but the arrestee reports that he or she has used the drug in the last three days. This type of error is referred to as overreporting of drug use.

Aggregated Comparisons. Using these definitions and methods, it is possible to examine the validity of self-reported drug use among arrestees. Table 3.6 compares the results of the urinalysis with self-reported drug use over the last three days. The percentages without parentheses show the proportion of arrestees who tested positive or negative and reported or denied drug use. The percentages in parentheses show the overall proportion of responses in each category for the entire sample.

The total concordance of response using the two measures is generally quite good. The percentages in parentheses show that the total concordance for cannabis (positive tests with use confirmed and negative tests with use denied) was 82 percent. The total concordance for the other illegal drugs was even higher. Among the recreational drugs, the concordance rates were 90 percent for benzodiazepines and 95 percent for amphetamines. The concordance among the more addictive drugs was also quite high, with heroin at 93 percent, methadone at 96 percent, and cocaine powder or crack at 88 percent. The lowest total concordance was for alcohol, which had an overall agreement of 66 percent. This much lower level of agreement can be explained in part by the faster rate that alcohol is metabolized by the body, as noted earlier. This means that in most cases, the urinalysis test would only detect alcohol consumed within the last few hours.

The results can also be investigated by looking at the percentage of users who overestimate (they say that they had consumed a drug when the urinalysis test was negative) and underestimate drug misuse (they say that they had not consumed a drug when the urinalysis test was positive).

TABLE 3.6. *Percentage of arrestees reporting drug use in the last three days by urinalysis result*

	Positive for drug	Negative for drug	TOTAL (*n*)
Used cannabis in last 3 days	77 (37)	14 (7)	1,249
Not used cannabis in last 3 days	23 (11)	86 (45)	1,584
TOTAL (*n*)	1,352	1,481	2,833
Used amphetamines in last 3 days	41 (2)	1 (1)	105
Not used amphetamines in last 3 days	59 (4)	99 (93)	2,728
TOTAL (*n*)	169	2,664	2,833
Used benzodiazepines in last 3 days[a]	51 (8)	4 (3)	307
Not used benzodiazepines in last 3 days	49 (7)	96 (82)	2,526
TOTAL (*n*)	432	2,401	2,833
Used heroin in last 3 days	79 (26)	1 (1)	749
Not used heroin in last 3 days	21 (7)	99 (67)	2,084
TOTAL (*n*)	921	1,912	2,833
Used methadone in last 3 days	64 (4)	2 (1)	162
Not used methadone in last 3 days	36 (2)	98 (92)	2,671
TOTAL (*n*)	187	2,646	2,833
Used cocaine/crack in last 3 days	64 (16)	4 (3)	541
Not used cocaine/crack in last 3 days	36 (9)	96 (72)	2,292
TOTAL (*n*)	732	2,101	2,833
Used alcohol in last 3 days	96 (22)	44 (34)	1,574
Not used alcohol in last 3 days	4 (1)	56 (44)	1,259
TOTAL (*n*)	647	2,186	2,833
TOTAL (*n*)	660	2,273	2,833

Note: Figures in parentheses are the number of cases.

[a] Self-reported use of benzodiazepines = use of temazepam, diazepam, or other tranquilizers in the last three days.

There is generally good correspondence between self-reported drug use over the last three days and the urinalysis results in relation to the negative test results, which examine overestimation. In other words, there is little evidence from these results of overreporting drug use. In relation to most drug types, the proportion of arrestees overreporting was no more than one or two percentage points. The biggest disparities occurred in relation to alcohol, with 44 percent of those testing negative saying that they had consumed alcohol in the last three days, and cannabis, with 14 percent of those who said that they had used cannabis in the last three days testing negative for the drug. In both cases, this difference could be a result of the inability of the test to detect certain kinds of drug consumption in the last three days. It could also be a result of genuine overreporting where for some reasons users said that they had consumed the drug when they had not. However, this did not appear to occur in relation to the more serious drugs. Overreporting of heroin was only 1 percent, and overreporting of crack or cocaine powder was 4 percent.

The correspondence between self-reported drug use and the urinalysis results is less strong in relation to the positive test results, which examines underestimation. In relation to most drug types, the proportion of arrestees underreporting their drug use was higher than the proportion of arrestees overreporting their drug use. In some cases, the underreporting rate was quite high. Twenty-one percent of users who tested positive for opiates denied that they had consumed heroin in the last three days (7% of the total responses given), and 36 percent of users who tested positive for cocaine denied that they had consumed either crack or cocaine in the last three days (9% of the total responses given).

Disaggregated Comparisons. It is possible that there might be some variation in discordance between urinalysis results and self-reported drug use by demographic characteristics. Although it is not wholly possible to determine whether any differences are a result of variations in the truthfulness of the respondents, it is nevertheless interesting to see whether any variations exist by gender, ethnicity, and age.

In relation to gender, there were no significant differences between males and females in terms of 'underreporting' (denying use but producing a positive test result) and 'overreporting' drug use (claiming use but producing a negative test result), with the exception of males who were more likely than females to overreport use of alcohol (45% compared with 36%; $p < .05$). However, the total concordance (under- and overreporting combined) was significantly worse for females than males in relation to heroin use (93% males and 89% females; $p < .01$). The results for ethnicity showed that nonwhite arrestees were significantly more likely than white arrestees to underreport use of cocaine/crack (33% whites and 46% nonwhites; $p < .01$) and use of alcohol (3% whites and 10% nonwhites; $p < .05$). However, whites were significantly more likely than nonwhites to over-report cocaine/crack (4% whites and 2% nonwhites; $p < .05$). Whites were also more likely than nonwhites to overreport use of benzodiazepines (4% compared with 1%; $p < .01$), amphetamines (2% compared with 1%; $p < .05$), and alcohol (45% compared with 38%; $p < .05$). In relation to age (split at 17–24 compared with 25 and older), younger arrestees were significantly more likely than older arrestees to underreport use of cocaine/crack (44% for young arrestees and 31% for old arrestees; $p < .05$). Younger arrestees were also more likely than older arrestees to overreport use of cannabis (20% compared with 10%; $p < .001$). However, older arrestees were more likely than younger arrestees to overreport methadone use (1% young compared with 2% old; $p < .05$).

Comment. The disparity between urinalysis results and self-reported drug use over the last three days might be explained by several reasons. It is not necessarily the case that differences are a result of intentional deception on the part of the arrestee. A certain proportion of all urinalysis responses will be false positives and false negatives. The methods used can differ in sensitivity to certain kinds of drugs and produce incorrect results. This has been estimated at around 2 percent of cases (Visher, 1991) but could be higher in relation to some drug types. It is also possible that a small quantity of a particular drug taken, say, three days earlier might have been sufficiently metabolized at the time of the test for it not to be detectable by the assay. It should also be noted that the test for opiates would detect heroin and also any other drugs with an opium base. The most common other drug

TABLE 3.7. *Proportion of arrestees reporting high, medium, and low rates of drug use in the last 30 days by drug type*

Drug type	High rate (15+ days)	Medium rate (5–14 days)	Low rate (1–4 days)	Total %	Total n
Cannabis	55	17	28	100	1,845
Amphetamines	17	17	66	100	277
Ecstasy	5	21	74	100	420
Heroin	81	8	12	100	891
Crack cocaine	47	20	33	100	719
Cocaine powder	12	20	68	100	403
Methadone	48	20	32	100	289
Alcohol	29	35	36	100	2,376

Note: Among all arrestees ($n = 3,135$).

that might trigger this test is codeine, which in sufficient quantities could generate a positive result. It also needs to be borne in mind that reporting errors on the part of the arrestee do not necessarily mean that they attempted deliberately to mislead the interviewer. Instead, the respondent might have misjudged the three-day window period or consumed a drug that was not what it was believed to be. McGregor and Makkai (2003) noted that in many cases of reported ecstasy use, the arrestee had in fact consumed methamphetamine and concluded that, in the case of ecstasy, few detainees were getting what they paid for.

RATE OF DRUG MISUSE

The previous analysis has been based wholly on the prevalence of drug use among arrestees. However, it is also important from the point of view of policy and in understanding the scale of drug use among arrestees to know something about the incidence or rate of drug misuse.

Table 3.7 displays the rate at which arrestees reported having used selected drug types over the last 30 days. The term 'high rate' is defined here to mean that the drug was used 15 days or more in the last 30 days, 'medium-rate' use is defined as the drug being used between 5 and 14 days in the last 30 days, and 'low-rate' use is defined as the drug being used between 1 and 4 days in the last 30 days. These rates can be interpreted to mean that high-rate users consume drugs at least every other day, suggesting substantial involvement in drug use, whereas low-rate users consume drugs less than once a week, suggesting occasional rather than compulsive use.

In total, 73 percent of drug users used one or more drugs at a high rate. The highest proportion of high-rate drug users was among heroin users. Over 80 percent of heroin users were high-rate users (using at least every other day). It is interesting that there does not appear to be a wholly direct relationship between the presumed addictiveness of the drug and the rate of use. The proportion of crack users classified as high rate was almost half that of heroin users (47% compared with 81%) and the proportion of cocaine powder users identified as high rate users was the second lowest percentage (12%). Conversely, the second highest proportion of high-rate users was found among users of cannabis. More than half (55%) of cannabis users consumed the drug at least every other day. The lowest proportion of high-rate users was found among users of ecstasy.

There were also some differences in involvement in high-rate drug misuse by demographic factors. Males were more likely than females to use cannabis at a high rate (57% compared with 42%) and females were more likely than males to use heroin and crack at a high rate (90% compared with 78% and 63% compared with 43%). Older arrestees (aged 25+) were significantly more likely than younger arrestees (aged 17–24) to use one or more drugs at a high rate (76% compared with 70%). They were also more likely to use heroin and cocaine powder at a high rate. Younger arrestees were more likely than older arrestees to use cannabis at a high rate (58% compared with 51%). All of these differences were statistically significant at the $p < .05$ level and all of the percentages were based on users of the drug only.

The rate of drug use is obviously of some importance when thinking about the connection between drug use and crime. The higher the rate of drug use, the higher the costs of the drug for the user. The following section explores the issue of amount spent on drugs in more detail.

EXPENDITURE ON DRUGS

The amount spent on drugs provides another indicator of involvement of drug misuse among arrestees. Expenditure on drugs can also indicate the regularity of drug use and the frequency of seeking and purchasing drugs. Levels of expenditure on drugs can also tell us something about the link between drug use and crime. Arrestees who use large quantities of drugs must find some way of generating the funds to pay for them. There is an obvious danger that at least some of these funds will be generated from crime.

Arrestees who reported that they had used at least one drug (excluding alcohol and tobacco) in the last 12 months were asked how much they had spent on drugs in the last seven days. Table 3.8 shows differences in expenditure patterns in relation to various types of drug use and the overall cost of drugs. On average, drug-using arrestees spent £161 in the last week on drugs. The average amount spent on drugs among drug users varied significantly across the areas. The highest weekly expenditure rates were in Bournemouth (£276) and in the Bethnal Green site in London (£264). The lowest weekly rates were in Sunderland (£76) and Southampton (£204). The difference in expenditure rates across areas can be the result of a number of factors, including the prevalence of use, rate of use, and cost of drugs. Estimates from the National Criminal Intelligence Service (NCIS) for

TABLE 3.8. *Mean expenditure on drugs in the last 7 days by drug type*

Drug type	£	n
Users of drugs other than heroin, crack, or cocaine	22	896
Heroin, cocaine, and crack	417	352
Heroin and crack	335	421
Heroin and cocaine	143	47
Crack and cocaine	148	96
Heroin only	143	194
Crack only	134	87
Cocaine only	61	312
Significance	***	
TOTAL	161	2,405

Note: Among arrestees who had used drugs in the last 12 months ($n = 2,443$). Some missing cases. Analysis of variance test: *** $p < .001$.

1999 suggest that heroin and crack prices were slightly higher in London than elsewhere (average costs were £60–£80 for heroin and £60–£120 for cocaine powder). Hence, it is possible that the higher rates of expenditure among users of heroin, crack, and cocaine in Bethnal Green were in part explained by higher prices.

Expenditure on drugs varied by drug type and drug type combination. Users of drugs other than heroin, crack, or cocaine powder reported the lowest weekly expenditure on drugs. On average, this group spent £22 in the last week on drugs. Arrestees who used heroin, crack, and cocaine in the last 12 months reported the highest levels of expenditure on drugs. Overall, the mean expenditure in the last seven days among this group was £417, which is nearly 20 times the expenditure of arrestees who used other drugs only. Mean expenditure was also high among users of heroin and crack (but not cocaine) at £335 per week. This was nearly double the amount spent by users of heroin and cocaine (but not crack). It is also considerably higher than the amount spent among users of just heroin, just crack, and just cocaine powder.

Table 3.9 presents the average levels of expenditure on drugs by demographic factors. On average, women reported significantly higher levels of expenditure on drugs than men, with an average expenditure of £258 per week among women compared with £145 among men. This finding is likely to be explained by the higher rate of use of opiates and cocaine (the most expensive and addictive drugs) among females, mentioned earlier. Younger arrestees (aged under 25) tended to report lower levels of expenditure than older arrestees (aged 25–59). Overall, the average expenditure on drugs among younger arrestees was £128 compared with £198 among older arrestees (the difference was statistically significant). There were also significant differences in expenditure on drugs by ethnic group. White arrestees reported spending an average of £171 per week compared with £118 among nonwhite arrestees.

Table 3.10 combines the total number of drug users and the average expenditure on drugs to determine the total amount spent on drugs among each group. The table shows that the greatest proportion of total expenditure on drugs was from among users of heroin, crack, and cocaine powder. This group spent 38 percent of the total amount

TABLE 3.9. *Mean expenditure on drugs in the last 7 days by sex, age, and ethnicity*

Drug type	£	n
Sex		
Male	145	2,074
Female	258	331
Sig. of difference	***	
Age		
17–19	98	578
20–24	152	694
25–29	205	472
30+	194	661
Sig. of difference	***	
Ethnic group		
White	171	1,945
Nonwhite	118	459
Sig. of difference	*	
TOTAL	161	2,405

Note. Among arrestees who had used drugs in the last 12 months ($n = 2,443$). Some missing cases.
Analysis of variance test: *** $p < .001$; * $p < .05$.

spent on drugs by all arrestees. The second largest proportion was from among users of heroin and crack, who spent 36 percent of the total amount spent on drugs among all arrestees. Combining these two groups shows that users of heroin, cocaine powder, and crack and users of heroin and crack purchased more than three-quarters of the money value of drugs of all arrestees. Hence, one-quarter (25%) of all arrestees spent three-quarters (74%) of the total expenditure on drugs of all arrestees.

DISCUSSION

The aim of the chapter was to determine the prevalence and incidence of drug misuse among arrestees in the United Kingdom. It was argued that arrestees represent a difficult-to-reach population that is likely to be excluded from national general population surveys. The issue of drug misuse among arrestees is also relevant to understanding the links between drug misuse and crime. If there were a link, it would

TABLE 3.10. *Mean expenditure on drugs in the last 7 days by drug type and total amount spent*

Drug type	£ Mean	£ Total	% Total spent	% Total n	n
Users of drugs other than heroin, crack, or cocaine	22	20,028	5	37	896
Heroin, cocaine, and crack	417	146,718	38	15	352
Heroin and crack	335	140,951	36	18	421
Heroin and cocaine	143	6,710	2	2	47
Crack and cocaine	148	14,220	4	4	96
Heroin only	143	27,703	7	8	194
Crack only	134	11,675	3	4	87
Cocaine only	61	19,027	5	13	312
Significance	***				
TOTAL	161	387,032	100	100	2,405

Note. Among arrestees who had used drugs in the last 12 months ($n = 2,443$). Some missing cases.
Analysis of variance test: *** $p < .001$.

be expected that arrestees would be more heavily involved in drug misuse than nonarrestees. The chapter also aimed to look at some of the variations in drug misuse in terms of drug type, drug combinations, and the demographic characteristics of arrestees.

The results of the urinalysis and self-report analysis show high levels of involvement in drug misuse among arrestees. More than two-thirds of arrestees who provided a urine specimen tested positive for one or more illicit drug, and about the same proportion of all arrestees reported consuming an illicit drug in the last three days. Prevalence of drug misuse was even higher over the last 12 months and whole lifetime. The most commonly used drugs were cannabis, with two-thirds of arrestees reporting cannabis use in the last 12 months, and heroin, with one-third reporting heroin use in the last 12 months. Males were more likely than females to test positive for cannabis and alcohol, whereas females were more likely than males to test positive for opiates, methadone, cocaine, and benzodiazepines. Younger offenders were more likely than older offenders to test positive for cannabis. However, for most other drugs, including opiates and cocaine, older offenders were more likely to test positive.

The results of the NEW-ADAM program provide evidence for the first time in the United Kingdom over multiple sites of the high levels of involvement of arrestees in drug misuse. These results are important for understanding the nature of the drug-crime connection in the United Kingdom. First, they provide a comparison with the results of drug use measured by national surveys of the general population. The results show that the prevalence of drug use among arrestees is many times that of the general population; for some drug types, such as heroin and cocaine, the proportion may be considerably greater. Second, they provide baseline evidence for the statistical association between drug misuse and crime. It would be expected, if drug use and crime were associated, that arrestees would be heavily involved in drug misuse. In fact, almost 90 percent of arrestees said that they had consumed at least one illicit drug in their lifetime, and more than half had consumed heroin, crack, or cocaine powder, the drugs more frequently implicated in the drug-crime connection

The findings are also important from the point of view of government policy and methods of tackling drug misuse. Knowledge about the most frequently used drugs among arrestees and the types of arrestees who most frequently use them can help target antidrug strategies.

CHAPTER FOUR

Drugs and Health

INTRODUCTION

A wide variety of health problems can be experienced by drug users including dependency, infectious diseases, harmful physiological effects of certain drugs, and risk of overdose and death. These problems are important not only for the individual drug user but also for those people (such as the police) who come into regular contact with them. They are also important in that they increase the burden on the health service and its personnel, including general practitioners and hospital-based services.

PREVIOUS RESEARCH

Previous research on the health problems of drug misusers has tended to focus on the problem of dependency and addiction. However, research has also been conducted on general health problems, the prevalence of injection and sharing equipment, the spread of infectious diseases such as HIV and AIDS, and the link between drug use and alcohol and tobacco consumption.

General Health Problems

Drug Side Effects. Most drugs that are commonly misused can cause short-term negative effects on mental and physical functioning. Heroin can produce various kinds of physiological change including dry mouth, drowsiness, impaired mental functioning, and slowed breathing. At high dosages, heroin consumption can lead to respiratory failure. Chronic users can develop collapsed veins, infection of the heart lining, abscesses, and liver disease. Street heroin is often mixed with various substances, including sugar, starch, and some poisons that may also have harmful physiological effects. Cocaine use can cause constricted blood vessels, increased temperature, heart rate, and blood pressure. Cocaine that is snorted might also cause permanent damage to the nose lining. Cannabis is associated with respiratory infections, impaired memory, increased heart rate, anxiety, and panic attacks. Regular cannabis smokers might experience the same health problems as regular cigarette smokers including persistent cough, lung infections, and cancer. LSD and other hallucinogens cause changes in perceptions and mood as well as physiological changes. These include elevated heart rate, increased blood pressure, high body temperature, sweating, sleeplessness, dry mouth, and tremors. They also include nausea, blurred vision, dizziness, convulsions, nausea, and vomiting. The main psychological effects are visual and auditory hallucinations, and emotional distress (Office of National Drug Control Policy, 2005).

Mental Health. Research on the health of drug misusers commonly reports much higher rates of mental health problems than found in the general population (Farrell et al., 1998). A study by Weaver et al. (2002) in the United Kingdom found that 75 percent of users of drug services experienced mental health problems. Most had affective disorders (depression) or anxiety disorders. Approximately one-third of the sample experienced comorbidity (co-occurrence of a number of psychiatric disorders or substance misuse problems). Another study of psychological health problems among patients in treatment in the United Kingdom found that one in five drug users had previously received treatment for a psychiatric health problem other than substance misuse (Marsden et al., 2000).

Physical Health. A study by Neale (2004b) on the health of Scottish drug users compared them with the UK general population on general health and found that drug users' health was consistently worse than that of the general population on the majority of measures

used. Brooke et al. (2000) examined differences between prisoners
on remand with substance misuse problems. The research showed that
prisoners with substance misuse problems reported more childhood
adversity, conduct disorder, self-harm, past psychiatric treatment, and
current mood disorder. There is also evidence of drug users contract-
ing infections at a higher rate than the general population. The Health
Protection Agency (2005) in the United Kingdom reported a range
of diseases including abscesses, skin infections, MRSA (Methicillin-
Resistant Staphylococcus Aureus), wound botulism, and tetanus. Gossop et al. (2002) found that the annual mortality rate among users
in treatment in the United Kingdom was about six times higher than
that for a general, age-matched population. Fourteen percent of the
deaths were due to self-inflicted injuries, accidents, or violence, and
18 percent were due to medical causes.

Dependence

One of the most common health effects of drug misuse discussed in
the literature is dependence. Dependence can lead to the continuation and exacerbation of some of the other problems associated with
drug misuse. However, it can also be regarded as a problem in its
own right. It makes desistance from drug use harder and can lead
to drug misuse dominating users' lives. Information provided by a
survey conducted by the Office of National Statistics (ONS) of psychiatric morbidity among 10,000 adults in Great Britain showed that the
lifetime prevalence of dependence in the general population for any
drug was 4 percent (Singleton et al., 2003). Most people who were
classified as dependent said that they were dependent on cannabis (3
percent of the population) and most scored 1 on a 5-point scale of
levels of dependence.

There is also some information on the offender population from
surveys of prisoners. A survey of female prisoners conducted in
2001 included questions on drug use and dependency (Borrill et
al., 2003). The study found that almost half of the women interviewed reported being dependent on at least one drug. The most
common drugs of dependence were heroin (33 percent of inmates)
and crack (24 percent of all inmates). There were strong ethnic

differences with 60 percent of all white inmates dependent on one
or more drugs compared with 29 percent of all black or mixed-race
inmates.

Information on alcohol dependency is more readily available. The
results of the General Household Survey for 2001 showed that 75 percent of men and 59 percent of women had drunk at least one unit of
alcohol in the last week. The report defined safe use (having no significant health risk) as regular consumption of three or four units a day
for men and two or three units a day for women. Using this definition,
it was found that 39 percent of men and 22 percent of women drank
more than the safe limit in the last week, and 21 percent of men and
10 percent of women drank at least twice the safe limit. Information
on alcohol dependence in the general population is available from the
ONS Survey of Psychiatric Morbidity among Adults in Great Britain.
Seven percent of adults were assessed as being dependent on alcohol.
Men were more likely to show signs of dependence than women (12%
compared with 3%) and younger people were more likely to have signs
of dependence than the older groups (24% of all 20- to 24-year-old
males were deemed to be dependent on alcohol compared with 2%
of all 70- to 74-year-old males). However, in most cases the form of
dependence was described as mild (Singleton et al., 2003).

Injection

Many drug users (especially those dependent on heroin) choose to
administer their drugs by intravenous injection – potentially a very
harmful way of administering drugs. It carries various kinds of health
risks to the user, including abscesses, blood clots, blood poisoning,
and the risk of overdose. It also carries various kinds of health risks
to others, including cross-infection when equipment is shared, health
problems relating to the disposal of used syringes, and the spread of
diseases such as the HIV virus.

The prevalence of injecting in the drug user population has been
investigated through the statistics collected as part of the Regional
Drug Misuse Database of clients attending treatment facilities. According to the published statistics, 65 percent of drug users had injected
a drug. Men were more likely than women to have injected a drug,

and older users were more likely than younger users to have injected (Department of Health, 2002a).

Sharing Equipment

One of the major problems with injection is the habitual sharing of syringes. There are a number of reasons users do this, including a shortage of syringes (heavy users might need three or more a day) and the social "nicety" of sharing something that is pleasurable to them. The regular series of surveys conducted by the Department of Health (the Unlinked Anonymous Prevalence Monitoring Program [UAPMP]) based on drug users attending selected agencies in the United Kingdom includes some information on self-reported sharing of injecting equipment. The surveys have shown that the prevalence of sharing needles and syringes increased in the late 1990s, but has remained stable since then with approximately one in three injectors reporting this activity in the last month (Health Protection Agency, 2005). The proportion reporting direct sharing has been found to vary by region and country. The most recent figures (for 2003 and 2004 combined) show that the level of sharing was highest among injectors in Northern Ireland (36%) and lowest in the northwest of England (21%). Data from the Regional Drug Misuse Database in the six months ending March 2001 found that just under half (49%) of users who injected in the last six months had shared their equipment. The study found that women were more likely to share than men, and younger users were more likely to share than older users (Department of Health, 2002a). Hence, the research shows that a notable proportion of injecting drug users (perhaps as much as half) share their needles or syringes.

Infectious Diseases

Another problem of injection is drug-related infectious diseases. The UAPMP of drug users attending agencies in the United Kingdom in 2004 showed that in London 1 in 29 male and 1 in 20 female injecting drug users were HIV infected (Health Protection Agency, 2005). Outside of London, in other parts of the United Kingdom, the rates were much lower (1 in 129 men and 1 in 298 women). Since 1998, the prevalence of HIV infection among injecting drug users has remained stable, which indicates a continuing low rate of HIV transmission through injecting drug use. The UAPMP also provides information on the prevalence of hepatitis B, one of the most prevalent diseases among drug users. The results show that one in three injecting drug users in London in 2004 had hepatitis B (one in three men and one in four women).

Alcohol and Tobacco

Some evidence suggests that the prevalence of alcohol and tobacco use is greater among drug users than among the general population (e.g., Richter et al., 2002; Australian Institute of Health and Welfare [AIHW], 2003). The harmful effects of alcohol and tobacco use are widely known, and drug users can become exposed to the health risks associated with them. The General Household Survey among adults in Great Britain in 2004 (Goddard and Green, 2005) showed that 25 percent of the adult population aged 16 or older, reported current smoking, and 65 percent reported consuming alcohol at least once in the last week. Eight percent of the population could be classified as heavy smokers (defined as 20 or more cigarettes per day) and 30 percent exceeded the daily benchmark for safe alcohol consumption (defined as more than 4 units for men and more than 3 units for women).

Surveys of offender and drug user populations tend to show higher rates of alcohol and tobacco use than surveys of the general population. The ADAM annual report of drug misuse among arrestees in the United States for 2000 showed that 61 percent said they drank alcohol heavily (drinking at least five or more drinks on a single occasion) in the last year and 52 percent said that they drank heavily in the last month (National Institute of Justice [NIJ], 2003). The Survey of Psychiatric Morbidity among Prisoners in England and Wales for 1997 (Singleton et al., 1999) also showed high levels of alcohol use among the offender population. Overall, 63 percent of males sentenced, 58 percent of male remands, 39 percent of females sentenced, and 36 percent of female remands reported hazardous drinking in the year prior to imprisonment (defined as a score of 8 or more on the

Alcohol Use Disorders Identification Test (AUDIT). Tobacco use was also found to be higher in the prison population than among the general population. Overall, 85 percent of the male remand population and 78 percent of the male sentenced population were current smokers. The figures for females were 83 percent and 81 percent, respectively.

High levels of smoking and drinking have also been found among samples of drug users. Figures from the National Drug Strategy Household Survey in Australia, for example, show that 57 percent of cannabis users compared with 18 percent of nonusers had recently used tobacco (AIHW, 2003). Cannabis users were also more likely than nonusers to have recently used alcohol (97% compared with 81%). A similar pattern of results was found when exploring tobacco and alcohol use among amphetamine users and nonusers. High levels of tobacco and alcohol use have also been found among drug users in treatment. Richter et al. (2002), for example, reported that estimates of cigarette smoking among people in drug treatment settings range from 74 percent to 88 percent.

GENERAL HEALTH PROBLEMS

In the remainder of this chapter, we investigate each of the issues discussed above in relation to UK arrestees using the data collected in the New English and Welsh Arrestee Drug Abuse Monitoring (NEW-ADAM) surveys. General health problems were investigated by asking all arrestees if in the last three days they had taken any drugs that had been prescribed by a doctor or purchased over the counter for the treatment of health problems. If they said that they had, they were asked which drugs they had taken and the nature of their health problems.

Table 4.1 shows that just over one-quarter of arrestees (26%) said they had recently taken drugs prescribed by a doctor and just under one-tenth (9%) said that they had consumed drugs that had been purchased over the counter. Arrestees who had reported using heroin or crack in the last 12 months were more likely (33%) than users of other drug types (21%) or no drug types (25%) to have been prescribed a drug by a doctor in the last three days. In contrast, arrestees who had

TABLE 4.1. *Proportion of arrestees reporting being under prescription from a doctor or buying drugs over the counter in the last 3 days by type of drug used in the last 12 months (years 2 and 3)*

	Heroin or crack in the last 12 months % (n)	Other drugs in the last 12 months % (n)	No drugs in the last 12 months % (n)	All arrestees % (n)
Arrestees who were prescribed a drug by a doctor in the last 3 days	33 (351)	21 (215)	25 (150)	26 (716)
Sig. of difference	***			
Arrestees who purchased drugs over the counter in the last 3 days	7 (78)	10 (107)	12 (70)	9 (255)
Sig. of difference	**			
All arrestees % (n)	100 (1,067)	100 (1,040)	100 (609)	100 (2,716)

Notes: Among all interviewed arrestees but excluding Liverpool (n = 210) and Plymouth (n = 209); n = 2,716. Some missing cases.
Chi-square test: *** $p < .001$; ** $p < .01$.

not used drugs in the last 12 months were more likely than those who had to have purchased over-the-counter medication in the last three days.

It is important to know whether these rates are higher than in the general population. The closest comparison that can be obtained is from the General Household Survey for 2004/2005, which asked respondents about visits to their general practitioner (GP) in the last 14 days (compared with 3 days in the NEW-ADAM surveys; Goddard and Green, 2005). The results showed that 14 percent of respondents (11% of males and 16% of females) had visited their GP during the two-week period before the interview. This rate is much lower than among arrestees (14% compared with 26%) over a longer period of time (14 days compared with 3 days). Hence, the results indicate that the arrestees interviewed as part of the NEW-ADAM program were substantially more likely than the general population to have recently visited a GP.

Arrestees were also asked about their reasons for visiting a doctor or purchasing drugs over the counter and the nature of their health problems. These were open-ended responses and have been coded into the response categories listed in Table 4.2. The most common reasons for visiting a GP for prescribed drugs were psychological/psychiatric health problems (32%) and drug-related health problems (30%). The most common drug-related reasons concerned problems associated with heroin addiction (85%) and the most common psychological/psychiatric health problems were depression (20%) and insomnia (9%). In contrast, the most common health problems associated with over-the-counter drug purchases was pain (64%) and the most common reasons for needing pain relief were headaches and migraine (38%). It is also worth noting that some arrestees reported quite severe health problems. Ten percent visited a doctor for some kind of asthma or respiratory problem and 10 percent reported some kind of medical condition including heart/lung problems, high blood pressure, epilepsy, and diabetes.

Typically, arrestees did not elaborate drug-related reasons for seeing a doctor. Instead, they tended to say that it had to do with their addiction or to assist with withdrawal. However, further insight into their health problems can be obtained by looking at the types of

TABLE 4.2. *Proportion of arrestees reporting being under prescription from a doctor or buying drugs over the counter in the last 3 days by type of health problem (years 2 and 3)*

		Prescribed a drug in the last three days, % (*n*)	Purchased drugs over the counter in the last three days, % (*n*)
Drug related	Heroin addiction related	26 (185)	1 (3)
	Other problems	4 (29)	1 (3)
	SUBTOTAL	30 (214)	2 (6)
Psychological/psychiatric	Depression	20 (140)	2 (6)
	Insomnia	9 (61)	2 (6)
	Anxiety	4 (29)	<1 (1)
	Other	5 (33)	<1 (1)
	SUBTOTAL	32 (229)	6 (14)
Infection/inflammation	Chest	1 (5)	0 (0)
	Cough/cold/flu	1 (7)	8 (21)
	Other	4 (26)	5 (12)
	SUBTOTAL	5 (38)	13 (33)
Pain	Recent surgery	<1 (3)	<1 (1)
	Headache/migraine	3 (18)	38 (96)
	Back	3 (22)	4 (10)
	Stomach	3 (18)	4 (10)
	Teeth/mouth	1 (10)	11 (28)
	Arthritis	1 (10)	<1 (1)
	Other	4 (29)	8 (21)
	SUBTOTAL	15 (109)	64 (164)

(continued)

TABLE 4.2 (*continued*)

		Prescribed a drug in the last three days, % (n)	Purchased drugs over the counter in the last three days, % (n)
Allergies	Hay fever	1 (6)	2 (6)
	Asthma	9 (64)	3 (7)
	Other	0 (0)	0 (0)
	SUBTOTAL	10 (70)	5 (13)
Conditions/abnormalities	Heart/lungs	1 (1)	1 (2)
	Kidneys/bladder/bowels	<1 (2)	0 (0)
	Epilepsy	2 (15)	0 (0)
	Diabetes	1 (8)	0 (0)
	Hypertension	2 (11)	0 (0)
	Other	4 (27)	1 (3)
	SUBTOTAL	10 (71)	2 (6)
Injury	Back	1 (4)	0 (0)
	Head	<1 (3)	0 (0)
	Other	4 (27)	2 (6)
	SUBTOTAL	5 (34)	2 (6)
Other problem	Other	<1 (1)	2 (6)
Not stated		3 (20)	5 (13)
All problems, n		716	255

Notes: Among arrestees who had been prescribed a drug and/or purchased over-the-counter drugs in the last three days (excluding Liverpool [$n = 210$] and Plymouth [$n = 209$]; $n = 886$). Totals do not add to 100% because multiple responses were possible. Of the total sample, 108 arrestees reported receiving a prescription in relation to more than one health problem. Eight arrestees reported purchasing drugs over the counter in relation to more than one health problem.

drugs prescribed for drug-related problems. The most common drug prescribed to this group of arrestees was a heroin substitute (81%), including methadone. Heroin substitutes are prescribed by doctors either for maintenance (to stabilize addiction and its problems) or as part of a withdrawal program. The next most common drug type prescribed to arrestees with drug-related health problems was some kind of tranquilizer (44%). These are typically prescribed to drug users for anxiety or to assist in sleeping. The third most common drug type was antidepressants (5%).

It is also possible that some of the other reasons given for seeing a doctor concern health problems related to drug misuse. Some health problems such as asthma, headaches, anxiety, depression, and stomach problems can also be a product of drug-taking. Hence, the proportion of arrestees visiting a doctor for drug-related reasons is possibly an underestimate of that shown.

DEPENDENCE

One of the many problems associated with drug misuse is drug dependence. Drug dependence might be regarded as a problem in its own right because it serves to perpetuate drug use and the problems associated with it. In fact, dependent users are commonly defined as problem drug users, and it is widely believed that such users are the main sources of the common problem behaviors associated with drug misuse, such as health and crime. In a medical sense, dependence refers to the development of a tolerance for a drug that results in withdrawal symptoms when the drug is removed. In the current chapter, the word 'dependence' is used more broadly to include psychological as well as physical dependence. The extent of drug dependence was investigated by asking arrestees who admitted taking any drug whether they thought they were currently dependent on the drug.

Prevalence of Dependence

Arrestees who said that they had used one or more illicit drugs in their lifetime were asked whether they had ever or recently been dependent on those drugs. Arrestees were asked 'Have you recently felt that you needed [the drug] or felt bad or ill when you did not have [the drug]?"

Using this definition, 35 percent of all interviewed arrestees said that they were dependent on one or more drug. The three drugs most frequently associated with dependence were tobacco (64%), heroin (23%), and cannabis (10%). Interestingly, only 6% of arrestees said that they were dependent on crack and only 1% said that they were dependent on cocaine. The drugs least frequently associated with dependence were LSD, amphetamines, and ecstasy (1%).

The proportion of dependent arrestees varied substantially across the 16 survey locations. The highest rate was shown for Middlesbrough (51% currently dependent) and the lowest rate was Southampton (16% currently dependent). There was no clear pattern to the variations in dependency across locations in terms of size or geographic location. However, there was a clear link between dependence and prevalence of consumption of drugs commonly associated with dependence. The highest rate of positive tests for any opiates was in Middlesbrough (57%), the site with the highest rate of dependency, and the lowest rate was in Southampton (13%), the site with the lowest rate of dependency.

It is possible that drug users are dependent on more than one drug type. This was analyzed by looking at reported dependence on each of the 19 illicit drug types investigated in the NEW-ADAM questionnaire. Twenty-three percent of arrestees said that they were dependent on one drug type. However, 8 percent said that they were dependent on two drugs and 3 percent said that they were dependent on four drugs. In total, 12 percent of the sample were dependent on two or more drug types. Hence, 12 percent of the sample could be defined as having multiple-drug dependency. The highest percentage of multiple-drug dependency was in Newport, where 18 percent of all arrestees said that they were dependent on two or more drugs.

Changes in Dependence Over Time
Changes in the prevalence of dependency over time are shown in Table 4.3. Trend data was obtained by comparing the eight sites that were surveyed in Year 1 (1999) and in Year 3 (2001). In both years, just under one-third of arrestees said that they were currently dependent on any drug.

TABLE 4.3. *Current dependency on selected drug types over time among users of that drug type (years 1 and 3)*

Drug type	Year 1, % (n) (n = 1,510)	Year 3, % (n) (n = 1,554)	Total, % (n) (n = 3,064)	Significance of difference
Amphetamines	9 (43)	4 (13)	7 (56)	*
Cannabis	15 (155)	17 (167)	16 (322)	ns
Cocaine	4 (16)	3 (12)	3 (28)	ns
Crack	12 (45)	19 (83)	15 (128)	**
Ecstasy	2 (8)	2 (7)	2 (15)	ns
Heroin	61 (253)	69 (303)	65 (556)	*
Methadone	24 (60)	22 (45)	23 (105)	ns
Temazepam	9 (28)	8 (22)	9 (50)	ns
Diazepam	17 (60)	14 (49)	15 (109)	ns
Tobacco	72 (956)	71 (944)	71 (1,900)	ns
Alcohol	10 (138)	9 (122)	10 (260)	ns
Any drug	40 (477)	42 (488)	41 (965)	ns

Note. Among users of the specified drug type in the last 12 months.
Chi-square test: ** $p < .01$; * $p < .05$; ns = not significant.

The table shows the proportion of arrestees reporting dependence among those who said that they used a particular drug in the last 12 months. There were three significant changes over time in the prevalence of drug dependence. Dependence on amphetamines among amphetamine users decreased from Year 1 to Year 3 from 9 percent to 4 percent. However, dependence on crack and heroin both increased over this period from 12 percent to 19 percent in relation to crack and from 61 percent to 69 percent in relation to heroin. Hence, the increases in use of these drugs shown in the previous chapter were matched by an increase in dependence on these drugs. This suggests that new users of these drugs are becoming addicted more quickly than users in the past.

Dependence on one or more drugs is sometimes used as a measure of problem drug use (Hough, 1996). Using this definition all arrestees were categorized as problem drug users, non-problem drug users, and non-drug users. A breakdown of the characteristics of these three groups is shown in Table 4.4. There are significant differences between the three groups of arrestees on each of the variables analyzed. Problem drug users were more likely than non-problem users and non-drug users to be female, aged 20 to 29, white, to have left school before age 17, and to have been in receipt of social security benefits in the last 12 months. Furthermore, problem drug users reported generating less legal income and more illegal income than non-problem users and nonusers. In fact, problem drug users reported a mean annual illegal income that was nearly 10 times higher than the mean illegal income reported by non-drug users (approximately £13,790 compared with £1,420).

INJECTION

One of the aims of the United Kingdom's drugs strategy is to reduce the number of drug users who inject and to reduce the number of injectors who share their equipment. Injection is potentially the most harmful way to administer drugs. It carries various kinds of health risks to the user (such as infection, abscesses, and risk of overdose) and various kinds of health risks to others (such as cross-infection when equipment is shared and health problems relating to disposal of

TABLE 4.4. *Characteristics of problem drug users, non-problem drug users, and non-drug users (years 2 and 3)*

	Problem drug users,[a] % (n)	Non-problem drug users,[b] % (n)	Non-drug users,[c] % (n)	All arrestees, % (n)
Sex				
Male	82 (884)	90 (1,224)	83 (574)	86 (2,682)
Female	19 (201)	10 (134)	17 (118)	14 (453)
Significance			***	
Age group				
17–19	17 (181)	30 (408)	20 (137)	23 (726)
20–24	30 (328)	28 (373)	17 (120)	26 (821)
25–29	23 (253)	16 (222)	15 (105)	19 (580)
30+	30 (323)	26 (355)	48 (330)	32 (1,008)
Significance			***	
Ethnic group				
White	85 (926)	78 (1,051)	73 (502)	79 (2,479)
Nonwhite	15 (159)	23 (306)	28 (190)	21 (655)
Significance			***	
Age left full-time education				
16 or under	88 (936)	77 (1,025)	65 (436)	78 (2,397)
17 or over	12 (125)	23 (309)	35 (239)	22 (673)
Significance			***	

(continued)

TABLE 4.4 (continued)

	Problem drug users,[a] % (n)	Non-problem drug users,[b] % (n)	Non-drug users,[c] % (n)	All arrestees, % (n)
On social security				
Yes	76 (825)	50 (684)	38 (263)	57 (1,772)
No	24 (260)	50 (674)	62 (429)	44 (1,363)
Significance			***	
Legal income[d]				
Mean (last 12 months)	£3,240	£5,979	£7,628	£5,394
Significance			***	
Illegal income[d]				
Mean (last 12 months)	£13,790	£4,042	£1,420	£6,821
Significance			***?	
TOTAL (n)	1,085	1,358	692	3,135

Note. Among all interviewed arrestees (n = 3,135).
[a]Problem drug users are arrestees who reported being recently dependent on one or more illicit drug type.
[b]Non-problem drug users are arrestees who said that they had used one or more illicit drugs in the last 12 months but reported that they had not been recently dependent on any of those drugs.
[c]Non-drug users are arrestees who said that they had not used any illicit drugs in the last 12 months.
[d]Outliers controlled by recoding the top 5 percent of responses to the next highest value. Some missing cases.
Chi-square test: *** p < .001.

used syringes). Injection also might escalate addiction and drug use as a result of the potential for increased perceived benefits on the part of the drug user and the possibility of consuming larger amounts of the drug than normal and more quickly.

Prevalence and Incidence of Injection

The prevalence of injection among all arrestees is shown in Table 4.5. About one-quarter (26%) of arrestees said that they had injected an illegal drug at some time in the lives, and one-fifth (20%) said that they had done so in the last 12 months. Seventeen percent had injected in the last 30 days, and 15 percent had injected in the last three days. The most frequently injected drug in the last 12 months was heroin (19% of arrestees had injected it) followed by crack (5%) and amphetamines (4%). The prevalence of injection can also be investigated in relation to users of specific drug types. The highest proportion of injectors among users of a particular drug was in relation to users of heroin. In total, 57 percent of heroin users injected it in the last year. This compares with 15 percent of crack users who injected crack and 18 percent of amphetamine users who injected amphetamines.

The incidence or rate of injection was measured by asking arrestees about the number of times that they had injected drugs in the last 30 days. This showed that the incidence of injection was highest among heroin injectors, who injected on average 24 of the last 30 days and among crack injectors, who injected on average 16 of the last 30 days. Amphetamine, methadone, and cocaine injectors injected about once every three days. These results can also be expressed in terms of the proportion of high-rate injectors (measured as those who injected 15 or more days in the last 30 days). This shows that more than three-quarters (80%) of injectors of heroin and over half (54%) of crack injectors could be classified as high-rate injectors.

Changes in Injecting Over Time

It is possible to use the results of the repeat surveys in Years 1 and 3 to determine the extent to which the practice of injecting drugs has increased or decreased over time. These show that the prevalence of

TABLE 4.5. *Proportion of arrestees who reported injecting selected drug types over various periods of time (years 2 and 3)*

Drug type	Ever injected, % (n)	Injected in last 12 months, % (n)	Injected in last 30 days, % (n)	Injected in last 3 days, % (n)
Heroin	23 (714)	19 (582)	15 (479)	14 (436)
Methadone	2 (66)	1 (21)	<1 (10)	<1 (3)
Cocaine	7 (206)	3 (85)	1 (43)	1 (20)
Crack	7 (210)	5 (144)	3 (96)	2 (59)
Amphetamines	13 (403)	4 (110)	2 (58)	1 (29)
Any drug (14 types)	26 (825)	20 (637)	17 (519)	15 (466)

Note. Among all interviewed arrestees (*n* = 3,135).

78

injection of any drug remained fairly constant over time at just under 20 percent (18% in Year 1 and 16% in Year 3). The only significant change was in relation to injecting amphetamines, which decreased from 8 percent of all arrestees interviewed in Year 1 to 3 percent of arrestees interviewed in Year 3. This in part was a result of a general reduction in amphetamine use. However, looking at changes in the prevalence of injection among amphetamine users only also shows a reduction from 24 percent of amphetamine users in Year 1 compared with 14 percent of amphetamine users in Year 3). Hence, not only did amphetamine use decrease among arrestees during the three-year period of the research, the prevalence of injecting the drug decreased as well.

SHARING EQUIPMENT

One of the main problems associated with injection as a method of administration is that users might share equipment. This is done not only out of convenience when injecting equipment is in short supply but also as a social activity as part of the culture of drug use. We asked all arrestees who had injected a drug at any time whether they had shared the equipment (including lending and borrowing). Overall, 8 percent of all arrestees interviewed said that they had shared syringes or needles at some time in their lives, and 5 percent said that they had done so in the last 12 months. Among arrestees who reported injecting drugs, almost one-third (30%) had shared their equipment at some time in their lives, and nearly one-quarter (24%) had done so in the last 12 months. These results are troubling in that they show a notable minority of drug users injects their drugs and a notable minority of those individuals share their needles or other pieces of drug-using equipment.

INFECTIOUS DISEASES

It has been shown that drug-dependent arrestees are at a greater risk of poor health and disease than non-drug-dependent arrestees. This might be as a result of injecting or sharing equipment or as a result of a general lifestyle that prioritizes drug misuse. All arrestees were asked whether they believed that they were HIV positive or had hepatitis. Those who said they had these diseases were asked whether they had been confirmed by testing.

Just over 1 percent of all arrestees thought that they were HIV positive (2% of heroin users and 2% of crack users) and three percent of the sample thought that they currently had Hepatitis (8% of heroin users and 7% of crack users). Injectors in the last 12 months were significantly more likely than noninjectors to say that they were HIV positive (3% compared with 1%). This rate is similar to that reported earlier in the UAPMP study showing that 3 percent injecting drug users in London were HIV positive (Department of Health, 2002). However, it is much higher than the rate shown for injecting drug users outside London. Injectors in the last 12 months were also significantly more likely than noninjectors to say that they had hepatitis (11% compared with 1%). Injectors who shared were as likely as those who did not share to say that they were HIV positive (3% for each) and significantly more likely to say that they had hepatitis (18% compared with 9%).

There was some variation across areas. In 7 of the 16 areas (Southampton, Wolverhampton, Bethnal Green, Hammersmith, Middlesbrough, Nottingham, and Brixton), there were no reports of HIV infection, whereas in 4 of the 16 areas (Bournemouth, Leeds, Liverpool, and London, Colindale), more than 5 percent of arrestees reported that they were HIV positive.

ALCOHOL AND TOBACCO

Use of alcohol and tobacco can have a further detrimental effect on the health of drug users. Drug users become exposed to all of the health risks associated with these products, including respiratory disease in relation to tobacco use and liver damage and stomach problems in relation to alcohol. In addition, some evidence shows that drug users are more likely to use alcohol and tobacco than the general population and to do so at a higher rate (e.g., AIHW, 2003; Richter et al., 2002).

All arrestees were asked if they had used alcohol and tobacco in the last 30 days and in the last 7 days. Overall, 61 percent of arrestees reported having used alcohol in the last 7 days (Table 4.6). The mean

TABLE 4.6. *Drug use in the last 30 days by type of alcohol use in the last 30 days (years 2 and 3)*

Drug use in last 30 days	No alcohol use, % (n)	Low rate alcohol use, % (n)	High rate alcohol use, % (n)	All arrestees, % (n)	Significance of difference
Heroin	51 (383)	22 (374)	20 (134)	28 (891)	***
Methadone	17 (127)	7 (110)	8 (52)	9 (289)	***
Cocaine	11 (84)	11 (193)	19 (127)	13 (404)	***
Crack	37 (279)	18 (303)	20 (137)	23 (719)	***
Amphetamines	7 (52)	8 (127)	14 (98)	9 (277)	***
Ecstasy	6 (43)	13 (224)	23 (153)	13 (420)	***
Cannabis	53 (401)	59 (1,006)	65 (438)	59 (1,845)	***
Any drug	76 (575)	69 (1,162)	75 (507)	72 (2,244)	***
All alcohol users	100 (759)	100 (1,697)	100 (679)	100 (3,135)	

Notes. Among all arrestees (*n* = 3,135). High rate use = 15+ days in the last 30 days. Low rate use = 1–14 days in the last 30 days.
Chi-square test: *** *p* < .001.

number of days that alcohol was used was 3.2 days, and the mean number of units consumed was 20 units per day. Given that the recommended weekly intake is 21 units for men and 14 units for women, it is evident that these arrestees were drinking in excess of these recommended amounts. This in itself can increase the risk of alcohol-related health problems. Most of the arrestees who had consumed alcohol in the last week reported having consumed beers and lagers (76%).

The majority of arrestees interviewed (80%) had smoked tobacco in the last week. On average, users reported smoking 30 cigarettes per day (or 0.4 ounces of tobacco). These rates are much higher than the national average (see earlier in this chapter) and increase the risk of smoking-related health problems.

It might be thought that users of more addictive drugs would consume alcohol at a higher rate than users of less addictive drugs. For example, it might be hypothesized that those who use one type of drug addictively will use other types of drugs in the same way. In fact, the findings do not support this view. High-rate alcohol users (those who have used alcohol on 15 or more days in the last 30 days) were less likely than nonusers to have consumed heroin, methadone, or crack in the last 30 days. By contrast, high-rate alcohol users were more likely than nonusers to have used "recreational" drugs such as cocaine powder, amphetamines, ecstasy, and cannabis.

DISCUSSION

It is widely known that drug use is associated with a range of personal, economic, and social problems. This chapter has investigated the extent to which drug-misusing arrestees experience health problems. It was argued that health problems are important not only for the drug user but also for the wider community. They are important to the drug users because of the serious nature of some drug-related diseases as well as the risk of overdose and death. They are important to others who come into contact with drug users, such as the police, who risk infection or direct contamination from used syringes. They are also important to society generally through the burden that drug users can place on emergency and treatment services.

The NEW-ADAM surveys aimed to investigate the issue of the prevalence and nature of health problems experienced by drug-misusing arrestees. The research has shown that arrestees are more likely to have health problems than the general population. More than one-quarter of all arrestees had visited a doctor in the three days before interview, and one-tenth had bought over-the-counter drugs. One in three reported heroin users had visited a GP in the last three days. Although the reasons for visiting a doctor were often drug-related, almost one-third visited a GP for psychological or psychiatric problems. One-third of all arrestees were dependent on one or more drugs. About one-quarter of arrestees had injected an illegal drug at some time in their lives, and more than half of heroin users had injected the drug in the last year. On average, one-third of arrestees who had injected drugs had shared their equipment with others at some time in their lives, and one-quarter had done so in the last year. About 1 percent of all arrestees said that they were HIV positive. This increased to 2 percent of heroin users and 3 percent of injectors.

The main research implication of these findings is that more research needs to be done on high-risk populations such as offenders. The health problems of drug-misusing arrestees are likely to be affected by the risk factors associated with being both a drug user and an offender.

The main policy implications concern the fact that arrestees can enter the first stage of processing in the criminal justice system with a wide range of health problems including drug dependency, infectious diseases, psychiatric problems, and physical ailments. The problems of offender health are already known to the police, and the prison services and facilities are already in place for monitoring these. However, the criminal justice system currently addresses only some of these problems in relation to some offenders. Offenders not convicted or those convicted and given community sentences are unlikely to experience the same level of health monitoring as those given a custodial sentence. This means that arrestees can be released back into the community with a wide range of drug-related health problems. These problems might be addressed by the user by unconventional means, such as self-medication from illegal drug purchases or pharmacy theft. They also include bullying general practitioners and antisocial behavior in doctors' surgeries. Alternatively, the problems might remain unaddressed and lead to further infections and spread of disease.

PART THREE

DRUG-CRIME AFFINITIES

CHAPTER FIVE

Drugs and Crime

INTRODUCTION

It is widely believed that drug use causes crime. The current UK drugs policy is based on this assumption and one of the aims of the strategy is to reduce crime by reducing the availability of drugs (Home Office, 2002). However, it is not wholly certain that there is a connection. Although many studies have shown a link between drug use and crime, many others have not. There have also been few systematic reviews of the literature as a whole which might help unravel these different findings. It is possible that drugs and crime are connected under certain conditions and not under others. The data collected as part of the New English and Welsh Arrestee Drug Abuse Monitoring (NEW-ADAM) program adds to this body of knowledge on the links between drug use and crime. In particular, it provides an opportunity to investigate variations in the association and some of the conditions that might affect it.

PREVIOUS RESEARCH

A considerable body of research has attempted to establish whether there is a statistical connection between drug use and crime. The association has been investigated in part by looking at samples of criminals to determine their level of drug use and, in part, at samples of drug users to determine their level of criminality. The following section summarizes selected research findings from different countries and a brief overview of some reviews of the literature.

Previous Studies

In a study conducted in the United States, Johnson et al. (1994) conducted interviews with more than 1,000 drug abusers. The authors found some differences between the user types. Crack users were found to be more likely than non–drug users to have committed shoplifting (21% compared with 9%) and handling offenses (20% compared with 5%) in the last year. Cocaine users were no more likely than non–drug users to report shoplifting offenses (10% compared with 9%).

In the United Kingdom, Best et al. (2001b) conducted a study that investigated the criminal behavior and drug use of 100 new entrants to a drug treatment service in London. The results show that the rate of offending was significantly higher among crack users than nonusers. The total number of acquisitive crimes committed in the last month was 41 among crack users compared with 13 among nonusers. The amount of illegal income derived from shoplifting was also significantly higher among crack users (£777) than nonusers (£229).

In a study of drug users in Greece, Kokkevi et al. (1993) found that arrest and conviction rates were higher among drug users than among a control sample of nonusers. Two-thirds of drug users reported at least two arrests in the last year compared with 15 percent of controls.

In Finland, Turpeinen (2001) used a sample of 119 drug-experimenting school children to investigate the association between intravenous drug use and offending. The results showed that subjects who had used opiates intravenously were significantly more likely than those who had not to have been in prison in the 20-year follow-up period. The same was also true for subjects who had used amphetamines intravenously during adolescence.

In a study in Spain, Morentin et al. (1998) conducted interviews with 578 police detainees. Just over half of the subjects were diagnosed as having heroin dependence. Heroin-dependent subjects had a significantly higher mean offense rate (1.8 offenses compared with 1.1) than nonusers. Heroin users committed more burglary offenses (1.1 compared with 0.2) and more robbery offenses (0.2 compared with 0.1). By contrast, there was no significant difference between the groups in terms of the rate of drug distribution offenses or theft offenses.

In Australia, Makkai and Feather (1999) used data from the Drug Use Monitoring in Australia (DUMA) program to explore the relationship between drug use and offending among arrestees. The prevalence of property offending was substantially higher among arrestees who tested positive for opiates than among those who tested negative (64% compared with 25%). By contrast, there was little difference between the two groups in terms of those charged with drug offenses (10% compared with 12%).

Hence, this brief review of selected studies shows that there are some differences across studies in the nature of the relationship. In particular, there are variations in results by type of drug used and type of offense committed.

Previous Reviews of the Literature

It is not possible to assess the results of the entire body of research on the drug-crime connection by looking at selected studies. The closest that we can get to this is to look at the results of reviews of the literature. As far as we know, there have only been two previous systematic reviews of the literature on the relationship between drug use and crime: one by Derzon and Lipsey (1999) on the relationship between marijuana use and juvenile delinquency and the other by Bennett, Holloway, and Farrington (in press) on the relationship between illicit drug use and property crime.

The review by Derzon and Lipsey (1999) used meta-analytic techniques to summarize the findings of research on the relationship between marijuana use and various problem behaviors, including delinquency. The review was based on 63 reports summarizing 30 independent studies. The research found a positive and significant correlation between marijuana use and various measures of delinquency, including aggressive behavior, property offending, and crimes against the person. However, the authors concluded that the strength of the relationship was not large with the majority of the mean correlations being less than 0.3. The review by Bennett, Holloway, and Farrington (in press) included a meta-analysis of the results of 30 studies that presented findings on the relationship between measures of drug use and measures of crime. The results showed that the odds of offending were about three to four times greater for drug users than non–drug users. The odds of offending were highest among crack users and lowest among users of 'recreational' drugs. Overall, the report concluded that the research showed a connection between drug use and crime. However, the relationship varied widely depending on the kinds of drug use and kinds of crime measured.

There have been a larger number of general reviews of the literature. One of the earliest was by Gandossy, Williams, Cohen, and Harwood (1980) who conducted a comprehensive survey of the English language research literature, covering studies from America, Australia, Canada, and Europe. The review focused mainly on the association between heroin use and crime, although the relationship between other drugs and crime was also considered. The authors found a strong correlation between drug addiction and reported criminal behavior and noted, 'it was difficult to avoid concluding that addicts engage in substantial amounts of income-generating crimes. This is true when analyzing the charges against drug-using arrestees, convictions of addicts in prisons, arrest records of treatment populations, or the observations of street addicts' (Gandossy et al., 1980, p. 52).

Chaiken and Chaiken (1990) reviewed the literature on the relationship between drug use and predatory crime (i.e., instrumental offenses committed for material gain). Their review found no evidence of a general association between drug use and participation in crime and no association between drug use and onset or persistence in criminality. They concluded that when behaviors of large groups of people were studied in aggregate, there was no coherent association between drug misuse and predatory crime. They also concluded that, for the majority of drug types other than heroin and cocaine, drug use was unrelated to the commission of crimes. The only consistent evidence of an association between drug use and predatory crime was that offenders who were daily users of heroin or cocaine and those who used multiple types of drugs committed crimes at significantly higher rates than did the less drug-involved offenders (Chaiken and Chaiken, 1990).

Hough (1996) conducted a review of British research investigating the drug-crime connection. This covered studies based on drug-user populations and offender populations and studies that estimated the proportion of crimes committed to finance drug use. He concluded that 'current knowledge about the volume and cost of drug-related crime is so patchy that all we can say with certainty is that problem drug misuse is responsible for a significant minority of crime in England and Wales' (Hough, 1996, p. 19).

These studies show some variation in the conclusions drawn. Although many studies show a relationship between drugs and crime, many others do not. There are two main reasons why reviews might arrive at different conclusions. They might vary in the studies selected for review. They might also vary in the way in which the authors weigh up and summarize the results.

EXPLANATIONS

Drugs and crime might be connected in a number of ways. These are sometimes referred to as causal models. Some of the most common causal models are the following: (1) the 'drug-use-causes-crime' model, (2) the 'crime-causes-drug-use' model, (3) the 'reciprocal' model, (4) the 'common-cause' model, and (5) the 'coincidence' model. The first two models (drug-use-causes-crime and crime-causes-drug-use) are the most straightforward. The relationship between the two might be direct or indirect. A direct relationship is one in which drug use leads directly to crime or crime leads directly to drug use with no intervening variables. An indirect relationship is one in which drug use leads to crime through an intervening variable. The third model (the reciprocal model), a more complex model, is based on the idea that drug use sometimes causes crime and crime sometimes causes drug use. This model presumes that the relationship between drug use and crime is bidirectional. Menard et al. (2001) argue that drug use and crime are causally linked and mutually reinforcing. Illegal behavior might lead to the initiation of drug use and serious drug use might lead to the continuity of illegal behavior. The fourth model (the common-cause model) proposes that drug use does not cause crime nor does crime cause drug use. Instead, they are both caused by a third or common variable. The fifth model (the coincidence model) could be described as a spuriousness model. This model purports that drug use and crime are not causally connected. Instead, they exist within a nexus of correlated variables and problematic behaviors.

MEASURES OF DRUG USE

One method of measuring recent drug use in the NEW-ADAM program was through urinalysis. The use of urinalysis to measure the prevalence of drug use is sometimes regarded as a more objective and more accurate measure than self-report measures. The specimens collected were tested for seven types of drugs: cannabinoid metabolite, opiates, methadone, cocaine metabolite, amphetamines, benzodiazepines, and alcohol. The results were returned for each specimen stating whether each of the seven tests was either positive (the drug was detected) or negative (the drug was not detected). A second method of measuring drug use was through self-reports. All arrestees were asked about their illegal drug use in their lifetime, in the last 12 months, in the last month, and in the last three days. The respondents were asked about the use of 19 types of drugs which are commonly used illegally, plus alcohol and tobacco.

MEASURES OF CRIME

The main measure of criminal behavior was self-report as part of the main interview. All arrestees were asked whether they had committed each of 11 common acquisitive crimes in the whole of their lifetime and over the last 12 months. All arrestees were asked to estimate their total illegal income over the last 12 months. Illegal income is a broader concept than acquisitive crime and covers a variety of ways in which arrestees might obtain income in cash or kind in addition to the normal legal routes of employment or state benefits. Some property crimes (such as joyriding or unsuccessful property offenses) do not generate illegal income, either in cash or in kind. Some forms of illegal income (such as undeclared earnings or prostitution) are not normally thought of as property crimes.

PREVALENCE AND INCIDENCE

In the following analysis, drug use is investigated using the concepts of prevalence and incidence. The prevalence of drug use or offending is used to refer to the proportion of the sample that was involved in certain kinds of behavior. The prevalence of drug use refers to the proportion of the sample that tested positive for, or reported use of, one or more drug types or certain kinds of drug types. The prevalence of crime refers to the proportion that committed one or more crimes or certain types of crimes over the last 12 months. The incidence of drug use or offending refers to the rate of these behaviors among those who reported being involved in them. The incidence of drug use refers to the number of positive tests or reported rate of drug use in the last 30 days. The incidence of crime refers to the number of offenses reported as being committed in the last 12 months.

The distinction between prevalence and incidence is important in assessing the drug-crime connection. However, the issue of potential differences in findings relating to prevalence and incidence is discussed only infrequently in the research literature. As a result, there is a danger that findings relating to prevalence and incidence might be confused. It is possible, for example, that the prevalence of drug use is associated with the prevalence of crime (those who use one or more drugs tend also to report committing one or more crimes), but the incidence of drug use is not associated with the incidence of crime (those who use drugs at a high rate do not necessarily commit crimes at a high rate). The former might be used to show that there is a drug-crime connection, and the latter might be used to show that there is not. To understand the association between drug use and crime, it is useful to know the connection between both prevalence and incidence.

Prevalence of Drug Use Versus Prevalence of Crime

In this section, we look at the relationship between prevalence of drug use and prevalence of crime. In other words, it considers whether there is an association between taking drugs and committing crimes. Specifically, the section aims to establish whether arrestees who use certain drugs are more likely than those who do not to report recent offending. The prevalence of drug use is measured using both urinalysis covering recent drug use and self-reports of drug use in the last 12 months. The prevalence of crime is measured by using self reports of 10 selected property offenses over the last 12 months.

Urinalysis. The urinalysis results show the association between drug use and crime by comparing offending among arrestees testing positive for drugs and those testing negative. Table 5.1 shows that arrestees who tested positive for one or more drugs were significantly more likely than those who did not, to report committing 1 of the 10 selected offenses types in the last 12 months (64% compared with 29%). The relationship was almost as strong for 'recreational' drug users as users of opiates, cocaine, or methadone. Sixty-one percent of arrestees who tested positive for cannabis and 75 percent of those testing positive for benzodiazepines reported offending in the last 12 months. The proportion reporting offending was lower among those testing positive for amphetamines (53%). The highest percentage involvement in offending was among those testing positive for opiates (79%) and those testing positive for methadone (80%). Overall, the results indicate that arrestees testing positive for any drug are more likely than those who do not, to report offending in the last 12 months.–>

Self-Report. Similar results were obtained when looking at self-reported drug use in the last 12 months and self-reported offending (see Table 5.2). Just over sixty percent of cannabis users reported offending compared with 16 percent of non–drug users. The highest prevalence rates of offending were among heroin, crack, and methadone users (all over 80%). Interestingly, cocaine users were slightly less likely than heroin or crack users to report offending in the last 12 months (70% reported one or more offenses). Hence, the results of the two methods show similar findings that drug users are more likely than non–drug users (of all or specific drug types) to report recent offending.

Prevalence of Drug Use Versus Incidence of Crime

The prevalence of drug use was measured using both urinalysis covering recent drug use and self-reports of drug use in the last 12 months. The incidence of crime was measured by using self-reports of offending over the last 12 months.

TABLE 5.1. *Proportion of arrestees reporting one or more income-generating offenses in the last 12 months by urinalysis results (years 2 and 3)*

Drug type	Offended in the last 12 months, % (n)	Not offended in the last 12 months, % (n)	All arrestees, % (n)	Sig. of difference
Cannabis	61 (819)	39 (533)	100 (1,352)	***
Amphetamines	53 (89)	47 (80)	100 (169)	ns
Benzodiazepines	75 (323)	25 (109)	100 (432)	***
Opiates	79 (722)	22 (198)	100 (920)	***
Cocaine	73 (532)	27 (199)	100 (731)	***
Methadone	80 (150)	20 (37)	100 (187)	***
Any drug	64 (1,242)	37 (715)	100 (1,957)	***
Multiple drugs[a]	73 (814)	27 (301)	100 (1,115)	***
No drugs	29 (250)	71 (625)	100 (875)	***
All arrestees	53 (1,492)	47 (1,340)	100 (2,832)	

Notes: Includes arrestees who provided a urine specimen (n = 2,833). One missing case.
Chi-square test: *** p < .001, ns = not significant.
[a]Multiple drugs = positive tests for two or more drug types.

TABLE 5.2. *Proportion of arrestees reporting one or more income-generating offenses in the last 12 months by self-report use of selected drug types (years 2 and 3)*

Drug type	Offended in the last 12 months, % (n)	Not offended in the 12 months, % (n)	All arrestees, % (n)	Sig. of difference, % (n)
Cannabis	62 (1,304)	38 (808)	100 (2,112)	***
Amphetamines	68 (412)	32 (191)	100 (603)	***
Ecstasy	66 (562)	34 (295)	100 (857)	***
Heroin	82 (828)	18 (187)	100 (1,015)	***
Crack	82 (785)	18 (171)	100 (956)	***
Cocaine	70 (566)	30 (243)	100 (809)	***
Methadone	84 (400)	16 (78)	100 (478)	***
Cannabis only	37 (180)	63 (301)	100 (481)	***
Any drug[a]	61 (1,496)	39 (945)	100 (2,441)	***
No drug	16 (109)	84 (583)	100 (692)	
All arrestees	51 (1,605)	49 (1,528)	100 (3,133)	

Notes: Includes all arrestees (*n* = 3,135). Two missing cases.
Chi-square test: *** *p* < .001.
[a] Any of 19 illicit drug types.

96

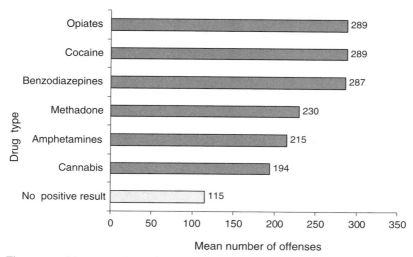

Figure 5.1 Mean number of offenses committed in the last 12 months by drug test results. *Notes*: Includes all arrestees who reported committing an acquisitive crime in the last 12 months (excluding prostitution) who provided a urine specimen ($n = 1,492$). Five missing cases. Outliers were controlled by recoding the top 5 percent of responses (to the 94.9% value of 1,177). This equates to a mean maximum rate of approximately three offenses per day every day for 365 days.

Urinalysis. The urinalysis results can be used to determine the association between drug use and crime by comparing offending among arrestees testing positive for drugs and those testing negative. Figure 5.1 shows that arrestees who tested positive for any of the six illicit drug types (opiates, cocaine, amphetamines, benzodiazepines, methadone, and cannabis) offended at significantly higher rates than those who tested positive for no illicit drug types. The highest rate of offending was among arrestees who tested positive for opiates or cocaine (an average of 289 offenses in the last 12 months). Those testing positive for cannabis also offended at significantly higher rates (194 offenses) than those who tested positive for no illegal drugs (115 offenses). Those who tested positive solely for cannabis reported much lower rates of offending (88 offenses) than those who tested positive for no illegal drugs (115 offenses).

Self-Report. A similar analysis was conducted using self-reported drug use in the last 12 months as the measure of substance misuse. The mean number of offenses committed among users of different types of drugs is shown in Table 5.3. Overall, arrestees who said that they had used 1 or more of the 19 drug types reported a significantly higher mean offending rate (an average of 211 offenses) than those who said that they had not used drugs (93 offenses). The highest offending rates were reported among users of heroin, crack, cocaine, and methadone (ranging from an average of 258 to 307 offenses). Heroin, crack, or cocaine users as a group reported a significantly higher number of offenses (251) than either nonusers (93) or users of cannabis only (88).

Hence, the results of these two methods of measuring drug misuse are very similar. They both show that drug users committed more crimes than non–drug users and that the highest rates of offending were among users of opiates (including heroin) and cocaine (including crack).

Incidence in Drug Use versus Prevalence of Crime

The foregoing analysis has shown a correlation between whether certain drugs were used and the prevalence or rate of offending. However, it has not yet been determined whether rate of drug use is associated with offending. It is possible that only high-rate users of drugs report offending whereas low-rate users do not. To test this hypothesis, the incidence of drug use and the prevalence of crime were compared using both urinalysis and self-report measures of drug use.

Urinalysis. Strictly speaking, it is not possible to determine the rate of drug use from urinalysis results because the test is designed only to determine the presence or absence of a drug. However, an alternative measure of incidence can be created by looking at the number of positive tests. This is a measure of multiple drug use rather than high-rate use. Nevertheless, they both suggest a high level of involvement in drug use. Hence, the association between the incidence of drug use and prevalence of crime can be examined by comparing the mean number of positive tests and whether or not the users reported offending in the last 12 months. Table 5.4 shows some consistent differences

TABLE 5.3. *Mean number of income-generating offenses committed in the last 12 months by self-reported use of selected drug types (years 2 and 3)*

Drug type	Mean no. of offenses in the last 12 months	Total no. of arrestees	Sig. of difference between users of drug type and non-drug users	Sig. of difference between users of drug type and users of cannabis only
Cannabis	199	1,299	***	n/a
Amphetamines	229	411	***	***
Ecstasy	214	560	***	***
Heroin	275	826	***	***
Crack	276	783	***	***
Cocaine	258	563	***	***
Methadone	307	399	***	***
Cannabis only	88	178	ns	
Any drug[a]	211	1,491	***	n/a
No drug	93	108		
All arrestees	203	1,599		

Notes: Includes all arrestees who reported committing an acquisitive crime in the last 12 months (excluding prostitution) ($n = 1,605$). Six missing values. 'n/a' signifies cases for which it is not possible to perform the statistical tests as the drug type is not independent of the comparison group. Analysis of variance test: *** $p < .001$, ns = not significant. Outliers were controlled by recoding the top 5 percent of responses (to the 94.9% value of 1,177). This equates to a mean maximum rate of approximately three offenses per day every day for 365 days.
[a]Any of 19 illicit drug types.

TABLE 5.4. *Proportion of arrestees who reported having committed an income-generating offense in the last 12 months by number of positive tests (years 2 and 3)*

No. of positive tests	Offended in the last 12 months, % (n)	Not offended in the last 12 months, % (n)	All arrestees
0 illicit drug types	29 (250)	71 (625)	100 (875)
1 illicit drug type	51 (428)	49 (414)	100 (842)
2 illicit drug types	67 (403)	33 (200)	100 (603)
3 illicit drug types	79 (267)	21 (70)	100 (337)
4+ illicit drug types	82 (144)	18 (31)	100 (175)
Sig. of difference		***	
All arrestees	100 (1,492)	100 (1,340)	100 (2,832)

Notes: Includes all arrestees who provided a urine specimen (n = 2,833). One missing case.
Chi-square test: *** p < .001.

between number of positive tests and whether the arrestee reported offending. Twenty-nine percent of arrestees who tested positive for no drugs said that they had offended in the last year compared with 51 percent of those who tested positive for one drug and 67 percent of those who tested positive for two drugs. Over 80 percent of users testing positive for four of more drugs reported offending in the last 12 months.

Self-Report. The results of self reported drug use and offending behavior are shown in Table 5.5. The rate of drug use has been divided into high-rate use (15 or more days in the last 30 days) and low-rate use (between 1 and 14 days in the last 30 days). The results relating to recreational drugs show that high-rate cannabis users were significantly more likely to report offending than low-rate cannabis users (66% compared with 60%). Similarly, high-rate amphetamine users and high-rate ecstasy users were more likely than low-rate users of these drugs to report offending. However, neither of these differences was statistically significant. This might be because the number of high-rate users of these recreational drugs was low, which might have affected the power of the statistical test to show a significant effect. The results relating to the heroin, crack, and cocaine showed higher rates of involvement in criminal behavior

TABLE 5.5. *Proportion of arrestees who reported committing an income-generating offense in the last 12 months among high and low rate drug users (years 2 and 3)*

Drug type	High rate (15+ days), % (n)	Low rate (1–14 days), % (n)	All users, % (n)	Sig. of difference, % (n)
Cannabis	66 (667)	60 (494)	63 (1,161)	**
Amphetamines	75 (35)	69 (158)	70 (193)	ns
Ecstasy	68 (15)	65 (257)	65 (272)	ns
Heroin	86 (612)	74 (129)	83 (741)	**
Crack	87 (293)	81 (307)	84 (600)	*
Cocaine	70 (33)	68 (243)	69 (276)	ns
Methadone	78 (108)	89 (135)	84 (243)	*
Cannabis only	45 (86)	32 (94)	37 (180)	**
Any drug[a]	71 (1,158)	45 (270)	64 (1,428)	***

Notes: Includes all arrestees who reported using the specified drug in the last 30 days. Chi-square test: *** $p < .001$; ** $p < .01$; * $p < .05$, ns = not significant.
[a]Any of 19 illicit drug types.

among high-rate than low-rate users. The results were significant in relation to heroin and crack but just failed to reach significance in relation to cocaine (perhaps because of the small number of high-rate users). Conversely, high-rate users of methadone were significantly less likely than low-rate users to report offending.

The second set of results based on self-reported drug use look at the relationship between expenditure on drugs and whether arrestees reported 1 or more of the selected 10 offense types in the last 12 months. Table 5.6 shows a fairly clear positive correlation between amount spent on drugs in the last seven days and the proportion of arrestees who reported offending. Just over one-third (39%) of arrestees who reported zero expenditure on drugs reported offending in the last year compared with 89 percent of those who reported spending £350 or more.

The comparisons show once again a strong connection between rate of drug use and the likelihood of offending. Generally speaking, drug-using arrestees who consumed their drugs at a high rate (on various measures) were more likely than those who consumed them at a low rate to report offending in the last 12 months.

TABLE 5.6. *Proportion of arrestees reporting having committed income-generating offenses in the last 12 months by expenditure on drugs in the last 7 days (years 2 and 3)*

Expenditure on drugs in last 7 days	Offended in the last 12 months, % (*n*)	Not offended in the last 12 months, % (*n*)	Sig. of difference, % (*n*)
£0	39 (270)	61 (417)	100 (687)
£1–19	52 (127)	48 (119)	100 (246)
£20–49	52 (191)	49 (180)	100 (371)
£50–139	71 (286)	29 (118)	100 (404)
£140–349	83 (300)	17 (63)	100 (363)
£350+	89 (309)	11 (38)	100 (347)
Sig. of difference			***
All arrestees (incl. zero expenditure)	61 (1,483)	39 (935)	100 (2,418)
All arrestees (excl. zero expenditure)	70 (1,213)	30 (518)	100 (1,731)

Notes: Includes all arrestees who reported having used any illicit drug in the last 12 months (*n* = 2,443). Some missing cases.
Chi-square test: *** $p < .001$.

Incidence in Drug Use versus Incidence of Crime
This final section investigates whether rate of drug use is related to rate of offending. It might be hypothesized that arrestees who consume drugs at a high rate might commit crimes at a high rate.

Urinalysis. The findings are shown in Table 5.7. The table shows that the rate of offending tends to increase as the number of positive tests increases. Reported offending was highest among arrestees who tested positive for four or more drug types (an average of 305 offenses reported in the last 12 months) and lowest among those who tested positive for no drug types (an average of 115 offenses). Overall, the offending rate tends to increase as the number of positive tests increase.

Self-Report. The comparison can be repeated using self-reported drug use. The incidence of drug use was measured using two measures. The first measure was based on the number of days in the last 30 that the drug was used. The second was the average expenditure on drugs

TABLE 5.7. *Mean number of income-generating offenses committed in the last 12 months by number of positive tests*

No. of positive tests	Mean no. of offenses in the last 12 months	Total number of arrestees
0 illicit drug types	115	250
1 illicit drug type	151	426
2 illicit drug types	237	403
3 illicit drug types	287	264
4+ illicit drug types	305	144
Any illicit drug type	226	1,237
Multiple illicit drug types	265	822
Opiates and/or cocaine	277	842

Notes: Includes all arrestees who reported committing an acquisitive crime in the last 12 months (excluding prostitution) who provided a urine specimen ($n = 1,492$). Five missing cases. Outliers were controlled by recoding the top 5 percent of responses (to the 94.9% value of 1177) This equates to a mean maximum rate of approximately three offenses per day every day for 365 days.

over the last seven days. This is not identical to rate of use because it is not known whether the drugs purchased were consumed, and it is not known whether a small number of expensive drugs were purchased or a large number of cheap drugs. Nevertheless, there is likely to be some association between amount spent and quantities of drugs consumed, and as such it provides a useful alternative measure of incidence.

The first set of results show the mean number of reported offenses by rate of drug use for various drug types (Table 5.8). For most drug types, the mean number of offenses reported is higher among high-rate than low-rate users. The only exception to this is the case of methadone users. High-rate methadone users tended to report fewer crimes than low-rate users. However, the difference in rates was not statistically significant and might have occurred by chance. It can also be seen from Table 5.8 that none of the differences in reported offending among cannabis, amphetamine, and ecstasy users was statistically significant. The only significant differences were those in relation to offending rates among high- and low-rate heroin and crack users.

The second set of results look at the association between the amount spent on drugs in the last seven days and the number of offenses reported. Table 5.9 shows that expenditure on drugs is strongly

TABLE 5.8. *Mean number of offenses committed in the last 12 months by high-and low-rate drug users*

Drug type	High rate (15+ days)	Low rate (1–14 days)	Total n	Sig. of difference
Cannabis	209	190	1,157	ns
Amphetamines	329	211	193	ns
Ecstasy	190	189	272	ns
Heroin	312	196	740	**
Crack	338	274	598	*
Cocaine	331	278	274	ns
Methadone	249	332	242	ns
Cannabis only	107	43	276	*
Any drug[a]	245	90	1,423	***

Notes: Includes arrestees who had used the specified drug type and who reported committing income-generating crimes in the last 12 months. Some missing cases. Outliers (for mean number of offenses) were controlled by recoding the top 5 percent of responses (to the 94.9% value of 1,177). This equates to a mean maximum rate of approximately three offenses per day every day for 365 days.
Analysis of variance test: *** $p < .001$; ** $p < .01$; * $p < .05$, ns = not significant.
[a]Any of 19 illicit drug types.

TABLE 5.9. *Mean number of income-generating offenses committed in the last 12 months by expenditure on drugs in the last 7 days*

Expenditure on drugs in last 7 days	Mean no. of offenses in the last 12 months	Total no. of arrestees
£0	186	269
£1–19	94	127
£20–49	182	189
£50–139	460	285
£140–349	495	299
£350+	865	309
Sig. of difference	**	
All arrestees (incl. zero expenditure)	435	1,478
All arrestees (excl. zero expenditure)	490	1,209

Notes: Includes arrestees who reported committing an acquisitive crime in the last 12 months (excluding prostitution) and who reported using any illicit drug in the last 12 months ($n = 1,496$). Eighteen missing values.
Analysis of variance test: ** $p < .01$. Outliers (for mean number of offenses variable) were controlled by recoding the top 5 percent of responses (to the 94.9% value of 1,177). This equates to a mean maximum rate of approximately three offenses per day every day for 365 days.

correlated with the rate of offending. As expenditure increases, offending rate increases. Hence, the highest rates of offending were reported among those spending the highest amounts in the last week. Those spending £350 or more in the last week reported an average of 865 offenses in the last year. The lowest rates of offending were reported among those spending the lowest amounts. Those spending less than £20 in the last week reported an average of 94 offenses in the last year and those spending between £20 and £50 reported an average of 182 offenses. It is interesting that these offending rates are actually lower than that of arrestees who had spent nothing on drugs in the last week (£186). This may reflect previous findings that certain kinds of drug use (such as cannabis only) might lead to a reduction in the risk of offending. This might be due to the demotivating effects of the drug or features of those arrestees who chose this pattern of drug use.

The results of this section are similar across different measures of rate of drug use. They all show that as measures of level of involvement in drug use increase measures of offending tend to increase. Hence, the results so far show that (1) drug use is associated with higher rates of reported offending than non–drug use and (2) higher rates of drug use are associated with higher rates of offending than lower rates of drug use.

DRUG-MISUSING REPEAT OFFENDERS

One of the key target groups in the UK drug strategy is the group of offenders who use heroin, crack, or cocaine frequently and commit crimes at a high rate. This group of high-rate users and high-rate offenders is referred to in the strategy documents as drug-misusing repeat offenders (DMROs). The NEW-ADAM program provided an opportunity to attempt to define and identify DMROs and to investigate their patterns of drug use and offending behavior.

In the NEW-ADAM program, DMROs were defined as arrestees who used heroin, crack, or cocaine at least once a week on average (i.e., on five or more days of the last 30 days) and who reported two or more income-generating offenses per month on average (i.e., 24 or more offenses in the last 12 months). One of the aims of identifying the highest rate drug users and offenders in this way was to learn more about their demographic characteristics and their patterns of drug use and offending.

Overall, 18 percent of arrestees interviewed could be classified as DMROs using these criteria. The proportion of arrestees identified as DMROs varied across the 16 sites from a low of seven percent to a high of 30 percent. The characteristics of DMROs are shown in Table 5.10. The table shows significant differences between DMROs and other arrestees. DMROs were significantly more likely than other arrestees to be female, to be aged over 20 years, to be white, to have left school before age 17, and to have been in receipt of social security benefits in the last 12 months.

DMROs were also significantly different from other arrestees in terms of their patterns of drug misuse (Table 5.11). In particular, they were more likely to be heroin users rather than crack or cocaine users. Thirty-four percent of all users of heroin only were classified as DMROs compared with fourteen percent of users of crack only and four percent of users of cocaine only. Heroin users were also more likely to be classified as DMROs when they combined their heroin use with other drugs. More than half of heroin users who also used crack were defined as DMROs. However, heroin users who also used cocaine were only slightly more likely than heroin users alone to be defined as a DMRO (36% compared with 34%).

It is also possible that DMROs might be different from other arrestees in terms of the type of suspected offenses for which they were currently held. In fact, DMROs were significantly more likely than other arrestees to have been arrested under suspicion of committing theft offenses (60% of DMROs compared with 34% of other arrestees). Conversely, DMROs were significantly less likely than other arrestees to have been arrested for offenses against the person, property damage offenses, drug offenses, alcohol offenses, and disorder offenses. The two groups did not differ significantly in terms of the proportions arrested for other offenses.

It is also possible to compare the two groups in terms of self-reported offending. Table 5.12 shows that DMROs were significantly more likely than other arrestees to report having committed each of eleven income-generating offenses in the last 12 months. More than 80 percent of DMROs reported that they had shoplifted in the

TABLE 5.10. *Sociodemographic characteristics of drug-misusing repeat offenders compared with other arrestees*

	Drug-misusing repeat offenders, % (*n*)	Other arrestees, % (*n*)	All arrestees, % (*n*)
Sex			
Male	83 (456)	86 (222)	86 (2,679)
Female	17 (95)	14 (357)	14 (452)
Sig. of difference	*		
Age group			
17–19	13 (72)	25 (654)	23 (726)
20–24	27 (149)	26 (670)	26 (819)
25–29	29 (159)	16 (421)	19 (580)
30+	31 (171)	32 (835)	31 (1,006)
Sig. of difference	***		
Ethnic group			
White	88 (484)	77 (1,991)	79 (2,475)
Nonwhite	12 (67)	23 (588)	21 (655)
Sig. of difference	***		
Age left education			
16 or under	92 (495)	75 (1,889)	78 (2,394)
17 or older	8 (43)	25 (630)	22 (673)
Sig. of difference	***		
On social security			
Yes	16 (86)	49 (1,275)	44 (1,361)
No	84 (465)	51 (1,305)	57 (1,770)
Sig. of difference	***		
All arrestees	100 (551)	100 (2,580)	100 (3,131)

Notes: Includes all arrestees (*n* = 3,135). Some missing cases. Drug-misusing repeat offenders are arrestees who had used heroin, crack, or cocaine on at least 5 days of the last 30 *and* who had committed at least 24 income-generating crimes in the last 12 months.
Chi-square test: *** $p < .001$; * $p < .05$.

last 12 months, compared with 17 percent of other arrestees. Handling offenses were also more prevalent among DMROs than other arrestees, with 48 percent of arrestees in this group reporting having committed this offense type in the last 12 months, compared with 18 percent of other arrestees. By contrast, fewer than 10 percent of DMROs reported committing robbery or theft from a person in the last 12 months, although these rates are still almost four times those of other arrestees.

TABLE 5.11. *Types of drug user among drug-misusing repeat offenders and other arrestees*

Types of drug used	Drug-misusing repeat offenders, n (%)	Other arrestees, n (%)	All arrestees, n (%)
No drugs	n/a	100 (692)	100 (692)
Other drugs	n/a	100 (929)	100 (929)
Cocaine only	4 (11)	97 (302)	100 (313)
Crack only	14 (12)	86 (75)	100 (87)
Crack and cocaine	21 (20)	79 (77)	100 (97)
Heroin only	34 (67)	66 (129)	100 (196)
Heroin and cocaine	36 (17)	64 (30)	100 (47)
Heroin and crack	55 (229)	46 (191)	100 (420)
Heroin, cocaine, and crack	56 (195)	44 (155)	100 (350)
All arrestees	18 (551)	82 (2,580)	100 (3,131)

Notes: Includes all arrestees ($n = 3,135$). Four missing cases. Drug-misusing repeat offenders are arrestees who have used heroin, crack, or cocaine on at least 5 days of the last 30 *and* who have committed at least 24 income-generating crimes in the last 12 months.

Although DMROs comprised approximately one-third of all offenders in the last 12 months, they were responsible for committing more than two-thirds of all offenses reported. In total, there were just over 500 arrestees classified as DMROs, and these reported committing just under 225,000 offenses in the last 12 months (an average of 406 offenses per offender). In contrast, there were just over 1,000 other offenders and these reported committing just over 100,000 offenses in the last 12 months (an average of 96 offenses per offender).

It is also possible that there are differences between DMROs and non-DMROs in terms of the type of offenses committed. In fact, DMROs were significantly more likely to report committing shoplifting, handling, theft from a person, and drug supply offenses than other offenders. Among arrestees who had shoplifted in the last 12 months, DMROs reported an average of 398 shoplifting offenses, which was approximately five times the rate for other offenders. Similarly, the rate of burglary from a dwelling, burglary from a nondwelling, and handling offenses was significantly higher among DMROs than among other offenders. There were no significant differences in the rate of

TABLE 5.12. *Proportion of drug-misusing repeat offenders and other arrestees reporting each of 11 income-generating crimes in the last 12 months*

Types of drug used	Drug-misusing repeat offenders, % (n)	Other arrestees, % (n)	All arrestees, % (n)	Sig. of difference
Theft of a motor vehicle	12 (65)	6 (162)	7 (27)	***
Theft from a motor vehicle	21 (116)	6 (141)	8 (257)	***
Theft from a shop	81 (448)	17 (439)	28 (887)	***
Burglary from a dwelling	11 (59)	3 (80)	4 (139)	***
Burglary from a nondwelling	13 (74)	4 (92)	5 (166)	***
Robbery	7 (37)	2 (48)	3 (85)	***
Theft from a person	8 (42)	2 (43)	3 (85)	***
Fraud/deception	21 (114)	7 (187)	10 (301)	***
Handling	48 (265)	18 (476)	24 (741)	***
Drug supply	31 (173)	8 (206)	12 (379)	***
Prostitution	5 (27)	2 (47)	2 (74)	***
Any offense[a]	100 (551)	41 (1,052)	51 (1,603)	***
Any offense[b]	100 (551)	42 (1,070)	52 (1,621)	***

Notes: Includes all arrestees (n = 3,135). Four missing cases. Drug-misusing repeat offenders are arrestees who had used heroin, crack, or cocaine on at least 5 days of the last 30 *and* who had committed at least 24 income-generating crimes in the last 12 months.
Chi-square test: *** $p < .001$.
[a]Excluding prostitution-related offenses.
[b]Including prostitution-related offenses.

offending of DMROs and non-DMROs in relation to theft of or from a vehicle, drug supply, fraud, and prostitution.

DISCUSSION

The chapter has investigated whether drug use is associated with crime. The issue of the connection derives from the widely held belief that either drug use causes crime and the less widely held view that crime causes drug use. It was not possible to investigate the causal connection between these two variables because this would have required measuring temporal order and the mechanisms that linked the two. It would also require controlling for other confounding factors. However, the NEW-ADAM data provides an opportunity to investigate the nature of the statistical association in some detail. The results of this analysis have been presented here, and a finer breakdown of the relationship is provided in the next chapter.

Previous research has provided some evidence on the nature and strength of the relationship. However, few systematic reviews of the research are available to help untangle the differences between studies in terms of methods used, types of analysis, and the findings obtained. It was noted that the distinction between prevalence and incidence of offending is rarely tackled directly in the research literature and current knowledge is based on a combination of different kinds of results, some based on prevalence and some incidence. However, it is possible that the association might be different depending on whether involvement in drug use and crime is being investigated or the level of involvement.

The chapter investigated the nature and strength of the relationship between drug use and crime by looking at the association between various combinations of prevalence and incidence of drug use and prevalence and incidence of criminal behavior. It also used at least two measures of drug use and crime for each comparison. The results showed that drug use and crime were strongly connected in terms of both prevalence and incidence. In other words, drug users were more likely than non–drug users to commit crimes and to commit crimes at a high rate, and high-rate drug users were more likely than low-rate drug users to commit crimes and to commit them at a higher rate.

In the concluding section, the chapter examined the demographic characteristics of the subgroup of offenders who were both high-rate drug users and high-rate offenders, referred to as drug-misusing repeat offenders (DMROs). The analysis showed that about one-fifth of arrestees were DMROs. In terms of demographic characteristics, they were more likely than other arrestees to be female, older, and white. This group was particularly problematic in that they were responsible for more than two-thirds of all offenses committed among the sample as a whole.

CHAPTER SIX

Disaggregating the Drug-Crime Relationship

INTRODUCTION

Disaggregating the drug-crime relationship refers to breaking down the association between drug use and crime by various types of drug use and various types of crime. A number of reasons might make it useful to disaggregate findings. One is that it can reveal variations in the drug-crime relation that might be obscured when looking at aggregated categories. It is possible, for example, that certain kinds of drugs might be associated with certain kinds of crimes. Another reason is that drug policy needs to be efficient as well as effective. It might be the case that a blanket policy covering all drug types or all crime types might be unnecessary and wasteful. Instead, a more focused approach on specific drug-crime combinations might be more cost effective.

The idea that there might be variations in the drug-crime relationship depending on the type of drugs and type of crimes being considered has been suggested before in the research literature. It has been argued that drugs vary substantially in terms of their pharmacological properties, their addictive qualities, and their costs. It is unlikely, therefore, that their impact on criminal behavior would be identical (Farabee et al., 2001). Parker and Auerhahn (1998) make a similar point in relation to the study of drugs and violence and note the tendency of research to "lump all illicit drugs together, as if all drugs might be expected to have the same relationship to violent behavior" (p. 293). In fact, they point out that different drugs have different pharmacological effects, which influence whether or not the user has a tendency toward violent behavior. In response, it has been proposed that the study of the drug-crime connection would be better served by investigating disaggregated forms of these variables (Best et al., 2001b; Farrabee et al., 2001). In practice, this means looking at various types of association between subcategories of drug misuse and subcategories of crime.

EXPLANATIONS

Information about variations in the connection between certain types of drug misuse and certain types of crime can also be found in explanations of the drug-crime relationship. Explanations sometimes draw attention to particular drug-crime affinities. Baumer et al. (1998), for example, argued that crack users prefer robbery as a source of income because of the immediacy of the results. However, heroin users prefer burglary because their need for drugs is less urgent. These differences are explained in terms of the differences in the rate at which the effects of the drugs wear off. The effects of crack can wear off in half an hour, whereas the effects of heroin can last half a day. Goldstein (1985) suggested that heroin users tend to avoid violence as it is not their primary motivation. Instead, they tend to view violent crime as more dangerous than other crimes and more likely to result in imprisonment. Other writers have also noted that heroin users tend to choose less serious offenses such as burglary and theft as they carry less severe sentences (Speckart and Anglin, 1985). Explanations also note variations in the psychopharmacological properties of certain drugs and the kinds of behavior that might result from them. It has been argued, for example, that amphetamines and cocaine might lead to violence as a result of the stimulant effect of the drugs (Goode, 1997). However, it has also been noted that marijuana and heroin might have a calming effect that could actually reduce the probability of certain kinds of offenses being committed (Brochu, 2001).

PREVIOUS RESEARCH

A number of studies have used disaggregated measures to investigate possible variations in the drug-crime connection. Makkai et al. (2000) used disaggregated measures of drug use and crime in the analysis of data collected as part of the Drug Use Monitoring in Australia (DUMA) program to investigate the relationship between drug misuse and the prevalence of offending. The study included urinalysis and interviews with arrestees to provide a breakdown of six types of drug misuse and eight categories of criminal behavior. The results showed some variations in the relationship between offense types and drug types. Property offenders were more likely to test positive for opiates (55%) than those charged with drug offenses (38%) or violent offenses (32%). Arrestees charged with drug offenses were more likely to test positive for cannabis (76%) than property offenders (52%) or violent offenders (46%).

Another study based on the DUMA data provided a fuller set of results on the drug-crime relationship and used different methods of analysis (Makkai, 2001). The study included urinalysis and interview data from four sites over a one-year period in 1999. The results were presented in terms of odds ratios and the likelihood of being charged with a particular offense depending on whether the arrestee tested positive or negative for six drug types. The results also showed some variation in the relationship depending on drug type and crime type. Overall, testing positive for any kind of drug resulted in a greater likelihood of being charged with a property offense and (with one exception) a drug offense. Arrestees who tested positive for opiates were 4.2 times more likely to be charged with a property offense than those who tested negative for opiates. However, testing positive for any kind of drug resulted in a lower likelihood of being charged with a violent offense (with one exception). The exception was that arrestees testing positive for cocaine (including crack) were 2.4 times more likely to be charged with a violent offense.

Some studies using disaggregated measures have investigated the relationship between drug misuse and the rate of offending. Johnston et al. (1978) used data from a national longitudinal high school survey conducted in the United States to correlate rates of use of seven drug types with rates of 15 types of criminal behavior. The results showed that virtually all drug measures correlated positively with measures of property crime. However, the relationship was strongest for minor theft, shoplifting, and trespassing. The drugs most strongly predictive of interpersonal violence were heroin, barbiturates, amphetamines, and cocaine. The drug least strongly associated with rates of criminal behavior, in relation to almost all delinquency items, was marijuana.

Hammersley et al. (1989) conducted a self-report survey of both an offender sample (Scottish prisoners) and a drug-user sample (clients of a number of drug treatment centers). They collected data on 16 types of drug, which they collapsed into a 'drug-level' scale based on type of drug misused and rate of use (alcohol use at the lower end of the scale and high-rate opioid use at the top end of the scale). They also asked questions on 21 classes of crime, which they collapsed into four crime types ('theft', 'fraud', 'delinquency and violence', and 'drug dealing'). They found that as 'drug level' increased, various measures of rates of criminal behavior increased. However, the relationship only held true for 'theft' and 'drug dealing'. There was no association between rates of drug misuse and rates of 'delinquency and violence' or 'fraud'.

As part of a self-report survey of prisoners in eight institutions in Australia, Dobinson and Ward (1984) collected information on rates of use of eight categories of drugs and rates of commission of 10 offense types in the period prior to arrest. They found a significant positive correlation between rate of heroin use and rate of armed robbery. However, they found no significant association between rate of heroin use and rate of burglary, larceny, fraud, handling (receiving stolen goods), or other kinds of robbery.

Overall, the research on the drug-crime connection shows the relationship varies by type of drug and type of crime. The strongest finding seems to be that heroin is commonly associated with shoplifting and general theft. However, there are too few studies currently available to identify any clear patterns in the relationship between specific types of drug misuse and crime.

DRUG-CRIME CONNECTIONS

Research based on disaggregated measures tends to show that the relationship varies by type of drugs used and type of offenses committed. Theoretical statements and explanations of the relationship also point to variations in offense types and drug types. The aim of this chapter is to investigate whether such relationships exist and to explore the nature of these variations using data collected from among arrestees held in custody suites in England and Wales.

The previous chapter noted that a distinction is sometimes made in the research literature between measures of prevalence (involvement in drug misuse or crime) and measures of incidence (rate of drug misuse or crime). The following sections look at disaggregated measures to investigate the connection between drug use using both measures of prevalence and incidence of offending.

Prevalence and Incidence

The difference between prevalence and incidence was discussed in the previous chapter. The distinction is important because the drug-crime connection might be different depending on whether prevalence or incidence of drug use and crime is measured. Prevalence refers to the extent to which a group is involved in some kind of behavior, whereas incidence refers to the intensity of involvement among those who engage in that behavior. Hence, there might be no association between those in a group who take drugs and those who commit crimes. However, there might be an association between those who use drugs at a high rate and those who commit crimes at a high rate.

As was the case in the previous chapter, the prevalence of drug use refers to the proportion of the sample that tested positive for, or reported using, certain kinds of drugs, and the prevalence of crime refers to the proportion that reported committing certain types of crimes in the last 12 months. The incidence of drug use refers to the number of positive tests or reported rate of drug use in the last 30 days and the incidence of crime refers to the number of offenses reported as being committed in the last 12 months.

Drug Misuse and Prevalence of Offending

The relationship between drug misuse and prevalence of offending concerns the extent to which drug misuse is associated with particular kinds of crime. In other words, it addresses the issue of whether there is some kind of connection between using certain kinds of drugs and committing certain kinds of crime.

Table 6.1 shows the relation between various forms of drug misuse and criminal behavior. The table is divided into two main sections. The first shows the relation between 4 common recreational drugs and 10 common offense types. The second section shows the relation between heroin, crack, and cocaine and the same common offense types. The lower part of the table provides a summary for various groups of drugs.

The first section of Table 6.1 gives the percentage of users of cannabis, amphetamines, ecstasy, and diazepam who reported committing each of the 10 offense types in the last 12 months. To distinguish recreational users from users of heroin, crack, and cocaine who might also use these drugs, cannabis, amphetamine, ecstasy, and diazepam users include only those who had not also consumed heroin, crack, or cocaine in the last 12 months. This part of the table can be used to determine whether there are any significant differences between users of specific recreational drugs and nonusers in their involvement in specific types of criminal behavior.

In relation to almost every drug type and every offense type, users were more likely than nonusers to have committed one or more offenses in the last 12 months. For example, 8 percent of arrestees who reported using cannabis in the last 12 months compared with 2 percent of those who reported using no drugs said that they had committed theft of a motor vehicle in the last year. Fourteen percent of cannabis users reported shoplifting compared with 5 percent of nonusers. Twenty-one percent of cannabis users reported handling stolen goods compared with 8 percent of nonusers. With the exception of burglary in a dwelling, cannabis users were significantly more likely than nonusers to report committing each of the 10 offense types. There were no clear affinities between involvement in particular drug types and particular offenses. Instead, the pattern of results showed that recreational drug misusers had a higher general tendency toward offending than non–drug users across most offense types. Hence, the table suggests that recreational drug use is associated with higher levels of involvement in offending than non–drug use. There do not appear to be any special affinities between specific drug types and specific offense types.

TABLE 6.1. *Percentage of arrestees who reported committing selected offense types in the last 12 months by type of drug used*

	Theft of motor vehicle	Theft from a motor vehicle	Shoplifting	Burglary in a dwelling	Burglary nondwelling	Robbery	Theft person	Fraud	Handling	Drug supply	Total
Cannabis[a,b]	8 ***	6 ***	14 ***	3 ns	4 ***	2 **	1 **	7 ***	21 ***	8 ***	837
Amphetamines	9 ***	11 ***	26 ***	6 **	6 ***	2 *	2 **	10 ***	27 ***	11 ***	176
Ecstasy	9 ***	8 ***	17 ***	6 ***	7 ***	1 ns	2 **	9 ***	23 ***	10 ***	235
Diazepam	14 ***	13 ***	25 ***	10 ***	9 ***	4 *	1 ns	16 ***	29 ***	8 ***	77
Heroin[c]	9 ns	14 ***	63 ***	8 ***	10 ***	5 ***	6 ***	15 ***	33 ***	19 ***	1015
Crack	10 *	16 ***	60 ***	9 ***	10 ***	5 **	6 ***	17 ***	35 ***	22 ***	956

	1	2	3	4	5	6	7	8	9	10	n
Cocaine[c,d]	10	14	39	7	9	4	5	16	38	25	809
	ns	***	***	***	***	**	***	***	***	***	
No drugs	2	1	5	1	<1	<1	0	3	8	<1	692
Recreational drugs only[b,d]	7	5	14	3	3	2	1	7	21	8	929
	***	***	***	ns	***	*	**	***	***	***	
HCC drugs[e]	10	13	48	7	9	4	5	14	33	20	1512
	*	***	***	**	***	**	***	***	***	***	

Note. $N = 3{,}133$ (two missing cases).

$*\ p < .05$; $**\ p < .01$; $***\ p < .001$; ns = not significant.

[a] The four drug types shown in this section include users of the drug type in the last 12 months who have not consumed heroin or crack or cocaine (HCC drugs). However, they may also have consumed other non-HCC drugs in the same period.

[b] The term *recreational drugs* refers to cannabis, amphetamines, ecstasy, or diazepam.

[c] The three drug types shown in this section include users of the drug type in the last 12 months. However, they may also have consumed other HCC drugs or non-HCC drugs in the same period.

[d] Chi-square test comparison of drug type or group with the 'No drugs' group.

[e] Chi-square test comparison of drug type or group with the 'Drugs other than HCC' group.

The second section of the table shows participation in offending among users of heroin, crack, and cocaine. In this section, participation in offending among hard drug users is compared with participation in offending among recreational drug users. The results also show generally higher levels of participation among heroin, crack, and cocaine users than recreational drug users in relation to almost every offense type. The only comparison between heroin, crack, and cocaine use and the 10 offense types that was not statistically significant was in relation to theft of a motor vehicle. Heroin and cocaine users appeared to be no more likely than recreational drug users to report committing this offense in the last 12 months. However, some of the other differences are striking. Fourteen percent of recreational drug users reported shoplifting in the last year compared with 63 percent of heroin users and 60 percent of crack users. Eight percent of recreational drug users reported drug supply offenses in the last year compared with 25 percent of cocaine users and 22 percent of crack users.

As before, there were no clear affinities between involvement in particular drug types and particular offenses. Almost every comparison of drug type and crime type was statistically significant. Hence, the table suggests that hard drug users are associated with a higher prevalence of offending than recreational drug users across a range of offense types. Although there are clear differences between recreational and hard drug users in their overall prevalence of offending, there is little indication that involvement in certain kinds of drugs is associated with involvement in certain kinds of crime. In other words, the findings suggest a general drug-crime connection rather than specific drug-crime connections. However, these findings relate only to prevalence, and they are based only on bivariate analysis. It is possible to investigate the relationship further using multivariate analysis.

To make a clearer comparison of differences in the strength of the relationship, the measures were reanalyzed using logistic regression. The results are shown in Table 6.2. The table shows the odds ratio for the independent variables of each significant drug-crime connection. The logistic regression was repeated using each offense type in turn as the dependent variable.

TABLE 6.2. *Odds ratios for likelihood of offending in the last 12 months*

	Theft of motor vehicle	Theft from a motor vehicle	Shoplifting	Burglary in a dwelling	Burglary nondwelling	Robbery	Theft person	Fraud	Handling	Drug supply
Drug variables										
Cannabis in last 12 months	2.15	1.87	1.63	1.88	2.27	2.05	ns	ns	1.65	2.51
Amphetamines in last 12 months	1.48	1.47	ns	1.70	ns	ns	ns	ns	1.27	1.87
Ecstasy in last 12 months	ns	ns	ns	ns	1.92	ns	2.41	ns	ns	1.34
Diazepam in last 12 months	ns	1.67	1.65	1.91	ns	1.89	1.91	1.73	1.65	1.43
Heroin in last 12 months	ns	ns	4.95	ns	1.91	ns	3.64	ns		ns
Crack in last 12 months	1.48	2.18	2.06	1.84	1.75	2.05	ns	1.77	1.40	2.00
Cocaine in last 12 months	ns	ns	ns	ns	ns	ns	ns	1.79	1.84	2.05

(*continued*)

TABLE 6.2 (continued)

	Theft of motor vehicle	Theft from a motor vehicle	Shoplifting	Burglary in a dwelling	Burglary nondwelling	Robbery	Theft person	Fraud	Handling	Drug supply
Demographic variables										
Sex (male)	4.19	2.55	0.61	2.31	5.33	ns	ns	0.60	.	1.70
Age group (25 or older)	0.37	0.44	ns	0.41	0.62	0.35	ns	0.58	0.52	0.74
Race (white)	1.86	ns	1.78	ns	ns	0.49	ns	ns	ns	ns
Marital status (single)	1.67	1.56	1.64	ns	ns	ns	2.10	ns	ns	ns
Employment status (unemployed)	1.54	1.36	1.55	1.77	1.49	ns	ns	1.46	1.25	ns
Home-owning status (not own)	ns	1.41	ns	ns	1.83	ns	ns	ns	1.33	ns
Age left school (under 16)	1.41	2.01	ns	2.24	2.11	2.19	1.75	ns	ns	ns
Lived on streets in last year (yes)	ns	1.59	1.70	1.75	ns	ns	ns	ns	ns	ns
Nagelkerke[a] R^2	0.14	0.20	0.42	0.17	0.18	0.11	0.14	0.10	0.14	0.19

Note: $N = 3,133$ (two missing cases).

All odds ratios shown are statistically significant at $p < .05$. ns = nonsignificant

[a] The Nagelkerke R^2 is the nonparametric test equivalent of the parametric test R^2.

Use of recreational drugs was a significant predictor of involvement in offending across a range of offense types. Cannabis and diazepam use made a significant contribution to explaining participation in eight of the 10 offense types, amphetamines 5 types, and ecstasy 3 types. For example, users of cannabis were 2.3 times more likely to report burglary in a nondwelling than were non–cannabis users and 2.2 times more likely to report theft of a motor vehicle. However, they were no more likely than non–cannabis users to report theft from a person or fraud. Overall, the findings suggest a general association between recreational drug use and a range of offense types in line with the findings of the bivariate analysis. The logistic regression adds to this analysis by providing an estimate of the difference in likelihood of offending among users and nonusers. In most cases, use of the drug increased the likelihood of offending between approximately 50 percent and 100 percent.

Use of crack was also associated with a higher general level of involvement in crime. Crack use explained participation in nine of the 10 offense types. However, use of heroin was associated with higher levels of involvement in relation to only three specific types of crime: shoplifting, burglary in a nondwelling, and theft from a person. Similarly, use of cocaine was associated with higher levels of involvement in only three offenses: fraud, handling, and drug supply. Heroin use increased the likelihood of committing shoplifting by almost five times that of nonusers of heroin. It also increased the likelihood of committing theft from a person by 3.6 times and burglary in a nondwelling by 1.9 times. Cocaine use approximately doubled the risk of committing fraud, handling stolen goods, and drug supply offenses. Hence, there is clearer evidence of specific drug-crime connections in relation to prevalence when looking at the results of the logistic regression analysis. The main difference between the bivariate and multivariate analyses is that the logistic regression controls for demographic variables and the results are presented in terms of odds ratios, which more clearly differentiate effect sizes.

Overall, the findings of the bivariate analysis show that recreational drug users are more likely than non–drug users to have committed a range of offense types and that hard drug users are more likely than recreational users to have done so. The bivariate analysis suggests a general drug-crime connection rather than specific ones. The findings of the logistic regression analysis also show that users of most recreational drugs (especially cannabis, amphetamines, and diazepam) are more likely than nonusers of these drugs to report committing a wide range of offense types. It also shows a general association between crack use and a range of crime types. However, the findings relating to heroin and cocaine tend to show some evidence of specific drug-crime connections.

Hence, there is some evidence of specific drug-crime connections. However, the dominant finding of this section is that drug use is associated with a general increased likelihood of offending that covers a range of offense types. Nevertheless, the analysis so far has concerned only whether involvement in drug use is associated with involvement in crime. In the next section, we look at the relationship between involvement in drug use and the rate of offending.

DRUG MISUSE AND THE INCIDENCE OF OFFENDING

The relation between drug misuse and incidence of offending concerns the extent to which drug misuse is associated with higher frequencies of offending among offenders. This means that the drug-crime connection is compared only in relation to those who have taken drugs and committed crime. The measure of interest is not whether drug users offend but whether drug users offend at a higher rate when they do offend.

The association between various kinds of drug misuse and rates of 10 offense types is shown in Table 6.3. The table shows the median number of offenses (the middle value of a ranked range) reported as being committed over the last 12 months among different kinds of drug misusers in relation to 10 offense types. The figure in parentheses next to the median value gives the number of cases.

The first set of results shown compare recreational drug users with non–drug users. In most cases, there is no significant difference in the median offending rate of the two groups. For example, the median number of burglary in a nondwelling offenses committed by cannabis users was two in the last 12 months, which is the same rate as non–drug users. The median rate of robbery among amphetamine users was two

TABLE 6.3. *Median number of 10 types of crime committed in the last 12 months by type of drug used*

	Theft of motor vehicle	Theft from a motor vehicle	Shoplifting	Burglary in a dwelling	Burglary nondwelling	Robbery	Theft person	Fraud	Handling	Drug supply
Cannabis[a,b]	2 (63)	4 (45)	3 (116)	3 (24)	2 (28)	3 (18)	2 (12)	3 (60)	5 (172)	8 (66)
Amphetamines	6 (15)	6 (18)	6 (44)	1 (11)	2 (10)	2 (4)	2 (4)	2 (17)	25 (46)	20 (19)
	ns	—	ns	—	—	—	—	ns	*	
Ecstasy	4 (21)	6 (18)	15 (39)	2 (14)	2 (15)	1 (3)	1 (5)	2 (22)	10 (53)	6 (22)
Diazepam	7 (11)	4 (9)	81 (18)	3 (8)	2 (6)	1 (3)	53 (1)	1 (12)	20 (21)	2 (5)
	—	—		—	—	—	—	ns		—
Cocaine[c,d]	3 (76)	10 (111)	88 (310)	2 (53)	4 (73)	2 (36)	2 (39)	4 (129)	15 (303)	93 (202)
	ns	ns	***	ns	*	ns	ns	ns	***	***
Crack	4 (97)	10 (148)	104 (562)	3 (78)	7 (97)	2 (47)	2 (56)	4 (158)	19 (331)	100 (211)
	ns	ns	***	ns	**	ns	ns	ns	***	***
Heroin	3 (93)	10 (142)	109 (635)	3 (78)	7 (97)	2 (46)	2 (60)	4 (149)	17 (330)	100 (191)
	*	*	***	ns	*	ns	ns	ns	***	***
No drugs[a]	2 (14)	6 (10)	2 (32)	1 (9)	2 (3)	1 (3)	0 (0)	2 (21)	6 (54)	6 (2)
Recreational drugs only[c,e]	2 (66)	4 (48)	4 (129)	2 (26)	2 (30)	3 (18)	2 (12)	2 (66)	5 (191)	9 (71)
HCC drugs	4 (146)	10 (196)	100 (719)	2 (100)	4 (132)	2 (62)	2 (71)	4 (213)	15 (491)	90 (300)
	*	*	***	ns	*	ns	ns	ns	***	***

Note. Offense rates have been adjusted to control for the number of months arrestees had spent in prison in the last 12 months.

$* p < .05; ** p < .01; *** p < .001$; ns = not significant; — = insufficient number of cases to conduct a significance test.

[a] Mann-Whitney test comparison of drug type or group with the 'No drugs' group.

[b] The five drug types shown include users of the drug type in the last 12 months who have not consumed heroin or crack or cocaine.

[c] Mann-Whitney test comparison of drug type or group with the 'Recreational drugs only' group.

[d] The three drug types shown include users of the drug type in the last 12 months. However, they may also have consumed other HCC drugs or non-HCC drugs in the same period.

[e] The term *recreational drugs* refers to cannabis, amphetamines, ecstasy, or diazepam.

in the last 12 months, compared with one among non–drug users. In many cases, the number of offenses committed was too small to conduct valid significance tests (represented by a dash in the table). The only significant difference in rate of offending among recreational drug users and non–drug users was in relation to handling stolen goods. Amphetamine users had a median rate of 25 offenses in the last 12 months compared with six offenses among non–drug users. Hence, the results provide little evidence of a general drug-crime connection in relation to rate of offending among recreational drug users. With the exception of amphetamine use and handling, they also provide little evidence of specific drug-crime connections between particular drug types and particular crimes.

The second set of results, which look at rate of offending among users of heroin, crack, and cocaine and recreational drug users, show quite a different picture. All three drug types were significantly associated with higher rates of shoplifting, burglary in a nondwelling, handling, and drug supply offenses than recreational drug users. For example, the annual rate of shoplifting among heroin users was 109 offenses compared with four offenses among recreational drug users and two offenses among non–drug users. Similarly, the annual rate of drug supply offenses among crack users was 100 offenses compared with nine offenses among recreational drug users and six offenses among non–drug users. Heroin users also had a significantly higher rate of vehicle crime than recreational drug users (10 per year compared with 4 per year). Hence, the pattern of findings is different in relation to incidence compared with prevalence. In the case of prevalence, there was a general association between the prevalence of drug use and the prevalence of crime with little evidence of specific drug-crime connections. In the case of incidence, there was less evidence of an overall connection between drug use and rate of commission of crime. Instead, there were a small number of very specific drug-crime connections.

To explore this finding further, a logistic regression analysis was conducted using a dichotomized version of offending rate, created by splitting the distribution at the median to produce a high (median or above) and low (below the median) rate of offending (see Table 6.4).

TABLE 6.4. *Odds ratios for likelihood of offending at a high rate in the last 12 months*

n^a	Theft of motor vehicle (n = 227)	Theft from a motor vehicle (n = 257)	Shoplifting (n = 889)	Burglary in a dwelling (n = 139)	Burglary nondwelling (n = 166)	Robbery (n = 85)	Theft person (n = 85)	Fraud (n = 301)	Handling (n = 742)	Drug supply (n = 379)
Drug variables										
Cannabis in last 12 months	ns	ns	0.6	—	—	—	—	ns	ns	ns
Amphetamines in last 12 months	ns	ns	ns	—	—	—	—	ns	ns	ns
Ecstasy in last 12 months	ns	ns	ns	—	—	—	—	ns	ns	ns
Diazepam in last 12 months	ns	ns	1.7	—	—	—	—	ns	ns	ns
Heroin in last 12 months	ns	ns	2.6	—	—	—	—	ns	ns	ns
Cocaine in last 12 months	ns	ns	ns	—	—	—	—	ns	ns	ns
Crack in last 12 months	ns	ns	ns	—	—	—	—	2.1	1.9	2.0
Demographic variables										
Sex (male)	ns	ns	ns	—	—	—	—	ns	ns	ns
Age group (25 or older)	ns	ns	ns	—	—	—	—	ns	ns	1.7
Race (white)	ns	ns	ns	—	—	—	—	ns	ns	ns
Marital status (single)	ns	ns	ns	—	—	—	—	ns	ns	ns

(continued)

TABLE 6.4 (continued)

n^a	Theft of motor vehicle (n = 227)	Theft from a motor vehicle (n = 257)	Shoplifting (n = 889)	Burglary in a dwelling (n = 139)	Burglary nondwelling (n = 166)	Robbery (n = 85)	Theft person (n = 85)	Fraud (n = 301)	Handling (n = 742)	Drug supply (n = 379)
Employment status (unemployed)	ns	1.8	ns	—	—	—	—	ns	ns	ns
Home owning status (not own)	ns	ns	ns	—	—	—	—	ns	ns	ns
Age left education (under 16)	2.0	ns	1.3	—	—	—	—	ns	1.5	1.7
Lived on streets in last year (yes)	ns	ns	ns	—	—	—	—	ns	ns	ns
Nagelkerke^b R^2	.04	.03	.12	—	—	—	—	.05	.06	.10
n^c	224	254	856	135	165	83	83	297	724	367

Note. Offense rates have been adjusted to control for the number of months arrestees had spent in prison in the last 12 months.

All odds ratios shown are statistically significant at $p < .05$. ns = not significant; — = insufficient number of cases to conduct a significance test.

^{a}Refers to the total number of arrestees who reported committing the specified offense type in the last 12 months.

^{b}The Nagelkerke R^2 is the nonparametric test equivalent of the parametric test R^2.

^{c}Refers to the number of arrestees included in the regression analysis (i.e., after cases with missing data relevant to this analysis have been excluded).

128

Table 6.4 shows that, after controlling for a range of demographic variables, there were few significant differences in rates of offending between users of recreational drugs and non–drug users. The only significant findings were that cannabis users were significantly less likely to be high-rate shoplifters than non–cannabis users and that diazepam users were significantly more likely than non–diazepam users to be high-rate shoplifters.

The results of the logistic regression analysis relating to heroin, crack, and cocaine users resulted in the loss of many of the significant findings reported in the bivariate analysis. The only significant finding remaining relating to heroin use concerns the link between heroin use and rate of shoplifting. Heroin users were 2.6 times more likely than non–heroin users to be high-rate shoplifters. The remaining significant findings concerned crack users. Crack use continued to be linked to handling and drug supply offenses (with the addition of fraud offenses). However, it was no longer found significant in relation to shoplifting. Cocaine use was not shown to be related significantly to high-rate offending of any offense type.

Hence, the analysis suggests that the association between drug use and rate of offending is limited to just a few connections between specific drug types and specific crime types. The strongest evidence of a connection in terms of size of the odds ratio is between heroin use and high-rate shoplifting.

At the aggregate level, there is evidence that drug users are more likely than nonusers to offend at a high rate. However, according to the disaggregated analysis, it is possible that this association is the product of just a few specific drug-crime connections. To test this, the aggregate level analysis for mean rate of offending was repeated with the strongest drug-crime connection (heroin and shoplifting) removed. This resulted in the mean offending rate for drug-using arrestees falling from 211 to 146. As a result, the mean offending rate for drug users was no longer significantly different to the mean offending rate for non–drug users. In other words, if there were no heroin-shoplifting connection, there would be no drug-crime connection.

Overall, the drug-crime connection is more meaningful in relation to the prevalence of offending (drug users tend also to be offenders). It is less meaningful in relation to the incidence of offending, which

appears to be restricted to only a few, highly specific drug-crime connections (specific kinds of drug users tend to commit specific kinds of
offenses at a high rate).

DISCUSSION

This chapter's introduction presented the argument that studies based
on aggregated data and studies based on single drug types might inad-
vertently hide possible variations in the relationship between drug
misuse and crime. However, it was not known whether such variations
existed. In practice, it was not known whether drug use was associated with crime generally or whether specific types of drug use were
associated with specific types of crime. In the case of the former, the
association might be referred to as a general 'drug-crime connection',
and in the latter, the association might be referred to as specific 'drug-
crime connections'.

The main aim of this chapter has been to examine the association using disaggregated data to investigate some of these possible
variations. Specifically, the chapter has examined disaggregated relationships between the prevalence of drug use and the prevalence and
incidence of crime.

In relation to drug use and the prevalence of offending, the findings of the bivariate analysis showed that recreational drug users were
more likely than non–drug users to have committed a range of offense
types. It also showed that hard drug users were more likely than recreational users to have committed a wide range of offense types. These
findings were supported by the results of the logistic regression analysis. These showed that users of most recreational drugs were more
likely than nonusers of these drugs to report committing a wide range
of offense types. It also showed that crack users were more likely to
report a range of crime types. The findings relating to heroin and
cocaine were less wide ranging and tended to show an increased likelihood of offending only in relation to specific offenses. Hence, there is
some evidence of specific drug-crime connections. However, the dominant finding of this section is that drug use is associated with a general increased likelihood of offending that covers a range of offense
types.

In relation to drug use and the incidence of offending, the findings of the bivariate analysis showed that there were few significant connections between recreational drug use and rate of offending of any of the offense types. There were a greater number of significant associations between hard drug use and rate of offending. However, these were limited to specific offense types (mainly shoplifting, burglary in a nondwelling, handling stolen goods, and drug supply offenses). A similar pattern was found in the results of the logistic regression analysis. This showed that there were few connections between use of recreational drugs and high-rate of offending. However, there was an association between use of heroin and rate of shoplifting and crack use and rate of fraud, handling stolen goods, and drug supply offenses. Hence, the dominant finding of this chapter is that drug use is associated with high-rate offending, but only in relation to specific drug-crime combinations.

It was mentioned earlier that the aim of the chapter was to determine whether there was a general drug-crime connection or whether there were specific drug-crime connections. It appears from these findings that the answer is that the relation appears to be general when talking about prevalence of offending and specific when talking about incidence of offending.

Prevalence Findings
The first general finding is that there appears to be a general drug-crime link when looking at drug use and the prevalence of crime. In effect, this means that arrestees who used drugs also tended to commit crimes. It also means that there was no clear pattern in terms of the drug-crime preferences. Instead, there appeared to be a generally elevated risk of offending among drug users compared with non–drug users.

How can a relationship between drug use and commission of a wide range of offense types be explained? One explanation is that drug users are more likely than nonusers to be offense generalists. In other words, drug users might, for whatever reason, commit a larger number of offense types than nonusers. As a result, their prevalence rate would tend to be inflated across a range of offense types. There is some evidence from the New English and Welsh Arrestee Drug Abuse

Monitoring (NEW-ADAM) data to support this view. Heroin, crack, and cocaine users were significantly more likely (24%) than nonusers of these drugs (7%) to be offense generalists (defined as committing 3 or more of the 10 offense types in the last 12 months). Hence, the higher involvement of heroin, crack, and cocaine users in a range of offense types might account for their greater involvement in any specific offense type.

Incidence Findings

The second general finding is that there appears to be a number of specific drug-crime links when looking at drug use and the incidence of crime. In practice, this means that certain kinds of drug use are associated with high rates of certain kinds of crime. In fact, the relationships found in the previous section were limited to just a few specific connections between heroin use and high rates of shoplifting and crack use and high rates of fraud, handling stolen goods, and drug supply offenses.

How can these relationships be explained? One possible explanation for the small number of connections between drug misuse and rate of offending is a result of the fact that only some offenses can be easily committed at high rates. Shoplifting is a good example of an offense that can be committed at a high rate should the user wish to do so. Bank robbery is an example of an offense that might be harder to commit at a high rate. Hence, it would be expected that high-rate offending would occur only in relation to offense types that can be easily committed at a high rate. This might be as a result of drug misuse causing high rates of offending or of high-rate offending causing drug misuse.

Another possible explanation is that there are certain affinities between particular types of drug misuse and particular types of crime. Crack use might be associated with drug supply offenses because crack use might provide an opportunity to be involved in illegal drug markets. Crack use might not be associated with residential burglary because of the time taken to execute the offense and convert the goods into cash. Heroin use might amplify rates of shoplifting because it provides a frequent and nonconfrontational source of illegal goods that can be sold or used to conserve cash for drug purchases. Heroin use might be less likely to be associated with robbery, which might require confrontation and physical force to execute successfully. This might be difficult to achieve when under the influence of depressant drugs.

Implications for Research

Research on the drug-crime connection generally has not examined disaggregated findings and has not distinguished clearly between prevalence and incidence of offending. Future research might redress this balance by looking at the association between specific drug-crime connections. There is also greater opportunity to develop specific drug-crime theories of the link. It is not necessarily the case that one theory explains all connections. The heroin-shoplifting link might be explained by the economic necessity argument. However, other links (especially those relating to drugs and violence or those relating to drugs and expressive crimes) might require different explanations. It would also be helpful if explanations distinguished between reasons for involvement in a particular crime (prevalence) and reasons for committing the crime at a certain rate (incidence).

Implications for Policy

The findings of the chapter are important for government antidrug strategies. They suggest that generalized approaches to the problem of drug misuse and crime might not be as effective as targeted approaches that reach the high-rate drug-misusing offenders. In fact, they suggest that there might be some benefits obtained from targeting specific drug-crime relationships. This might include targeting specific types of drugs (such as heroin and crack) or specific types of offenses (such as shoplifting, fraud, and drug dealing). It might also include focusing on particular drug-crime combinations and the particular offenders responsible for them. In practice, this might mean tackling heroin-using shoplifters or crack-using drug dealers as a means of tackling both drug misuse and crime.

CHAPTER SEVEN

Multiple Drug Use and Crime

INTRODUCTION

Research on the connection between drug misuse and crime has tended to focus on either aggregated measures of drug misuse and criminal behavior or specific types of drugs and specific types of offenses. Little attention has been paid to the extent to which combinations of drug misuse might be connected to crime. This is surprising for at least two reasons. First, there has been considerable attention paid in the research literature to what is sometimes referred to as poly-drug or multiple drug misuse. However, much of this discussion has focused on explaining the phenomenon of multiple drug misuse or the implications of multiple drug misuse for treatment. Second, there are a number of plausible reasons to suspect that drug use combinations might be important in explaining crime. These include direct effects, such as the potential interactive or additive effects of drug mixing on judgment or behavior, and indirect effects, such as the potential amplifying effect of involvement in drug misuse on offending.

Research that has investigated the association between specific drug types, and crime has tended to investigate the use of the specific drug type in isolation from other drugs. Many studies, for example, have investigated the association between heroin misuse and criminal behavior. However, few have investigated the association between heroin use in combination with other drugs and criminal behavior. The main problem with this is that it cannot be assumed that the association between heroin use and crime will be the same regardless of the additional drugs consumed. Instead, it is likely that the nature of the drug-crime connection will be governed by the particular combination of drug types used in conjunction with heroin.

MULTIPLE DRUG USE

Before discussing the effects of multiple drug use on crime, it is useful to consider what is meant by the term multiple drug use. There are several terms of similar meaning including *polydrug use, multiple drug use, drug mixing, consecutive drug use, concurrent drug use, simultaneous drug use, co-use, co-occurrence, supplemental drug use, subsidiary drug use,* and *sequential drug use.*

Some writers have defined polydrug use to apply to drug users in treatment. Fountain et al. (1999), for example, used the term polydrug user to refer to users who supplement their prescribed drugs with additional nonprescribed drugs. Best et al. (2001b) also referred to polydrug use in the context of users in treatment whose consumption of heroin is supplemented with a combination of prescribed and nonprescribed drugs.

There is also some variation in whether multiple drug or polydrug use refers to concurrent use (drugs used at the same time) or sequential use (one drug followed by another). Pennings et al. (2002) defined concurrent use as occurring when both drugs are consumed at the same time in such a way that they might interact in terms of their physiological effects. Leri, Bruneau, and Stewart (2003) provided an example of the simultaneous use of heroin and cocaine in which cocaine is injected as a mixture with heroin or is injected immediately before or after heroin (sometimes without removal of the syringe). Leri et al. (2003) also referred to sequential use as one drug being used shortly after another to offset or enhance the effects. Other writers have argued that multiple drug or polydrug use includes both concurrent and sequential forms. Wilkinson et al. (1987) used the term polydrug use to mean use of more than one drug type, either over time or at a point in time. They defined polydrug users as 'users of a variety of psychoactive substances, either concurrently or sequentially' (p. 259).

Other writers have used the concept of multiple drug use to refer to the variety of drugs consumed over a set period of time. In these cases, multiple drug use might include concurrent and sequential use over a fixed period of time. In other words, a user who had used heroin, crack, and cannabis over, say, a one-month period might be defined as a multiple drug user during that period. The specific time period used in the literature tends to vary. Simpson and Sells (1974) investigated 'multiple drug use' over a two-month period before admission to treatment. Darke and Hall (1995) investigated 'polydrug' use over the last 6 months. Wilkinson et al. (1987) examined 'multiple drug use' over the last 12 months before interview. Schifano et al. (1998) investigated 'multiple drug use' over the whole lifetime.

In the current chapter, we have used the term multiple drug use rather than polydrug use because the latter term tends to be associated with treatment diagnoses and is sometimes used to refer to the use of subsidiary drugs in addition to prescription drugs. It is used in preference to simultaneous drug use because the chapter aims to investigate drug use and criminal behavior over various periods of time. In most cases, the term multiple drug use is used to mean use of two or more drugs over a 12-month period of time.

THEORIES OF MULTIPLE DRUG USE AND CRIME

There has been little discussion in the literature about the links between multiple drug use and crime. As a result, there has been little attempt to develop any theories relating to the link. However, a number of generalized statements can be found in the literature concerning the connection between multiple drug use and crime. The most common explanations are economic explanations, psychopharmacological explanations, and lifestyle explanations.

Economic Explanations

Economic theories of the association between drug use and crime are based on the idea that greater involvement in drug use leads to greater expenditure on drugs and greater involvement in acquisitive crime to pay for these drugs. Some writers have made generalized statements about the relation that include multiple drug use. Leri et al. (2003) argued that opioid users who also use cocaine will have drug habits that are even more expensive, which, in turn, might lead some individuals to engage in income-generating crime. They also noted that opioid addicts sometimes use amphetamines to sustain the activity level needed to 'hustle' the necessary funds to pay for their opioid habit. Chaiken and Chaiken (1990) reported that a large body of research shows that high-rate offenders who commit predatory crimes are likely also to use many different types of drugs. The main principle of economic theory is that regular drug use is expensive, and some users will seek funds for their drug use from illegal sources. This argument is usually made in relation to heroin addiction and the costs of habitual drug use (Brochu, 2001). However, the theory can be applied to any costly form of drug use. Users of multiple drugs (especially when two or more of them are expensive drugs) may face additional financial pressures to commit acquisitive crime.

Psychopharmacological Explanations

Psychopharmacological explanations are based on the idea that drugs can have a direct or indirect effect on behavior as a result of their chemical properties. These explanations are typically directed at drug use and violent crime and in most cases refer to the effects of individual drugs. However, some writers have discussed the interaction, protective, or additive effects of multiple drugs on the nature or rate of criminal behavior. Hammersley and Morrison (1987) noted that multiple drugs used simultaneously may increase intoxication. One reason for this is that drug combinations might create unique metabolites that are absent when the drugs are used individually. These metabolites may have greater toxicity than those formed when the drugs are used individually. Pennings et al. (2002) discussed theories about the possible mechanisms by which alcohol and cocaine in combination might lead to greater violence than from use of either drug alone. These include the idea that alcohol and cocaine each elevate extraneuronal dopamine and serotonin levels, which may lead to deficits in impulse control and to violent behavior.

Lifestyle Explanations

Lifestyle explanations are sometimes referred to as 'systemic' explanations in that crime is seen as an intrinsic (or systemic) part of the drug-using lifestyle. Lifestyle explanations are also sometimes referred to as 'spuriousness' explanations in that there may be no direct causal connection between drug use (including multiple drug use) and crime. Instead, they coexist within the same lifestyle context. Leri et al. (2003), for example, noted that addicts may use a wide range of drugs as part of a more general deviant lifestyle that includes both drug use and crime. The lifestyle perspective rejects the view that drug use can be seen as a cause of crime or that crime can be seen as the cause of drug use. However, some writers conceive of lifestyle as a common cause that explains both drug use and crime. Walters (1994) argued that lifestyles evolve out of predisposing factors, initiating factors, and maintenance factors. The maintaining factors help reinforce and escalate forms of behavior. In the case of drugs and crime, common maintaining factors encourage the convergence and reinforcement of both drug using and criminal lifestyles.

RESEARCH ON MULTIPLE DRUG USE AND CRIME

There has been little research on the relation between multiple drug use and crime of any kind. However, some studies have addressed specific aspects of the relationship.

Prevalence of Multiple Drug Use and Crime

The link between multiple drug use and crime has been investigated by studies based on arrestee surveys. Smith and Polsenberg (1992) found, in a study based on adult arrestee data for the District of Columbia, that 81 percent of arrestees testing positive for two or more drugs had a prior criminal record, compared with 71 percent of those who tested positive for one drug, and 52 percent of those who tested positive for no drugs. Makkai (2001) reported from a study of arrestees in Australia that the odds of being charged with a property offense were three times greater among those who tested positive for two or more drugs than those who tested positive for one or no drugs.

Incidence of Multiple Drug Use and Crime

Few studies have looked at the relation between multiple drug use and the rate of offending. Some studies have looked at the incidence of criminal behavior among multiple drug users from data derived from general population surveys. Chaiken and Chaiken (1990) recalculated Elliott and Huizinga's (1984) data from the US National Youth Survey (NYS) to show that crime commission rates per year were between 10 and 20 times higher among multiple drug users (who used alcohol, marijuana, and other drugs four or more times each) than among nonusers.

Number of Drug Types Used and Crime

It is fairly rare for studies to report the connection between a precise number of drug types used and number of crimes committed. Smith and Polsenberg (1992) examined the relationship between the number of positive tests for different drug types among a sample of arrestees and the average number of prior arrests. They found that as the average number of positive tests increased the average number of prior arrests increased. Those who tested positive for no drug type recorded an average of 1.95 prior arrests, those who tested positive for just one drug type had an average of 2.75 prior arrests, and those who tested positive for two or more drug types had an average of 4.64 prior arrests. Hammersley, Forsyth, and Lavelle (1990) found no association among a sample of drug users in Scotland when they attempted to predict crime from drug use variables. They found that the number of drug types used was not a significant predictor of any of the five types of crime under investigation.

Combinations of Drug Types Used and Crime

There is also little research on the relation between specific combinations of multiple drug use and crime. However, there has been some research on the effect of different combinations of heroin, crack, and cocaine, plus subsidiary drugs, on crime. Shaw et al. (1999) found from among a sample of arrestees in Los Angeles that those who had used cocaine only or crack only in their lifetimes had lower prevalence rates of criminal activities (10% and 14%, respectively) than those who used both cocaine and crack (16% among those who used cocaine first and 24% among those who used crack first). Other research has confirmed the effect of heroin, crack, and cocaine combining on crime. Sanchez, Johnson, and Israel (1985) found among a sample of incarcerated females that those who used heroin and cocaine in the last year had higher mean rates of drug and prostitution offenses than users of heroin only. In a study of entrants into publicly funded drug abuse treatment programs in six US cities, Collins, Hubbard, and Rachal (1985) found that daily users of both heroin and cocaine reported higher levels of illegal income in the last year than those who reported daily use of heroin only or cocaine only.

RESULTS

The New English and Welsh Arrestee Drug Abuse Monitoring (NEW-ADAM) data were investigated to determine the various kinds of relationships between multiple drug use and crime among our sample of arrestees. The first part of the analysis involved identifying the characteristics of multiple drug users within the sample. The remaining results have been divided into the four main methods of investigating the relationship found in the literature: (1) multiple drug use and prevalence of crime, (2) multiple drug use and the incidence of crime, (3) number of drug types used and crime, and (4) drug-use combinations and crime.

The Characteristics of Multiple Users

Table 7.1 summarizes some of the main characteristics of single and multiple drug users. Females were more likely than males to be multiple drug users ($p < .05$). Similarly, older arrestees (aged 25 or more) were more likely than younger arrestees (aged 17–24) to be multiple drug users. There were also substantial differences in multiple drug use in terms of ethnic group status. Eighty percent of white drug users were defined as multiple drug users compared with 57 percent of non-white users ($p < .001$). The remaining three variables cover socioeconomic status. Arrestees who left school early, who were recently unemployed, and who were receiving social security benefits were all significantly more likely than their counterparts to be multiple drug users.

Multiple Drug Use and Prevalence of Crime

The association between multiple drug use and prevalence of offending is shown in Table 7.2. The findings indicate that there is a

TABLE 7.1. *Sociodemographic characteristics of multiple and single drug users*

	Multiple drug users (two or more drug types), %	Single drug users (one drug type), %	Total, % (*n*)
Sex			
Male	75	25	100 (2,109)
Female	81	19	100 (334)
Sig. of difference			*
Age group			
17–24	74	26	100 (1,290)
25+	78	22	100 (1,153)
Sig. of difference			*
Ethnic group			
White	80	20	100 (1,977)
Nonwhite	57	43	100 (465)
Sig. of difference			***
Age left education			
16 or under	79	21	100 (1,961)
17 or older	62	39	100 (434)
Sig. of difference			***
Employment status			
Unemployed	80	20	100 (1,241)
Other	72	28	100 (1,196)
Sig. of difference			***
On social security			
Yes	82	18	100 (1,509)
No	66	34	100 (934)
Sig. of difference			***

Note: Includes drug users only (*n* = 2,433).
Chi-square test. ***p < .001, *p < .05, ns = not significant.

significant difference in the proportion of multiple drug users and non–multiple drug users who reported acquisitive offending in the last 12 months. About one-third of single drug users (38%) compared with two-thirds of multiple drug users (69%) said that they had committed one or more acquisitive crimes in the last 12 months (p < .001).

The prevalence of offending was higher among female multiple drug users (72%) than male multiple drug users (68%). Conversely, younger (aged 17–24) multiple drugs users were significantly more

TABLE 7.2. *Percentage of arrestees reporting offending in the last 12 months by type of drug use*

	Multiple drug users (two or more drug types)	Single drug users (one drug type)	Significance of difference in proportion of offending
Sex			
Male	68	38	***
Female	72	33	***
Age			
17–24	72	46	***
25+	66	26	***
Ethnic group			
White	70	36	***
Nonwhite	60	41	***
TOTAL	69	38	***

Note: Includes arrestees who used one or more drugs in the last 12 months ($n = 2,443$). Chi-square test. *** $p < .001$; ns = not significant.

likely than older (aged 25 or more) multiple drug users to report committing one or more acquisitive crimes in the last 12 months. Finally, white multiple drug users were more likely than nonwhite multiple drug users to report offending (70% compared with 60%).

Multiple Drug Use and Incidence of Crime

The next research question investigated was whether multiple drug users committed crimes at a higher rate than single drug users. The results indicate a significant difference in the mean number of offenses reported among multiple and non–multiple drug users. On average, multiple drug users reported 229 of the selected property offenses in the last 12 months compared with a mean of 104 for single drug users. Hence, multiple drug users reported on average twice as many offenses as single drug users.

A breakdown of the relationship by demographic factors showed that the rate of offending was higher among multiple than single drug users among all groups except one. Among female arrestees, the difference in offending rate did not reach the .05 level of statistical significance (probably because of small sample sizes). However, male arrestees who had used multiple drug types in the last 12 months

TABLE 7.3. *Mean number of offenses reported in the last 12 months by type of drug use*

	Multiple drug users (two or more drug types)	Single drug users (one drug type)	Significance of difference in proportion of offending
Sex			
Male	229	98	***
Female	231	157	ns
Age			
17–24	199	104	***
25+	265	104	***
Ethnic group			
White	232	102	***
Nonwhite	210	108	*
TOTAL	229	104	***

Notes: Includes only arrestees who reported one or more of the selected offenses in the last 12 months. Outliers (for mean number of offenses) were controlled by recoding the top 5 percent of responses (to the 94.9% value of 1177). This equates to a mean maximum rate of approximately three offenses per day every day for 365 days. Analysis of variance. *** $p < .001$, * $p < .05$; ns = not significant.

reported a mean offending rate of 229 offenses compared with a rate of 98 among male arrestees who had used just one drug type. Arrestees in both age groups and arrestees in both ethnic groups who had used multiple drug types reported approximately twice the mean offending rate as their counterparts who had used just one drug type.

The results of these first two sections show a statistically significant association between multiple drug use and crime both in terms of the proportion of drug users who offended and the mean rate of offending. However, it has not yet been established whether the number of drug types consumed is correlated with the number of crimes committed.

Number of Drug Types Used and Crime

The method of grouping drug use or criminal behavior into dichotomized variables (single drug users or multiple drug users) is useful in summarizing findings, but it loses important information about the details of the relationship. The association between multiple drug use and crime can be revealed more fully by examining variations

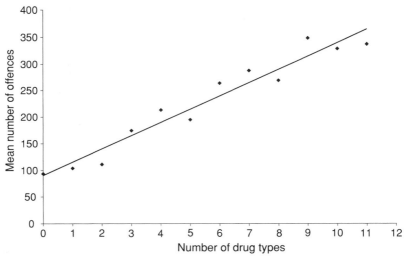

Figure 7.1 Mean number of offenses by mean number of drug types used in the last 12 months.

in both the number of offenses committed and the number of drug types used over the same period of time.

The relationship is presented as a line graph in Figure 7.1. The figure shows a positive correlation between number of drug types consumed and number of offenses committed (Pearson correlation coefficient based on an analysis of the individual cases = .23; $p < .01$). Among arrestees who had offended in the last 12 months, 7 percent had not used drugs in the last 12 months, 14 percent had used just one drug type, 9 percent had used two drug types, and 12 percent had used three drug types. The remaining 58 percent had used four or more drug types. The mean number of reported offenses was 93 among nonusers compared with 104 among users of one drug type, 195 among users of five drug types, and 337 among users of 11 drug types.

Hence, these results suggest a statistical association between the number of drug types used and the number of offenses committed. In this case, the results show that the association exists across a range of values and not just across specific groupings of values (e.g., single drug users vs. multiple drug users).

Combinations of Drug Types Used and Crime

Perhaps the most revealing way of looking at the relationship between multiple drug use and crime is through the particular combination of drug types used. There are a number of ways to identify and investigate drug type combinations. One method is to base the analysis on all combinations of all drugs found in the data. This is feasible with a small number of drug types. However, it becomes less feasible as the number of drug types increases. This was particularly problematic in the current study, which was based on 19 drug types. The main problem is that as the number of cells increases, the sample size per cell decreases. Another method is to combine the drug types into a small number of categories and to base the analysis on combinations of all drug groups found in the data. This would have the advantage that the number of groups would be small. However, it has the disadvantage of losing information as a result of grouping drug types. A third method (and the method preferred here) is to conduct a cluster analysis. This has the advantage that the number of clusters can be kept small while keeping the number of cases per cluster sufficiently high to conduct statistical analyses.

The cluster analysis described here was conducted only for recreational drug users and for hard drug users who might also have used recreational drugs. The first stage involved using hierarchical cluster analysis to determine the initial cluster means for the K-means analysis. This was done separately for users of drug combinations that did not include heroin, crack, or cocaine (the recreational drug [RD] sample) and for users of drug combinations that did include heroin, crack, or cocaine (the heroin, crack, or cocaine [HCC] sample). The analysis was conducted on a random 25 percent sample of the main data set to generate a sample size close to that recommended for this method. In each analysis, five clusters were requested. This number was chosen to strike a balance between a large enough number of groups to provide sufficient differentiation and a small enough number to ensure that the differences were interpretable. Our main aim was to identify a small number of interpretable groups that varied for the purpose of our analysis. It was not our aim to identify a definitive grouping of drug user types. A K-means cluster analysis was then conducted on the full data set. The cluster means generated from the hierarchical

TABLE 7.4. *Mean number of offenses in the last 12 months by drug type cluster*

Recreational drug clusters	Drug combinations	Mean offending rate
Cluster RD4	CA+AM	61
Cluster RD1	CA+DI+TE	44
Cluster RD5	CA+EC	43
Cluster RD3	CA+EC+AMY	35
Cluster RD2	CA	29
TOTAL	All	36
Significance		ns

Notes: Analysis of variance. Includes all drug users ($n = 2{,}443$). CA = cannabis; AM = amphetamines; DI = diazepam; TE = temazepam; EC = ecstasy; AMY = amyl nitrite.

analysis were used as the initial cluster means. In each analysis, five clusters were specified. This procedure was conducted separately for the recreational and hard drug samples.

The recreational drug analysis generated one cluster with one dominant drug (cannabis), two clusters with two dominant drugs (cannabis plus amphetamine and cannabis plus ecstasy), and two clusters with three dominant drugs (cannabis plus diazepam plus temazepam and cannabis plus ecstasy plus amyl nitrite; see Table 7.4). The hard drug analysis generated (when looking just at heroin, crack, and/or cocaine) two clusters of one HCC drug type (cocaine only and heroin only), two clusters of two HCC drug types (both heroin and crack), and one cluster of three HCC drug types (heroin, crack, and cocaine). Each HCC cluster included additional drug types (see Table 7.5).

The aim of the multiple-drugs-and-crime analysis was to determine whether there were any significant differences in the offending rate of users in each of the drug combination clusters. It was not essential that the clusters identified could be extrapolated to other samples of arrestees or other populations of offenders. The aim was simply to identify whether, within the current sample, different combinations of drug use were associated with significant differences in rates of offending.

The results for the recreational drug clusters are shown in Table 7.4. The analysis shows no significant difference in rate of offending between the five cluster types. However, the highest rate was recorded for users of cannabis and amphetamines (mean number of offenses =

TABLE 7.5. *Mean number of offenses in the last 12 months by drug type cluster*

Hard drug clusters	Drug combinations	Mean offending rate
Cluster HCC1	HE+CR+HS+RD+TR	265
Cluster HCC2	HE+CR+CO+HS+RD+TR	240
Cluster HCC3	HE+HS+RD	154
Cluster HCC5	CR+RD	135
Cluster HCC4	CO+RD	93
TOTAL	All	176
Significance		$p < .001$

Notes: Analysis of variance. Includes all drug users ($n = 2,443$). HE = heroin; CR = crack; CO = cocaine; HS = heroin substitutes; RD = recreational drugs; TR = tranquilizers.

61) and the lowest rate was recorded for users of cannabis alone (mean number of offenses = 29).

The results for the hard drug clusters are shown in Table 7.5. The results show that there were significant differences in the mean number of offenses committed across the hard drug type clusters ($p < .001$). The highest offending rates occurred among users of heroin and crack when combined with heroin substitutes, recreational drugs and tranquilizers (mean offending rate = 265). The lowest offending rates were found among users of cocaine who used no other drugs apart from recreational drugs (mean offending rate = 93).

These findings suggest that the particular drug-type combination is important. The knowledge that a user consumed cocaine in the last 12 months provides only a partial insight into their offending rates. Cocaine users who consumed only recreational drugs had a lower rate (mean = 93 offenses), whereas cocaine users who also consumed heroin, crack, and a range of other drug types had an offending rate twice that number (mean = 240 offenses). Similarly heroin users who consumed only recreational drugs or heroin substitutes had a mean offending rate of 154 offenses, whereas heroin users who also consumed crack and cocaine had a mean offending rate of 240.

DISCUSSION

The study has shown a correlation between multiple drug use and crime in relation to the arrestee sample. Almost twice as many multiple drug users as single drug users reported offending in the previous 12 months. Multiple drug users who offended reported on average twice as many offenses as single drug users who offended. Multiple drug users who used a large number of drug types reported committing a greater number of offenses than multiple drug users who used a small number of drug types. Multiple drug users, who included heroin, crack, or cocaine (or a combination of these) in their drug use committed a greater number of offenses on average than multiple drug users who used only recreational drugs. Multiple drug users who used heroin and crack and who also used heroin substitutes, recreational drugs, and tranquilizers had higher offending rates than multiple drug users who used heroin and crack without these additional drug types. These results have implications for both research and policy.

The relation between multiple drug use and crime is relevant to criminological research and understanding of criminal behavior. In the past, criminology has acknowledged the links between drug use and crime. However, little attention has been paid to the number or the specific combination of drug types used in explaining the drug-crime connection. It would be useful if more research were conducted in this area. In particular, it would be useful if research were conducted across different countries and among different groups to identify variations in the links between multiple drug use and crime. It is likely that the relationship will vary by drug-use preferences at particular times and locations. More research also needs to be done on the nature of drug-type combinations and their relationship with crime. The current analysis has explored the association between broad clusters of drug-type combinations and crime. Future research might investigate in more detail the association between specific combinations of drug types and crime. It is possible, for example, that heroin users who also use other specific drug types (such as temgesic or DF118 s) might commit crimes at a different rate from those who use other specific drug types (such as methadone or amyl nitrite).

There is also more that can be done to explain the links between multiple drug use and crime. Some explanations can be found in the literature, but the topic area is largely unexplored. In the main, theories of multiple drug use and crime are adaptations or extensions of existing theories of drug use and crime (such as the 'economic necessity' argument). However, other explanations of the relationship are possible that focus more precisely on the nature of multiple drug use. Concurrent multiple drug use (two or more drugs used at the same time) or sequential drug use (one drug used after another) might have different kinds of links with crime than use of multiple drug types over a period of time. The former might be explained by psychopharmacological factors and the effects of drug mixing on the motivation to offend. Conversely, the latter type of multiple drug use might be better explained by social factors such as lifestyles or the progress of drug use or criminal careers.

The connection between multiple drug use and crime is relevant to government policy on drugs and crime. Drug strategies aimed at reducing drug-related crime typically focus on users of heroin and crack without taking into account use of other drugs. However, the results of the current research have shown that heroin and crack use is not universally associated with high rates of offending. Heroin or crack users who use few other drugs (according to our results) are likely to have lower offending rates than those who use many other drugs. Further, even among heroin and crack users who are multiple drug users, there are likely to be variations in their offending rates depending on the particular multiple drug-type combination. Heroin and crack users who use only recreational drugs committed offenses at about half the rate of heroin and crack users who used heroin substitutes, recreational drugs, and tranquilizers. Hence, the nature of multiple drug use (in particular, the nature of other drugs used by heroin and crack users) might be useful in guiding intervention strategies.

Knowledge about multiple drug use is also relevant to treatment services provided as part of an antidrug strategy. Heroin users who also use crack might require a different treatment approach than heroin users who use only heroin. Similarly, heroin users who use many other drug types might require a different approach from those who use only a few. In many countries (notably the United Kingdom and the United States) treatment services have grown up around the treatment of heroin addiction. As a result, knowledge about the treatment of cocaine and crack addiction and multiple drug dependency is less well developed. Understanding and responding to the treatment needs of the most problematic drug users might help reduce the social problems associated with it and help reduce drug-related crime.

CHAPTER EIGHT

Users' Perceptions of the Drug-Crime Link

INTRODUCTION

The previous chapters have focused mainly on the statistical association between drug use and crime. We have not yet discussed whether drug use and crime are causally connected. It might be the case that the two are statistically associated (when you get one, you tend to get the other) but not causally connected (one does not cause the other).

There has been no shortage of theories of the possible causal connection between drug use and crime. These include economic explanations (e.g., crimes are committed to fund drug use), psychopharmacological explanations (e.g., crimes are committed as a result of judgment impairment from drugs), and sociological explanations (e.g., drugs are purchased from the proceeds of crime) mentioned earlier. However, little is known about whether these explanations are valid, whether some are linked to certain conditions or apply only to certain individuals, or whether some are more common than others. It is possible that the causal connection between drug use and crime is different for women compared with men, younger people compared with older people, heroin users compared with amphetamine users, or car thieves compared with street robbers. Common sense tells us that different circumstances will involve different causal processes. However, it is still unclear when one explanation might apply compared with another.

The New English and Welsh Arrestee Drug Abuse Monitoring (NEW-ADAM) surveys were not designed to investigate causality directly because this would have required determining the main elements of a causal process including establishing a statistical association, identifying the temporal order between the presumed cause and effect, and ruling out any rival hypotheses (other events that might have caused the changes). This type of investigation is better suited to longitudinal, which allow each of the causal elements to be monitored over time, rather than cross-sectional research designs. However, it was still possible to investigate whether drug use caused crime or crime caused drug use by asking the arrestees whether they thought the two were causally connected in their own case.

In this chapter, we investigate the connection between drug use and crime as perceived by drug users and offenders. In particular, we focus on drug-users' accounts of the connection between their own drug use and crime. We look at what previous research has said on this topic and the results of the NEW-ADAM research on arrestees in the United Kingdom.

MODELS AND EXPLANATIONS

A number of causal connections have been described in the literature. These include the causal models mentioned earlier that identify whether drug use causes crime or crime causes drug use. These include the 'drug-use-causes-crime model', the 'crime-causes-drug-use model', the 'reciprocal model', and the 'common-cause model' (Brownstein and Crossland, 2002; White, 1990).

The first model (the drug-use-causes-crime model) is based on the principle that drug use is a direct or indirect cause of crime. The second (the crime-causes-drug-use model) is based on the reverse principle that crime is a direct or indirect cause of drug use. The third (the reciprocal model) argues that drug use sometimes causes crime and crime sometimes causes drug use. Menard et al. (2001), for example, argued that drug use and crime are mutually reinforcing. Illegal behavior leads to early drug use and later (perhaps more serious) drug use leads to an escalation of illegal behavior. The fourth (the common cause model) proposes that drug use does not cause crime, nor does crime cause drug use. Instead, they are both caused by a third or common variable.

Causal connections can also be found in the main explanations of the drug-crime relationship. These include economic explanations (crimes are committed to fund drug use), psychopharmacological explanations (crimes are committed as a result of judgment impairment), sociological explanations (drugs are purchased from the proceeds of crime), and lifestyle explanations (deviant lifestyles generate a context for both drug use and crime) (Brochu, 2001; Goldstein, 1985; Menard et al., 2001; White and Gorman, 2000).

The first (the economic necessity argument) is based on the view that serious drug users will be unable to support their habit through legitimate activities and will resort to crime to fund their drug use (Goldstein, 1985). The second (the psychopharmacological explanation) is based on the idea that the intoxicating effects of drug use might lead to judgment impairment, which in turn might lead to the commission of crime (White and Gorman, 2000). The third is based on the view that criminals might use drugs as a form of chemical recreation to celebrate the successful commission of a crime (Menard et al., 2000). The fourth is sometimes referred to as a noncausal or spurious connection because drug use does not cause crime and crime does not cause drug use.

PREVIOUS RESEARCH

Research based on users' accounts has made good progress in listing explanations but has made less headway in identifying when, where, and how often they might apply. However, some progress has been made in the research literature in imposing order on the current body of knowledge. The research on this topic has generated evidence that can by summarized under five main headings: (1) the proportion of drug users who believe that there is a connection, (2) the proportion of drug users who report different types of connections, (3) variations between types of drug users and types of connections, (4) variations between types of drug use and types of connections, and (5) variations between types of crimes and types of connections.

Proportion of Drug Users Who Believe There Is a Connection

Studies of arrestees have been particularly productive in quantifying the frequency of use of explanations for drug use and crime. In most of these studies, the respondents are asked whether they believe that their drug use and crime are connected. Milner et al. (2004), for example, interviewed almost 3,000 arrestees as part of the Drug Use Monitoring Program in Australia (DUMA) program of detainees in Australia and asked them to report on the proportion of their offenses that were drug related in the past 12 months. Almost half (45%) of arrestees who said that they had used illegal drugs in the past 12 months said that at least some of their offenses were drug related.

Studies of prisoners have also provided insights into the proportion of drug-misusing offenders who report that their drug use and crime are connected. Liriano and Ramsay (2003) in a survey of prisoners in the United Kingdom asked inmates who reported taking drugs in the 12 months before entering prison whether they thought that their drug use and crime were connected. Fifty-five percent said that they thought that their drug use and crime were connected. In another study of prisoners, Makkai and Payne (2003) interviewed incarcerated offenders in three territories in Australia and asked them to describe whether their use of alcohol or drugs had had an effect on their criminal activities. Among the property offenders who answered the question, 71 percent thought that drugs or alcohol were connected to their offending. Among those who quantified the relationship, 26 percent thought that *all* of their offenses were drug or alcohol connected, 33 percent thought that *most* of their offenses were connected, and 12 percent thought that *some* were connected.

Studies based on other samples have also found high levels of perceived connection between drug use and crime. Wincup et al. (2003) interviewed 160 homeless young people in the United Kingdom about various aspects of their lifestyles, including their use of drugs and their criminal behavior. Over half of those who had a history of drug use thought that there was a link between drug use and their offending. Even higher correlations have been found in studies of drug-using populations. Hammersley and Morrison (1987) conducted interviews with 28 active heroin users. They reported that almost all of them said that their offending and drug-misuse were causally connected.

Proportion of Drug Users Who Report Different Types of Connection

Studies of arrestees and prisoners have also been useful in identifying the frequency of use of various explanations. These typically involve asking those offenders who reported a connection to tell the interviewer about the kind of connection.

In the study of prisoners mentioned earlier, Liriano and Ramsay (2003) found that 82 percent of prisoners who thought there was a connection between their drug use and their crime gave explanations that fell into the 'drug-use-causes-crime' category. Thirty-five percent said that it was 'through the effect of drugs on their judgment' and 22 percent said that it was 'drugs were one of the things that they bought with the money from crime'. Makkai and Payne (2003) found in their study of incarcerated offenders that among those who responded, 31 percent thought that the relationship was driven by economic necessity and 29 percent thought that the relationship was psychopharmacological. A further 27 percent thought that drug use caused crime but did not say in what way. The study by Wincup et al. (2003) of homeless young people mentioned earlier found that the most common explanations for the link between drug use and crime was financing drug use and committing offenses while under the influence of drugs.

Hence, the small amount of research on this topic has shown that a large proportion of drug-misusing offenders tend to see their drug use and crime as connected, and a large proportion of these tend to believe that the connection between drug use and crime is a result of the need for money to buy drugs.

Variations Between Types of Drug Users and Types of Connections

These general findings mask possible variations in the types of reasons given for the connection among various kinds of drug users. It is important to find out, therefore, what these variations are and when they apply. The main information that is currently available in the research concern variations by age.

Menard et al. (2001) used data from the National Youth Survey (NYS) to investigate the relationship between drug use and crime and concluded that 'the drugs-crime relationship is different for different ages and for different stages of involvement in crime and drug use' (p. 295). Faupel and Klockers (1987) made a similar point when they argued that different patterns are evident at different phases of the addiction career. During the 'occasional user' phase, they suggested, drug use and crime are spuriously related, during the 'stabilized junkie' and 'free-wheeling junkie' phases, drug use is facilitated by criminal income, and during the 'street addict phase', drug use appears to cause crime. Johnson et al. (1986) also identified age differences in the use of explanations for the drug-crime connection. They noted that 'The economic motivation explanation has not been supported among adolescents. Intensive drug users and highly delinquent youths do not report committing crimes to raise money for drugs' (Johnson et al., 1986).

Variations Between Types of Drug Use and Types of Connections

Goldstein (1985) concluded in his own review of the literature that different drug types are related to different types of connections. He noted that alcohol, stimulants, barbiturates, and PCP are more likely to be related to violent behavior, whereas heroin and cocaine are most likely to be related to economic crimes because they are expensive and are typified by compulsive patterns of use. There is some support for this view in the research literature.

One of the most common drug-crime connections discussed is the relationship between heroin and cocaine and crime. Many of these studies report an economic association between these drugs and crime. The study by Hammersley and Morrison (1987) mentioned earlier of 28 heroin users included questions on the nature of the connection. When asked why they committed economic crimes, 26 gave money for drugs as a reason, eight suggested money for other purposes, six said that it was for excitement or enjoyment, and two said that they committed drug-dealing as a favor for someone else (multiple responses were possible). Most of the sample thought that the link between their economic crimes and their drug-abuse was causal. Cromwell et al. (1991) looked at differences in the drug-crime connection among heroin and cocaine users. They concluded from their study of drug-using burglars that heroin-using burglars were more controlled and approached burglary as an occupation, whereas cocaine-using burglars showed less control over their drug use and offending and frequently committed burglaries under the influence of cocaine.

Some studies have looked at the variations in drug use and crime in relation to recreational drugs. Klee (1997) used data from the North

West England longitudinal study to explore the drug-crime relationship among a sample of amphetamine users. They found that the majority of amphetamine users in the sample reported that property crime preceded the use of drugs and concluded that their criminal activities had little or nothing to do with the use of amphetamines.

Variations Between Types of Crimes and Types of Connections

The importance of the type of crime in explaining the drug-crime connection was made by Welte et al. (2001) in relation to drug users in Canada. They reported that the relationship between substance use and delinquency depends on the type of offense. They found that the relationship between drug use and crime was less pronounced for the more serious types of delinquency and concluded that further research was needed to unravel these differences.

There has been some research that has looked at differences in explanation by differences in offense. The study by Wincup et al. (2003) of homeless young people mentioned earlier found that the most common explanation for committing shoplifting, burglary, and theft was to obtain money to fund drug use. However, there have been few studies that have looked at systematic differences between offenses and explanations. Some additional information can be found from studies that have focused on particular types of drug-using offenders. Erickson et al. (2000) conducted research on 30 female crack users working as prostitutes in Toronto and asked them about the relationship between their crack use and crime. The authors concluded that although some women started prostitution to support themselves or to pay for other (noncrack) drugs, most started after they had begun crack use. All women interviewed said that they spent most of what they earned from prostitution on crack. Hough (1996) drew attention to what he described as a 'complex dynamic' between prostitution and drug dependence in that prostitution is a method of financing drug use and drug use is a palliative to prostitution. In the study of burglars by Cromwell et al. (1991) mentioned earlier, they found that many of their respondents reported that crime caused drug use in that they celebrated a successful burglary by purchasing alcohol and drugs. A similar finding was reported in a study of street robbers by Wright and Decker (2001), who noted that for many of the sample the main aim of robbery was to 'keep the party going', which included the purchase of drugs.

RESULTS

The same five areas of investigation found in the research literature were examined using the NEW-ADAM data. The results of the research are summarized in this chapter under the following headings: (1) the proportion of drug users who believe that there is a connection, (2) the proportion of drug users who report different types of connection, (3) variations between types of drug users and types of connections, (4) variations between types of drug use and types of connections, and (5) variations between types of crimes and types of connections. In addition, we include a sixth section examining patterns in explanations of drug use and crime based on variations by sociodemographic, drug use, and crime characteristics that might help identify drug-crime connection profiles.

Proportion of Drug Users Who Believe There Is a Connection

All arrestees who reported using at least one drug and committing at least 1 of 10 selected offenses in the last 12 months were asked the following question:

In the last 12 months, do you think that your drug use was in any way connected to your offending?

Overall, 63 percent of arrestees who used drugs and reported crimes in the last 12 months thought that their drug use and crime were connected (see Table 8.1). Among those who thought there was a connection, 71 percent thought that *all* of their offenses were linked with drug use, 14 percent thought *most* of their offenses were connected, and 13 percent thought *some* of their offenses were connected. These percentages are in the higher range of the studies reported earlier in the chapter. This might be because we included only respondents who reported at least one offense and one crime in the last 12 months. We also excluded alcohol from the question and asked only about the drug-crime relationship. Nevertheless, the research clearly shows that a majority of drug-using offenders thought that their drug use and crimes were connected.

TABLE 8.1. *Perceived nature of the connection between drug use and crime by demographic factors*

	% Reporting connection between drug use and crime[a]	Type of connection[b]		
		Judgment impairment	Crimes committed for money for drugs	Drugs purchased from proceeds of crime
Sex	61***	24*	83**	6 ns
Male	61***	24*	83**	6 ns
Female	74	15	94	5
Age				
17–19	47***	27 ns	70***	7 ns
20–24	63	25	87	7
25–29	76	18	90	4
30 or older	69	20	88	4
Ethic group				
White	65***	23 ns	86***	5 ns
Nonwhite	52	17	74	9
TOTAL %	63	22	85	6
TOTAL n	1,455	914	914	914

Note: Multiple responses are possible.
[a]Respondents who reported committing at least one offense and taking at least one drug in the last 12 months ($n = 1,455$).
[b]Respondents who said that there was a connection between using drugs and committing crimes in the last 12 months ($n = 914$).
Chi-square test: * $p < .05$; ** $p < .01$; *** $p < .001$; ns = not significant.

It is possible that there may be differences among different kinds of drug-misusing offenders. Some may be more likely than others to see a connection between their drug use and crimes. There is some evidence to support this view. Table 8.1 shows that females were significantly more likely than males to see a connection between their drug use and crimes (74% females compared with 61% males). Similarly, older arrestees were more likely than younger arrestees to say that the two were connected (69% aged 30 or more compared with 47% aged 17–19). White drug users (65%) were also significantly more likely than nonwhite users (52%) to report a connection.

These differences are important and show it cannot be assumed that evidence of a statistical association is evidence of a causal connection.

All of the arrestees included in the analysis were both drug users and admitted offenders in the 12 months before the interview. However, more than one-third of them thought there was no connection between their drug use and crimes. Nevertheless, two-thirds of arrestees reporting drug use and crime thought that there was a drug-crime connection in their case. Hence, it is useful to investigate further the nature of these connections.

Proportion Who Report Different Types of Connections

All arrestees who said that there was a connection between their drug use and crimes were asked the following supplementary question:

In what way do you think that your drug use was connected to your offending?

Their responses were coded into four response categories: (1) judgment impairment, (2) crimes committed for money for drugs, (3) drugs purchased from the proceeds of crime, and (4) other connections. The first three categories were designed to match the main explanations of the connections found in the literature. The fourth category ('other' connections) included all other connections. These explanations were variable and have been excluded from the analysis ($n = 62$). Hence, the following analysis is based on those arrestees whose responses were coded as falling into one of the first three categories.

Table 8.1 shows that the main explanation given by arrestees for the drug-crime connection in their case was that they committed crimes for money for drugs (given by 85% of arrestees mentioning a connection). The second most common explanation was judgment impairment mentioned by 22 percent arrestees, and the third most common was that crime resulted in cash or goods that were used to purchase drugs (mentioned by 6% of arrestees).

Variations Between Types of Drug User and Types of Connections

The results in the previous section show that some explanations are more common than others. However, it is still unknown in what way the explanations vary among different types of drug users. It is possible that the type of connection varies by the demographic characteristics of the user.

When looking at gender differences (see Table 8.1), males were significantly more likely than females to mention judgment impairment as a reason for the connection (24% of males compared with 15% of females). Conversely, females were significantly more likely than males to report committing crimes for money for drugs (94% of females gave this as a reason compared with 83% of males). There were no gender differences in terms of the other explanation that drugs were purchased from the proceeds of crime.

With respect to age, older arrestees (aged 25 or over) were significantly more likely than younger arrestees (aged 17–24) to report committing crimes for money for drugs, whereas younger respondents were significantly more likely than older respondents to say that drugs were purchased from the proceeds of crime. Younger arrestees (aged 17–24) were also significantly more likely to describe the drug-crime connection in terms of 'judgment impairment'. There was little variation in use of explanations by ethnic group. The only significant difference was that white respondents were more likely than non-white respondents to say that they committed crimes for money for drugs.

Hence, there is some evidence that there are systematic differences in explanations of the drug-crime connection by demographic characteristics of the drug user. The extent to which it is possible to build up a picture of these variations into clearer group differences is explored in the following sections.

Variations Between Types of Drug Use and Types of Connections

It is also possible that the relationship between drug use and crime might vary by type of drug used. It might be assumed, for example, that drug users who consume relatively cheap drugs are less likely to report economic connections than those who consume relatively expensive drugs. To test this, the proportion of users who reported consuming each of nine common drugs of abuse in the last 12 months were compared in relation to each of the explanations offered.

Users who reported that their drug use and crime were connected as a result of 'judgment impairment' were significantly *more* likely than those who did not mention this connection to be users of ecstasy (see Table 8.2). Among users who mentioned this connection, 47 percent reported use of ecstasy in the last 12 months compared with 34 percent of those who mentioned committing crimes for money to buy drugs and 44 percent of those who mentioned purchasing drugs from the proceeds of crime. It should be noted that the comparison group mean (those who did not mention this connection) will be influenced most strongly by the group with the largest sample size. Hence, the comparison percentages are given below only for the larger of the two comparison groups (in this case, those who mentioned committing crimes for money for drugs). Users who mentioned 'judgment impairment' were also slightly more likely to be users of amphetamines (32% compared with 29%) and LSD (8% compared with 6%), although neither of these differences was statistically significant. Conversely, respondents who gave this explanation were significantly less likely to be users of heroin (72% compared with 88%). They were also less likely to be users of crack (68% compared with 77%) and methadone (36% compared with 45%). However, neither of these latter two differences was statistically significant. Hence, the pattern of responses suggests that arrestees who report that their drug use and crime are linked through judgment impairment are more likely to be recreational drug users who tend not to use hard drugs such as heroin.

Drug users who said that they committed crimes for 'money for drugs' had almost the reverse drug-use profile. This group was significantly *more* likely to be users of diazepam, crack, heroin, and methadone. For example, 88 percent of those who reported 'money for drugs' as a connection said that they had used heroin compared with 72 percent of those who reported 'judgment impairment' and 48 percent of those who reported 'drugs purchased from the proceeds of crime'. Similarly, 77 percent said that they had used crack compared with 68 percent of those who reported 'judgment impairment'. This group was also significantly *less* likely to be users of ecstasy (34% compared with 47% who mentioned 'judgment impairment') and LSD (6% compared with 8%). There was no relationship between membership of this group and whether the respondents said that they had used cannabis, amphetamines, or cocaine. The broad characteristic

TABLE 8.2. *Proportion of arrestees reporting use of selected drug types in the last 12 months among arrestees reporting specific drug-crime connections*

	Judgment impairment, % (n = 204)	Sig.	Crimes committed for money to buy drugs, % (n = 774)	Sig.	Drugs purchased from the proceeds of crime, % (n = 50)	Sig.	All connections, % (n = 914)
Cannabis	87	ns	84	ns	90	ns	85
Ecstasy	47	** (+)	34	*** (−)	44	ns	37
Amphetamines	32	ns	29	ns	30	ns	29
LSD	8	ns	6	** (−)	6	ns	7
Diazepam	54	ns	58	*** (+)	34	** (−)	54
Cocaine	44	ns	42	ns	56	ns	43
Crack	68	ns	77	*** (+)	64	ns	72
Heroin	72	** (−)	88	*** (+)	48	*** (−)	79
Methadone	36	ns	45	*** (+)	24	* (−)	41

Notes: Among respondents who said that there was a connection between using drugs and committing crimes in the last 12 months (n = 913). Sig. = statistical significance of difference between specified connection and the other connections combined. Totals do not add up to 914 because multiple responses were possible. (−) = significantly less likely; (+) = significantly more likely.

Chi-square test: $* p < .05$; $** p < .01$; $*** p < .001$; ns = not significant.

of this group is, therefore, of mainly hard drug users who are involved in recreational drug use at about the same level or (in the case of ecstasy and LSD) slightly lower level than other drug-using arrestees.

The third group includes those who reported that the 'proceeds from crime' were used to buy drugs. This group had a similar drug-use profile to that of the first group. Users who gave this explanation were slightly *more* likely than those who said that they committed crimes for money for drugs to use cannabis (90% compared with 84%), ecstasy (44% compared with 34%), and amphetamines (30% compared with 29%). However, none of these differences was statistically significant (which is likely due to the small sample sizes and low statistical power). Users who gave this explanation were also significantly *less* likely to report using diazepam, methadone, and heroin. Forty-eight percent of users of this group reported use of heroin compared with 88 percent of those who mentioned the 'money for drugs' motive. Hence, the pattern suggested by this group is of arrestees who are either as likely or more likely to use recreational drugs but less likely to use hard drugs such as heroin and methadone.

Variations Between Types of Crimes and Types of Connections

It is also possible that explanations of the drug-crime connection might vary depending on the types of crimes committed. It is likely, for example, that those who say they commit crimes for money for drugs are going to choose crimes that generate cash or sellable goods in sufficient quantities to pay for their drugs.

The findings of the current research show that respondents who say that their drug use and crimes are connected through 'judgment impairment' were more likely to commit theft from a person and handling offenses than those who suggested other connections (Table 8.3). However, they were no more likely than other arrestees to report having committed any of the eight other offense types in the last 12 months. Those who said that they committed crimes for money for drugs were significantly more likely than those who gave other reasons to report shoplifting in the last 12 months (77% compared with 66% of those who mentioned 'judgment impairment'). Conversely, they

TABLE 8.3. *Proportion of arrestees reporting selected offense types in the last 12 months among arrestees reporting specific drug-crime connections*

	Judgment impairment, % (n = 204)	Sig.[a]	Crimes committed for money to buy drugs, % (n = 774)	Sig.[a]	Drugs purchased from the proceeds of crime, % (n = 50)	Sig.[a]	All connections, % (n = 914)
Theft of a vehicle	15	ns	13	ns	24	* (+)	14
Theft from a vehicle	23	ns	20	ns	36	** (+)	20
Shoplifting	66	ns	77	*** (+)	58	ns	71
Burglary dwelling	14	ns	11	ns	12	ns	11
Burglary nondwelling	15	ns	13	ns	20	ns	13
Robbery	8	ns	5	* (−)	14	* (+)	6
Theft from a person	11	* (+)	8	ns	6	ns	8
Handling	52	* (+)	42	*** (−)	72	*** (+)	44
Fraud/deception	22	ns	20	ns	30	ns	21
Drug supply	32	ns	25	*** (−)	48	** (+)	29

Notes: Among respondents who said that there was a connection between using drugs and committing crimes in the last 12 months (n = 914).

[a]Sig. = statistical significance of difference between specified connection and the other connections combined. Totals do not add up to 914 because multiple responses were possible. (−) = significantly less likely; (+) = significantly more likely.

Chi-square test: * $p < .05$; ** $p < .01$; *** $p < .001$; ns = not significant.

were significantly less likely to report robbery, handling, and drug supply offenses. Users who said that they purchased drugs from the proceeds of crime were significantly more likely to report committing robbery, theft of a vehicle, theft from a vehicle, handling, and drug supply. They were no more likely to report burglary, fraud/deception, shoplifting, or theft from a person.

Hence, the pattern of findings suggest that arrestees who report 'judgment impairment' as a link between drug use and crime are more likely than others to report theft from a person and handling offenses. However, there are few other differences in involvement in other offense types. Those who report committing crimes for money for drugs are more likely than others to report committing shoplifting and less likely to report robbery, handling, and drug supply offenses. Arrestees who report purchasing drugs from the proceeds of crime are more likely to report a range of offenses including theft of, and from, a vehicle, robbery, handling, and drug supply.

Patterns in Explanations of Drug Use and Crimes

This final section considers whether there is some overall pattern of drug use and offending that is linked to the types of motives given for the drug-crime connection in particular cases. A summary of all of the significant findings presented is shown in Table 8.4. The table indicates that there are some variations in the profiles of arrestees across the various kinds of connection.

Users who mention judgment impairment as an explanation are more likely to be male, aged 17 to 24, and to use ecstasy. They are less likely to use hard drugs. They are also more likely to commit theft from a person and handling offenses. Users who state that they commit crimes for money for drugs tend to be white, female, and older than those who mention other reasons. They are also more likely to use hard drugs such as heroin, crack, and methadone and more likely to commit shoplifting. Those who say that they buy drugs as one of the items purchased from the proceeds of crime are more likely to be younger people (both male and female). They are also more likely to report a wide range of offense types, including, drug supply, robbery, handling, and vehicle crime.

TABLE 8.4. *Summary table of significant differences in the perceived nature of the connection between drug use and crime*

Significantly *more likely* to be/used/have committed . . .	Judgment impairment	Crimes committed for money for drugs	Drugs purchased from proceeds of crime
Demographics			
Male	✓		
Female		✓	
Aged 17–24	✓		✓
Aged 25 or more		✓	
White		✓	
Nonwhite			
Drug use			
Cannabis			
LSD			
Ecstasy	✓		
Amphetamines			
Cocaine			
Heroin		✓	
Crack		✓	
Methadone		✓	
Diazepam		✓	
Offending			
Drug supply			✓
Robbery			✓
Theft from a person	✓		
Burglary (dwelling)			
Burglary (nondwelling)			✓
Theft from a vehicle			✓
Theft of a vehicle			✓
Fraud/deception			
Handling	✓		✓
Shoplifting		✓	

Note. ✓ = Statistically significant finding; chi-square test; $p < .05$.

DISCUSSION

The main aim of the chapter was to investigate variations in users' explanations of the link between drug misuse and crime in their particular case. Understanding the nature of the causal connection between drug use and crime is important for both research and policy. Some governments (for example, the US and the UK governments) have adopted the view that drug use causes crime (rather than the other way around) and have developed policies to tackle various versions of this relationship. Conversely, some writers have argued that crime causes drug misuse and have generated explanations of the causal mechanisms by which drug use might lead to the commission of crime (White and Gorman, 2000).

The review of previous research showed that about half the drug-misusing offenders sampled thought that their drug use and crime were connected. The most common explanation was that drug use generated a need for illegal funds. However, other common explanations were that drug use impaired judgment, which led to crime, and that the proceeds of crime were sometimes spent on drug use. Little published research is available on variations in these explanations by user characteristics.

The findings of our own research supported many of these previous results. Most drug-misusing offenders reported that their drug use and crime were connected. The most common reasons concerned economic need, judgment impairment, and the fact that drugs just happened to be purchased from the proceeds of crime. The research also made some progress in identifying variations in the characteristics of drug users and the types of explanation given. Users who stated that they committed crimes for money for drugs were more likely to be white females and were, on average, older than those who mentioned other reasons. They were also more likely to use hard drugs such as heroin, crack, and methadone. Users who mentioned judgment impairment as an explanation were more likely to be male and to use recreational drugs.

Previous research has also suggested that there are some fairly common types of drug-misusing offenders. Some drug-misusing types mentioned in the literature are crack-using prostitutes who continue prostitution for money for drugs, heroin-using female shoplifters who commit shoplifting for money for drugs, robbers who operate as part of a 'street culture' and consume drugs for pleasure from the proceeds of crime, and young recreational drug users who occasionally commit crime as a result of drug-induced intoxication and judgment impairment. Although all of these might be viewed as drug-misusing offenders, they are clearly different in terms of the processes by which their drug use and crimes are connected.

There are two main implications that arise from this study: the first concerns understanding of the phenomenon and the direction of future research and the second concerns government drug policy and methods for tackling the relationship between drug misuse and crime.

The first implication is that some additional progress might be made if the study of the connection between drug use and crime attempted to document variations in users' accounts of the nature of the relationship. Many studies have demonstrated that there are variations in relation to particular drug-misusing groups (e.g., studies of prostitutes and studies of robbers). However, far fewer studies have looked across groups in the search for patterns in the nature of the connection. This type of investigation would be particularly suited to qualitative research that could investigate both between- and within-subject variations. Variations between subjects could be studied by selecting across different drug-using groups, combining perhaps samples drawn from treatment sources and criminal justice sources. Variations within subjects could be studied by asking respondents about different time periods in their drug-using career or by investigating different contexts in which drugs and crime coexisted.

The second implication is relevant to government policy. The current UK antidrug strategy (and that of many other countries) is based firmly on the principle that drug use causes crime and that drug users commit income-generating crimes to fund their drug habits (see Home Office, 2002). The strategy makes few distinctions between types of users or types of crimes and makes no reference to possible variations in the relationship. As a result, the policy might be described as 'one size fits all'. However, a greater appreciation of the variations in the drug-crime connection might help inform more focused strategies. The research suggests that government strategy aimed at reducing drug-related crime might be more effective if it responded differently to the various kinds of drug-misusing offenders and the various kinds of connections. For example, programs designed to reduce drug-related crime by reducing street prostitution might focus on outreach services, whereas programs to reduce shoplifting among heroin addicts might focus on treatment services or situational crime prevention. Similarly, programs designed to reduce crime among young recreational drug users might include educational programs, whereas strategies to reduce drug use among street robbers might focus on gang formations and street culture. In other words, a targeted strategy that took into account the various causal connections might be more productive than a general strategy that did not.

PART FOUR

SPECIAL TOPICS

CHAPTER NINE

Gender, Drugs, and Crime

INTRODUCTION

The relationship between gender and drug use has been referred to as 'the big neglected question' in the field of substance misuse (Measham, 2003, p. 22). Historically, the addiction literature has focused on male drug users, and less attention has been given to the problems of female users (Neale, 2004a). During the 1990s, this focus began to change, and female drug users became a topic of interest among researchers (Broom, 1994). However, it did not wholly answer the question of whether there were gender differences in drug misuse (Broom, 1994). As a result, relatively little research was done on the broader issue of whether women and men were fundamentally different in any way in the characteristics of their drug misuse and the problems associated with it.

Nevertheless, information relating to gender differences is now emerging. Recent research has shown that female and male drug users differ in terms of the nature of their drug use and in associated problems, including patterns of drug use (Neale, 2004a), the development of drug-use careers (Kandel, 2000), drug-use initiation (Eaves, 2004), and treatment outcomes (Hser, Huang, Teruya, and Anglin, 2004). These findings are important and suggest that both the nature of the problem and the nature of the solution might be different for women and men. However, the number of studies investigating any single issue within this broad area is small and the results obtained so far are contradictory (Hser et al., 2004). Hence, generalization is difficult and few definitive findings have emerged. Consequently, our knowledge of the specific problems raised by female and male drug consumption is limited.

RESEARCH ON GENDER DIFFERENCES IN DRUG MISUSE

In recent years, a number of studies have investigated gender differences in drug misuse. The main focus of this research has been on (1) differences in patterns of drug misuse, (2) developmental aspects of drug-misusing careers, (3) problems associated with drug misuse, and (4) differences in female and male treatment needs.

Patterns of Drug Use

Some studies of gender differences in patterns of drug misuse have shown higher levels of involvement among women than men. Parry, Pluddeman, Louw, and Leggett (2004), for example, reported findings from the 3-Metros study of drug use and crime among arrestees in South Africa. Urinalysis results revealed that women were more likely than men to test positive for cocaine, amphetamines, and opiates, whereas men were more likely than women to test positive for cannabis, mandrax, and benzodiazepines. Similar differences in the types of drugs used by male and female arrestees have also been found in Australia (Schulte, Mouzos, and Makkai, 2005) and in the United States (Zhang, 2004). Interviews with arrestees as part of the United States Arrestee Drug Abuse Monitoring (US-ADAM) program showed that female arrestees were more likely than males to report having used crack cocaine and heroin in the last month, whereas male arrestees were more likely than females to report having used cannabis, cocaine powder, and methamphetamines (Zhang, 2004). Gender differences in drug use have also been found among samples of prisoners. Peters, Strozier, Murrin, and Kearns (1997), for example, found that female prisoners were more likely than males to have ever used cocaine. However, women were less likely than men to have ever used cannabis and amphetamines.

Some evidence suggests that female and male drug users are different in terms of the rate at which they consume certain drugs and in the amount that they consume. Langan and Pelissier (2001), for example, reported that female prisoners were more likely than male prisoners to reach daily use of heroin and cocaine. Conversely, research among heroin and cocaine users has shown that women tend to use smaller daily amounts of these drugs than men (Powis, Griffiths, Gossop, and Strang, 1996).

There might also be differences among female and male drug users in their use of drug combinations. Some research has reported that multiple drug use (use of two or more drug types) is more prevalent among women than men (Langan and Pelissier, 2001). Kim and Fendrich (2002), for example, found in a study of juvenile arrestees, that women were more likely than men to be multiple drug users. The research also suggests that there are gender differences in terms of the types of drugs used in combination. Hser, Anglin, and Booth (1987a) noted that women more often than men combined opiates with other psychoactive drugs. However, Grella and Joshi (1999) showed that women were less likely than men to combine heroin with alcohol.

Other possible gender differences include the setting of drug use. Powis et al. (1996) reported that women cocaine users were more likely to use cocaine on a more "recreational basis" than men (p. 535). They found that women users were more likely than men to use cocaine at a party or at a club, whereas men were more likely to use cocaine at home alone or with a partner. Another study indicated, however, that once the addiction process has begun, women tend to use private locations for their drug use, whereas men more frequently use these substances in public places (Kauffman, Silver, and Poulin, 1997).

Drug-Use Careers

Research on gender differences in drug-use careers has examined the three main stages in the progress of the career: onset, continuation, and cessation. Drug use careers, however, do not always follow a clear pattern and can include multiple periods of abstinence, relapse, and escalation (DiClemente, 2003).

Some research on initiation has shown that male drug users start earlier than females (Hser, Huang, Teruya, and Anglin, 2003). There is also evidence of gender differences in relation to the situational factors precipitating drug use. Initial drug use among women has been found to be influenced by spouses or sexual partners, whereas first drug use among men tends, among other things, to be influenced by peer pressure (Hser, Anglin, and McGlothlin, 1987b).

Women and men might also be different in the speed with which they progress from initial use to daily use. Among cocaine-dependent users, McCance-Katz, Carroll, and Rounsaville (1999) found that women experienced a more rapid progression from first drug use to dependence. Anglin, Hser, and McGlothlin (1987a) also identified a similar pattern of rapid escalation among female heroin users. In relation to cessation of drug use, some research has shown that men find it harder to stop dependent drug use than women. DeWit, Offord, and Wong (1997), for example, reported that male drug users in Canada were significantly less likely than female users to stop using marijuana and hallucinogens. In the United States, Chen and Kandel (1995) found that, for most drug types, men were more likely than women to continue using drugs.

Problems of Drug Misuse

Research on the problems associated with drug misuse has focused mainly on dependency, health, and criminal behavior. In relation to dependence, the findings of research are mixed. Schulte et al. (2005) examined data from the Drug Use Monitoring Program in Australia (DUMA) and found that dependence on illicit drugs was more prevalent among female arrestees than among males. With regard to specific drug types, Lo (2004) reported findings from the US-ADAM program showing that dependence on cocaine was more common among female than male arrestees. However, dependence on cannabis was more prevalent among males. Neale (2004) found, in a study of drug users in treatment, that men were more likely than women to report that cannabis use had been a problem for them at some point in their lives. However, there were no gender differences in 'problematic' use of heroin, methadone, diazepam, cocaine, or crack.

Other problems of drug misuse include the health risks involved. Some research has shown that women drug users are at greater risk of physical and mental health problems than men (Becker and Duffy, 2002). Gossop, Marsden, and Stewart (2001), for example, found that women in drug treatment in the United Kingdom scored higher than their male counterparts across all psychological symptom scales. Pelissier (2004) reported a higher prevalence of depression among women prisoners receiving drug treatment in the United States.

One of the most frequently researched problems of drug misuse is crime. Several studies have looked at differences between men and women drug users and their involvement in offending behavior. Neale (2004) discovered that male drug users in treatment were significantly more likely than females to have recently committed drug-supply offenses, handling, assault, theft offenses, and criminal damage. Davis, Johnson, Randolph, and Liberty (2005) examined gender differences among a sample of 657 users and sellers of crack, powder cocaine, and heroin in central Harlem and concluded that more women than men participated in drug-supply offenses.

Treatment

Another area of research relevant to gender is drug treatment. A wide range of techniques and approaches have been used in the treatment of drug misuse (e.g., detoxification programs, methadone maintenance and reduction, therapeutic communities, psychological counseling, and twelve-step programs). Some forms of treatment are specific to drug misusers (e.g., substitute prescribing), whereas other forms are used to treat a variety of conditions and problems (e.g., cognitive-behavioral therapy). Drug treatment methods also vary in terms of their goals. Some forms of treatment aim to stabilize users and control their drug use, whereas other forms endeavor to help users abstain from drug misuse altogether.

Research that has examined gender differences in the use of treatment services and treatment effectiveness has shown that women are less likely than men to present themselves to drug treatment services (Becker and Duffy, 2002). Figures from the UK National Drug Treatment Outcome Research Survey (NTORS) showed that the ratio of men to women entering drug treatment in the United Kingdom is three to one (Department of Health, 2002b). One argument presented to explain this is that drug services have developed largely around the needs of men (Home Office, 2002). Hence, women often experience 'significant shortcomings' in the support available in terms of child care, transport facilities, women-only services, provision for minority ethnic women, and services within the criminal justice system (Home Office, 2002, p. 51). As a result, it is possible that they are less likely to seek treatment.

Research has also examined the time taken from onset and regular drug use to seeking treatment. Anglin, Hser, and McGlothlin (1987) reported that there was generally a shorter time interval between regular drug use and first treatment entry among women than men. Further, men were more likely than women to be referred into drug treatment through criminal justice agencies, whereas women were more likely to be referred into treatment by a medical provider (Anglin, Hser, and Booth, 1987).

Research on gender differences in treatment effectiveness has produced mixed results. Weisner, Ray, Mertens, Satre, and Moore (2003) examined treatment outcomes among outpatients in a managed care chemical dependence program and found that women were significantly more likely than men to be abstinent in the 30 days prior to the 5-year follow-up. In a study of patients receiving treatment in Los Angeles, Hser et al. (2004) also found that women reported lower levels of drug use following treatment than men. However, there were no significant gender differences in terms of crime reduction. Stewart, Gossop, Marsden, Kidd, and Treacy (2003) concluded that gender was not predictive of any outcome measures and that both men and women made significant improvements in their problem behaviors. Alterman, Randall, and McLellan (2000) also found no significant gender differences in alcohol or drug outcomes at 7-months follow-up of nine community treatment programs.

Although there have been many studies on gender differences in various aspects of drug misuse, the number of studies conducted in any particular area is still relatively small and the results are often mixed.

RESULTS

Some of the research issues discussed in the literature were investigated using data from the New English and Welsh Arrestee Drug

TABLE 9.1. *Gender differences in the proportion of arrestees testing positive for selected drug types*

	Male, % (*n*)	Female, % (*n*)	Total, % (*n*)	Sig. of difference
Cannabis	50 (1,214)	34 (138)	48 (1,352)	***
Alcohol	25 (599)	12 (48)	23 (647)	***
Amphetamines	6 (143)	7 (26)	6 (169)	ns
Opiates[a]	30 (736)	46 (185)	33 (921)	***
Cocaine[b]	24 (591)	35 (141)	26 (732)	***
Benzodiazepines	14 (348)	21 (84)	15 (432)	**
Methadone	6 (150)	9 (37)	7 (187)	*
Any drug	69 (1,686)	68 (272)	69 (1,958)	ns
Multiple drugs	38 (926)	47 (190)	39 (1,116)	**
Opiates and/or cocaine	39 (943)	53 (211)	41 (1,154)	***
All arrestees	100 (2,432)	100 (401)	100 (2,833)	

Note. Includes arrestees who provided a urine specimen (*n* = 2,833).
Chi-square test. * $p < .05$; ** $p < .01$; *** $p < .001$; ns = not significant.
[a]Including heroin.
[b]Including crack.

Abuse Monitoring (NEW-ADAM) program. In the following, we examine (1) gender differences in drug use, (2) gender differences in health-related issues, and (3) gender differences in criminal behavior.

Gender Differences in Drug Use

Urinalysis. Over two-thirds (69%) of all arrestees tested positive for at least one of the seven illicit drug types investigated. There were significant gender differences in the proportions testing positive for six of these seven drug types (Table 9.1). Significantly more women than men tested positive for cocaine (including crack), opiates (including heroin), methadone, and benzodiazepines. In contrast, significantly more men than women tested positive for cannabis and alcohol. Hence, according to the urinalysis results, female arrestees were more likely than males to have recently used certain hard drugs, whereas male arrestees were more likely than females to have used certain recreational drugs.

Self-Reported Drug Use in the Last 12 Months. The higher prevalence of the use of opiates and cocaine among female arrestees found in the

TABLE 9.2. *Gender differences in the proportion of arrestees reporting having used selected drug types in the last 12 months*

	Male, % (n)	Female, % (n)	Total, % (n)	Sig. of difference
Alcohol	87 (2334)	84 (380)	87 (2714)	ns
Cannabis	69 (1855)	57 (258)	67 (2113)	***
Ecstasy	28 (757)	22 (101)	27 (858)	*
Amphetamines	19 (516)	19 (87)	19 (603)	ns
Cocaine powder	27 (715)	21 (94)	26 (809)	**
Crack cocaine	30 (791)	37 (167)	31 (958)	**
Heroin	31 (830)	41 (187)	32 (1017)	***
Cannabis only	16 (441)	9 (40)	15 (481)	***
Any drug	79 (2,109)	74 (334)	78 (2,443)	*
Multiple drugs	59 (1,584)	60 (270)	59 (1,854)	ns
All arrestees	100 (2,682)	100 (453)	100 (3,135)	

Note: Includes all arrestees ($n = 3,135$).
Chi-square test: * $p < .05$; ** $p < .01$; *** $p < .001$; ns = not significant.

urinalysis results was also found when using the self-report questionnaire data. Table 9.2 shows that a significantly greater proportion of female than male arrestees reported having used heroin and crack in the last 12 months. By contrast, a significantly higher proportion of male than female arrestees reported having used cannabis, ecstasy, and cocaine powder.

One advantage of using self-report questionnaires is that they provide an opportunity to identify differences in the use of crack cocaine and powder cocaine (urinalysis is not able to distinguish between these two forms of cocaine). The results show that females were more likely than males to report use of crack cocaine, whereas males were more likely than females to report use of powder cocaine. DrugScope (2006) noted that cocaine powder tends to be used on a recreational basis, whereas crack cocaine tends to be used on a more dependent basis. Hence, this finding is consistent with the results of the urinalysis, which showed that females were more frequently involved in the use of hard drugs, and males were more likely to be involved in the use of recreational drugs.

Overall, significantly more male than female arrestees reported having used at least one illicit drug type in the last 12 months (79% compared with 74%). However, this finding is largely the result of the higher proportion of males reporting cannabis use. Removing cannabis from the calculation shows that women were more likely than men to report having used at least one illicit drug type in the last 12 months. There was no significant difference in the proportion of male and female arrestees that reported use of multiple drug types in the last 12 months.

Hence, male and female arrestees are clearly different in terms of the types of drugs most commonly used. This finding could have implications for the provision of appropriate treatment programs. Women, for example, might benefit more from programs that focus on heroin and crack use, whereas men might benefit more from programs designed to treat cocaine and cannabis use.

Rate of Drug Use in the Last 30 Days. Previous research has suggested that men and women might differ in the rate at which they misuse drugs (see Langan and Pelissier 2001). To test this idea, the number of days on which male and female arrestees reported using selected drug types in the last 30 days were compared. Among arrestees who had used cannabis in the last 30 days, male arrestees were significantly more likely than female arrestees to have used it at a high rate (i.e., on 15 or more days). By contrast, female arrestees who had used heroin or crack were more likely than male arrestees who had used these drugs to have used them at a high rate. However, there were no significant gender differences in the proportion of high-rate ecstasy, amphetamines, or cocaine powder users.

A similar pattern of findings was identified when investigating daily drug use (i.e., when the drug was reported as being used every day for the last 30 days). Male arrestees who had used cannabis were significantly more likely than females to report daily use (42% compared with 31%), and female arrestees were significantly more likely than males to report daily use of crack (49% compared with 27%) and heroin (84% compared with 69%). There were no significant gender differences in reported daily use of ecstasy, amphetamines, or cocaine powder.

Multivariate Analysis of Prevalence and Rate of Drug Use. A logistic regression analysis was used to explore whether gender had a significant effect on drug use and rate of drug use while controlling for the effect of other sociodemographic factors. The results showed that gender was a significant predictor of heroin use in the last 12 months. After controlling for other factors, women were 1.4 times more likely than men to have used heroin. Six of the seven other variables used in the analysis were also found to have a significant independent effect on heroin use: legal income (less than £5,000 per year), tenure (not a home owner), ethnic group (white), age (25 or over), age left full-time education (under 17), employment status (unemployed). The strongest predictors were legal income in the last 12 months and tenure. Marital status was the only variable that was not a significant predictor of heroin use.

Gender was also found to have a significant independent effect in explaining the rate of heroin use in the last 30 days. Female heroin users were found to be 2.1 times more likely than male heroin users to have used heroin every day for the last 30 days. Legal income (under £5,000), tenure (not a home owner), and age (over 25) were also found to be significant predictors of daily heroin use. By contrast, ethnic group, marital status, employment status, and age left full-time education did not have a significant independent effect on rate of heroin use. A similar pattern of results was found when exploring the prevalence and incidence of crack use. Hence, the results of multivariate analyses indicate that, even after controlling for other variables, gender was a significant predictor of rate of use of heroin and crack.

Injecting. Given that gender differences were found in the prevalence and rate of drug use, it is plausible that there might also be gender differences in the method of administering these drugs. Overall, about one-quarter of all arrestees who had used an illicit drug in the last 12 months had injected a drug on at least one occasion. The rate of injecting was highest among arrestees who had used heroin (58%) and lowest among ecstasy users (3%). However, there were no significant gender differences in the prevalence of injecting of any of the selected drug types. Hence, female arrestees were more likely than male arrestees to have used heroin and crack, but they were no more likely to have injected these drugs.

Sharing Equipment. As part of the interview, arrestees who reported having injected drugs were asked whether they had ever shared injecting equipment. Overall, nearly one-quarter (24%) of all arrestees who had injected drugs in the last 12 months said that they had shared injecting equipment. However, no significant gender differences were found in the proportion of arrestees reporting sharing injecting equipment. Hence, although females were more likely than males to have used heroin and crack, they tended to administer their drugs in roughly the same way.

In summary, the results described here show that there are some notable differences between male and female arrestees in terms of their drug use. Female arrestees were more likely than males to use the most addictive drugs and were also more likely to use them at a higher rate. However, female drug users were no different from males in the way in which they administered their drugs or in their willingness to share injecting equipment.

Gender Differences in Health-Related Issues

Dependence. Previous research has found that men and women differ in terms of the prevalence of dependency on illicit drugs (see Lo, 2004; Neale, 2004). The results of the current research lend support to this finding (Table 9.3). Overall, female arrestees were significantly more likely than males to report current dependence on one or more drug types (60% compared with 42%). There was a significant gender difference in the proportion of arrestees who had used these drugs to report being dependent on heroin and crack. Overall, female arrestees were significantly more likely than males to report dependence on crack (31% compared with 18%) and heroin (81% compared with 67%). However, there was no significant gender difference in the proportion of arrestees who reported dependence on ecstasy, cannabis, amphetamines, and cocaine. This finding is consistent with the earlier results which showed that women were more likely than men to use heroin and crack at a high rate. Hence, female drug users were more likely than male users of these drugs to use heroin and crack at a high rate and to be dependent on them.

TABLE 9.3. *Gender differences in the proportion of arrestees reporting current dependence on selected drug types*

	Male, % (n)	Female, % (n)	Total, % (n)	Sig. of difference
Ecstasy	2 (13)	2 (2)	2 (15)	ns
Cannabis	15 (270)	14 (36)	15 (306)	ns
Amphetamines	5 (24)	5 (4)	5 (28)	ns
Cocaine	3 (24)	3 (3)	3 (27)	ns
Crack	18 (141)	31 (52)	20 (193)	***
Heroin	67 (557)	81 (151)	70 (708)	***
Any drug	42 (884)	60 (201)	44 (1,085)	***

Note. Includes only those arrestees who reported use of the specified drug type in the last 12 months.
Chi-square test: *** $p < .001$; ns = not significant.

Perceived Need for Treatment. Arrestees who reported using drugs in the last 12 months were asked whether they had a current need for drug treatment. Table 9.4 gives the proportion of male and female arrestees who were either currently in treatment or who were not in treatment but wanted to be. The results show that significantly more female than male arrestees reported a current need for drug treatment. Twelve percent of female arrestees compared with eight percent of males reported that they were currently in treatment. A further 43 percent

TABLE 9.4. *Proportion of male and female arrestees who reported a current need for drug treatment*

	Male, % (n)	Female, % (n)	Total, % (n)	Sig. of difference
Currently in drug treatment	8 (166)	12 (38)	8 (204)	*
Would like drug treatment	27 (527)	43 (125)	29 (652)	***
Either in drug treatment or would like drug treatment	33 (693)	48 (163)	35 (856)	***

Note. Includes only those arrestees who reported use of any illicit drug in the last 12 months ($n = 2,443$).
* $p < .05$; *** $p < .001$; ns = not significant. Chi square test.

TABLE 9.5. *Gender differences in the proportion of arrestees who reported committing specified offense types in the last 12 months*

	Male, % (*n*)	Female, % (*n*)	Total, % (*n*)	Sig. of difference
Theft of vehicle	10 (204)	3 (9)	9 (213)	***
Theft from vehicle	11 (229)	5 (18)	10 (247)	**
Shoplifting	33 (690)	50 (167)	35 (857)	***
Burglary dwelling	6 (119)	3 (11)	5 (130)	ns
Burglary nondwelling	8 (158)	2 (5)	7 (163)	***
Robbery	4 (75)	2 (7)	3 (82)	ns
Theft person	3 (66)	6 (19)	4 (85)	*
Fraud	10 (220)	18 (60)	12 (280)	***
Handling	28 (596)	28 (92)	28 (688)	ns
Drug supply	16 (340)	11 (36)	15 (376)	*
Prostitution	1 (17)	17 (57)	3 (74)	***
Any offense[a]	61 (1,282)	64 (214)	61 (1,496)	ns
Any offense[b]	61 (1,285)	69 (229)	62 (1,514)	**
All arrestees	100 (2,109)	100 (334)	100 (2,443)	

Notes: Includes all arrestees who reported using any illicit drug in the last 12 months ($n = 2{,}443$). Some missing cases.
* $p < .05$; ** $p < .01$; *** $p < .001$; ns = not significant. Chi square test.
[a]Any offense excluding prostitution-related offenses.
[b]Any offense including prostitution-related offenses.

of female arrestees compared with 27 percent of male arrestees said that they were not currently in treatment, but wanted to be. Hence, the results show that, among arrestees, women are more likely than men to be in drug treatment and more likely to have an unmet need for treatment.

Gender Differences in Criminal Behavior

Prevalence of Offending. In addition to questions on drug misuse and drug-related health issues, arrestees were also asked to report the frequency and rate of offending in relation to 11 income-generating crimes. Overall, 62 percent of drug-using arrestees reported committing one or more income-generating crimes in the last 12 months (Table 9.5). In terms of gender differences, a significantly higher proportion of women than men reported committing at least one of the selected income-generating crimes in the last 12 months (69% compared with 61%). Female drug-using arrestees were also significantly more likely than males to report having committed shoplifting, theft from a person, fraud, and prostitution-related offenses in the last 12 months. By contrast, male arrestees were significantly more likely than females to report having committed vehicle theft, burglary of a nondwelling, and drug supply offenses.

Rate of Offending. To explore whether men and women differed in terms of their rate of offending, the mean number of crimes committed in the last 12 months were compared. The results showed that the mean rate of offending was highest among users who reported drug supply offenses (852 offenses) and shoplifting (246 offenses). However, there were no significant gender differences in terms of the mean rate of offending for any offense type. Hence, although there were gender differences in the prevalence of offending for various offense types, there were no differences in the rate of offending among those who reported committing these crimes.

Perceived Connection. The topic of the perceived connection between drug use and criminal behavior was discussed in the previous chapter. Arrestees who had used drugs and committed crimes in the last 12 months were asked whether they thought that their drug use and offending were connected in any way. Those arrestees who thought that there was a connection were asked about the nature of the connection. The results showed that women were more likely than men to report a connection between their drug use and offending behavior (74% compared with 61%). Among those who reported a connection, a significantly higher proportion of women than men described the connection in terms of a need for money to fund their drug use (94% of females compared with 83% of males). By contrast, male arrestees were significantly more likely than females to describe the connection in terms of the effect of drug use on their judgment (24% of males compared with 15% of females).

In summary, male and female arrestees differed in terms of the types of offenses committed but not in the rate at which they committed them. Gender differences were also found in the nature of the connection between drug use and offending behavior, with female arrestees more likely to describe the connection in terms of economic necessity and males more likely to describe the connection in terms of poor judgment.

DISCUSSION

The results show that there are clear gender differences in drug use and associated problem behaviors among arrestees in the United Kingdom. Female arrestees were significantly more likely than males to have used heroin and crack, and male arrestees were significantly more likely to have used cannabis, ecstasy, and cocaine powder. In addition to their higher prevalence of hard drug use, female arrestees also used heroin and crack at a higher rate than male arrestees. These findings remained significant even after controlling for other demographic factors such as age, ethnic group, marital status, and employment status. The research also found that female arrestees were more likely than males to report being dependent on these more serious drug types.

Gender differences were also found in terms of treatment needs. Among arrestees who had used drugs in the last 12 months, women were significantly more likely than men to be in treatment or to want treatment. In terms of offending behavior, male arrestees were more likely than females to report having committed vehicle offenses, burglary from a nondwelling, and drug supply offenses. By contrast, women were more likely to report having committed shoplifting, theft from a person, fraud, and prostitution offenses. Overall, the results suggest that female arrestees experience greater problems in their drug use and associated behaviors than male arrestees.

There are at least three explanations for these results. One is that women are generally more deviant than men. It would be expected, therefore, that women would be more heavily involved in drug use and associated problem behaviors than men.

Another explanation is based on the idea that when women are deviant, they are very deviant and far more deviant than their male counterparts. This idea is summarized in a poem by Henry Wadsworth Longfellow who, in connection with a story about a little girl, wrote, 'when she was good she was very, very good, but when she was bad she was horrid' (Hirsch, Kett, and Trefil, 2002). This would explain why general population surveys find relatively less deviant activity among women than men, whereas studies of deviant populations (such as arrestees or prisoners) tend to find relatively more deviant behavior among women than men (Kim and Fendrich, 2002; Langan and Pelissier, 2001).

A third explanation is based on the idea that there is bias in the mechanisms by which people are arrested on suspicion of committing crimes. This is sometimes referred to as the 'chivalry hypothesis' and is based on the idea that the police and other agents in the criminal justice system will tend to treat female offenders more leniently than males (Heidensohn and Brown, 2000; Pollak, 1950). As a result, women who do not match the criminal stereotype are less likely to be arrested and are less likely to enter the criminal justice system. It follows, therefore, that those women who are arrested are likely to be the most deviant female offenders. Hence, in a sample of the criminal justice population, women will appear to be more deviant than men because they have been selected that way.

Implications for Research

This chapter raises a number of issues relevant to future research on gender differences in drug misuse. It was mentioned in the introduction that historically there has been little research on gender differences in drug misuse. This has changed recently with the number of studies on the topic gradually increasing. However, the number of studies conducted on any single issue remains relatively small, and there are few definitive findings. Hence, there is a need for more research generally in the broad area of gender differences in drug misuse and associated problem behaviors. There is also a specific research need to investigate those topic areas that are particularly underresearched. These include studies of differences in types of drugs used, the rate of use, dosages, and the methods of administration, which to date have produced few consistent findings. Another research priority is to investigate those topic areas that are particularly important in terms of treatment and practice. In particular, it is important to determine whether women and men are different in terms of health-related issues, including dependency, unmet treatment needs, and equipment sharing and whether they are affected by these problems in different ways.

Implications for Policy

There are also a number of policy implications that flow from the research findings. The first is the difference in treatment needs of men and women. Almost twice as many female arrestees as male arrestees said that they had an unmet need for treatment. Hence, some attention needs to be paid to matching more closely treatment need and treatment provision in terms of gender. Attention might also be given to ensure that drug treatment is more widely available and to ensure that adequate child-care facilities and transport provisions are available for users seeking treatment. It might also mean that attention should be given to developing 'women-friendly' treatment programs designed to tackle heroin and crack use.

The second policy issue concerns the difference in patterns of drug misuse among male and female arrestees and the implication that this might have for drug and crime prevention. Women were more likely than men to report committing shoplifting, theft from a person, fraud, and prostitution-related offenses. Women were also more likely than men to report using heroin and crack. Government strategies designed to reduce drug-related crime might focus more precisely on the differences in the drug-crime connection between men and women. This might mean ensuring that prevention efforts target both male and female drug users. It might also mean that policing strategies should ensure that sufficient attention is paid to offenses that might be linked to drug misuse such as shoplifting and related offenses such as handbag snatches and credit card fraud.

CHAPTER TEN

Ethnicity, Drugs, and Crime

INTRODUCTION

There is surprisingly little research in the United Kingdom on drug misuse and associated problems among members of ethnic minority groups. In 1998, the Advisory Council on the Misuse of Drugs (1998) reported that the influence of ethnicity on illicit drug use in the United Kingdom was an 'under-researched topic' (p. 25). This lack of information on ethnicity and drugs also has been reported in other countries. Fountain and colleagues (2004) noted the following in relation to Europe:

> In several European Union countries drug use amongst black and minority ethnic communities is largely unacknowledged, ignored, unrecognised, or hidden by some policy-makers, drugs researchers, drug service planners and commissioners and by some members of some black and minority ethnic communities themselves. (p. 362)

Rounds-Bryant, Motivans, and Pelissier (2003) claimed that even in studies where ethnic minorities had been included, many investigators fail to report findings for individual ethnic groups. Others have criticized drug research for focusing on some ethnic groups and ignoring others (Fountain, Bashford, Winters, and Patel, 2003). The absence of research in this area has been attributed in part to the differing cultural values of ethnic groups. Reid, Crofts, and Beyer (2001) state that illicit drug use in minority ethnic communities is often associated with denial, shame, stigma, and loss of face. As a result, there might be some reluctance among researchers to investigate these sensitive topic areas.

The gap in research knowledge has several important implications. Rounds-Bryant et al. (2003) believe that the lack of empirical research on ethnic minority substance misuse is, 'an obstacle for providing empirically driven, culturally-relevant substance abuse treatment to minorities' (p. 333). It is possible that certain treatment approaches are suitable for some ethnic groups, but not others. A better understanding of drug misuse and related problems among ethnic groups could lead to more effective treatment services and reductions in drug use and associated problem behaviors.

In recent years, however, there has been a notable increase in research on ethnicity and drug misuse. This includes studies on ethnicity and methods of administration, patterns of drug use, drug preferences, age of onset, treatment retention and outcome, and criminal behavior (Reid et al., 2001; Sangster et al., 2002; Wanigaratne et al., 2003; Young and Harrison, 2001).

The aim of this chapter is to review recently published research in this area and to determine what is currently known about ethnic group variations in drug misuse and related problem behaviors. We then present the findings of our own research based on data collected from the New English and Welsh Arrestee Drug Abuse Monitoring (NEW-ADAM) program with the aim of contributing additional knowledge to the current research base.

ETHNIC GROUP DIFFERENCES IN THE PREVALENCE OF DRUG USE

Wanigaratne et al. (2003) referred to the problems created by the absence of reliable statistical data on substance misuse in Britain. They cited Baker (1997), who described how lack of data can lead to 'wishful thinking, anecdotal assertions, propaganda, rumor, exaggeration and potentially wildly inaccurate guesswork' (p. 40). As a consequence, some drug-user stereotypes have developed that imply that most drug users are black people (Wanigaratne et al., 2003). However, the stereotype of drug users as being largely from ethnic minority communities is not supported by the research. In fact, research findings tend to indicate that drug use is actually more prevalent among whites than among any other ethnic group.

General Population

The results of the 2000 sweep of the BCS found that lifetime prevalence of drug use was lower among ethnic minority groups than among the white population (Ramsay et al., 2001). Lifetime prevalence of any illicit drug use was 34 percent among white people, 28 percent among black respondents, 15 percent among Indian people, and 10 percent among Pakistani/Bangladeshi respondents. However, self-reported use in the last year was higher among black groups (13%) than white groups (11%). Drug use prevalence over the last year was lowest among Indians (5%) and Pakistani/Bangladeshis (5%).

The latest figures for the BCS that provide ethnic group breakdowns for drug use prevalence over the last 12 months are for the 2001–02 sweep (Aust and Smith, 2003). These results show that people from a mixed background were more likely than any other group to have taken an illicit drug in the last year. More than one-quarter of people from a mixed race background reported using an illicit drug in the last year compared with 12 percent of white people, 12 percent of black people, 8 percent of Chinese/other people, and 5 percent of Asian people. People from a mixed background were also more likely to have used Class A drugs (7% of mixed and 3% of whites).

The Offending, Crime, and Justice Survey (OCJS) also provides information about ethnic group differences in drug misuse among the general population. The OCJS is a national longitudinal, self-report offending survey among people aged 10 to 65 living in private households in England and Wales (Sharp and Budd, 2005). As with the BCS, figures from the OCJS identified a higher rate of drug use in the last 12 months among white and mixed ethnicity respondents than among other ethnic minority groups (Sharp and Budd, 2005). Seventeen percent of respondents of mixed ethnicity and thirteen percent of white respondents reported having used any drug in the last year, compared with eleven percent of black respondents and four percent of Asians. Class A drug use was also higher among mixed and white respondents (4% each) and lowest among black (2%) and Asian (1%) respondents (Sharp and Budd, 2005).

In addition to the BCS and OCJS, school surveys also provide information about ethnic group variations in drug misuse. As with studies of adults, school surveys have also shown that respondents of mixed ethnicity are more likely than white and black respondents to have recently taken drugs. Fuller (2005), for example, reports findings from a national survey of children aged 11 to 15 in 305 schools in England. The results show that pupils of mixed ethnicity were more likely than pupils from white or black ethnic groups to have used illicit drugs in the last month (17% compared with 11% and 12%, respectively). White pupils, however, were more likely than pupils from other ethnic groups to have drunk alcohol in the last week (25% white, 20% mixed, 10% black, and 6% Asian).

Parker, Aldridge, and Measham (1998) reported findings from the North-West Longitudinal Study of school children in England. Although their results are based on small numbers, the pattern of results shows that Asians were less likely than either white or black respondents to have ever taken an illicit drug. There were no differences, however, between white and black respondents. Best et al. (2001) also found ethnic group variations in substance use among a sample of children. They found that white children were more likely to have tried alcohol or tobacco than Asian or black children. White children were also more likely to progress from initiation to regular use than black or Asian children. Asian children reported the oldest ages of onset and lowest prevalence rates for both drinking and smoking.

The lower prevalence of drug use among ethnic minority groups has also been found in other countries. In the United States, for example, results of the Monitoring the Future school surveys have consistently shown lower usage rates of both alcohol and illicit drugs among blacks than among whites and Hispanics (Barnes, Welte, and Hoffman, 2002). Rate of cannabis use, however, was found to be similar across the three ethnic groups.

Offender Population

Prisoners. The higher prevalence of drug use among white people has also been found within samples drawn from offender populations. Budd, Collier, and colleagues (2005a) reported findings from the Criminality Survey of prisoners in England and Wales. Their results showed that white prisoners were more likely than black and Asian prisoners to have used any illicit drug (74% compared with 64% and 50%, respectively). White prisoners were also more likely to have used Class A drugs, to have used heroin, crack, or cocaine, to have injected a drug, and to have experienced problems staying off drugs.

Boys and colleagues (2002) examined drug use and initiation in prisons in England and Wales using data from a national survey of more than 3,000 prisoners. White prisoners were found to be more likely to report ever having used heroin, cocaine, or both than those prisoners categorized as black. Among those who had used heroin in prison, blacks were significantly more likely to have initiated use in prison. By contrast, being from an 'other' ethnic group significantly reduced the likelihood of initiation of cocaine use in prison.

Borrill and colleagues (2003) conducted a quantitative survey of prisoners and a qualitative survey of prison staff to explore differential substance misuse treatment needs of women, ethnic minorities, and young offenders in prison. The most important finding, according to the authors, was the finding that white women had problems relating to opiates, whereas black women were more likely to report problems relating to crack. The qualitative findings supported the survey results and confirmed that black women needed more interventions focused on crack use. Overall, 90 percent of white women were dependent on heroin and 25 percent on crack. By contrast, just 10 percent of black/mixed race women were dependent on heroin and 21 percent were dependent on crack. Ethnic differences in injecting behavior were also found among the sample. A higher rate of injecting was found among white women than among black/mixed race women (45% compared with 9%). White women were also more likely to be dependent on two or more drug types (46% compared with 28%).

Arrestees Arrestee surveys in various countries have also found a lower overall prevalence of drug use among ethnic minority groups. In South Africa, for example, urinalysis results revealed that white arrestees were more likely than nonwhite arrestees to test positive for any illicit drug (67% whites, 64% coloreds, 38% Africans, 48% Indians/Asians;

Parry et al., 2004). Ethnic group differences were also found in the use of individual drug types. Arrestees of color were the most likely to test positive for cannabis, mandrax, and benzodiazepines, whereas white arrestees were more likely to test positive for cocaine, amphetamines, and opiates (Parry et al., 2004).

Ethnic group differences in drug use were also identified in the US-ADAM program (National Institute of Justice, 2003). Urinalysis results for 1999 showed that black arrestees were more likely than white arrestees to test positive for cannabis and cocaine but were less likely to test positive for methamphetamines. In fact, only 0.8 percent of black arrestees tested positive for methamphetamines (lower than all other groups). There was little difference between white and Hispanic arrestees, although 15 percent of white arrestees tested positive for methamphetamines compared with 6 percent of Hispanics. Peters and colleagues (2002) also used data from the ADAM program and explored heroin use among arrestees in the southern states of the United States. The figures showed that African Americans had the lowest prevalence of heroin use among the three ethnic groups investigated. In 1997, the prevalence of heroin use was 10 percent among Hispanics, 9 percent among whites, and 4 percent among African Americans.

Summary

Research on general and offender populations has identified substantial ethnic group differences in the prevalence of drug misuse. Contrary to stereotypes, the prevalence of drug misuse is reported as being greater among whites than among ethnic minority groups.

ETHNIC GROUP DIFFERENCES IN RELATION TO DRUG-RELATED ISSUES

Researchers have also investigated ethnicity in relation to a range of drug-related issues including drug type preferences, methods of administration, age of onset, health, treatment utilization, perceived treatment needs, and treatment effectiveness.

Types of Drug Use

Research indicates that different types of drugs are more common among different ethnic groups. Sangster et al. (2002) found that, generally speaking, levels of drug use in the general population were similar among black Caribbean and white people. However, this was largely a result of the widespread use of cannabis among both groups. A focus on individual drug types shows that use of amphetamines, ecstasy, LSD, magic mushrooms, and amyl nitrate was less common among black Caribbean people than among whites (Sangster et al., 2002). Ethnic group differences were also found in patterns of problematic drug use. The results showed that problematic drug use among African Caribbean users focused mainly on crack. Black and minority ethnic opiate users were also less likely to inject than whites.

Wanigaratne et al. (2003) described how some African communities in the United Kingdom, such as the Somali community, were known to chew khat (a plant that contains a drug with stimulant properties). Khat is currently legal in the United Kingdom but illegal in the United States. Griffiths et al. (1997) explored patterns of khat use among approximately 200 Somalis living in London. They found that more than three-quarters of the sample had used khat at some stage in their lives and two-thirds had used the substance in the week before interview (cited in Wanigaratne et al., 2003, p. 42).

Method of Administration

Ethnic group variations in the method of administering drugs have been reported in several studies. Injecting is reportedly much less common among people from ethnic minority groups (see, e.g., Borrill et al., 2003; Budd et al., 2005a; Sangster et al., 2002). Fountain et al. (2003) used data from needle exchange programs in the United Kingdom to show that few ethnic minority groups attended these services. Injecting has been found to be particularly rare among Asian users. Siddique (1992) reported that the preference for smoking rather than injecting among Pakistanis can be partly explained by historical differences in the method of administering drugs in Pakistan.

Age of Onset

A few studies have explored the age of onset of drug misuse among different ethnic groups. Young and Harrison (2001) examined ethnic group differences in the sequences of drugs used by women using data from the 1995 National Household Survey on Drug Abuse in the United States. White females were found to have started using cigarettes earlier than black and Hispanic females (16.3 years compared with 17.5 and 17.7 years, respectively). White females also started using alcohol earlier than black and Hispanic women (18.3 compared with 18.7 and 19.2 years). Hispanic women, by contrast, started using cannabis at age 17.0 (compared with 18.7 for white and black women). Hispanic women also reported a younger age of onset for cocaine use and crack use.

A similar pattern of results has been found among drug-using offenders. Braithwaite et al. (2003) looked at alcohol and drug use among adolescent detainees in the United States. More than 2,000 male and female participants aged 11 to 18 were recruited from two juvenile justice detention facilities. The results showed that African American youth were significantly older than those in other ethnic groups at age of first use of cannabis (13.1 years compared with 12.3 for white and 12.2 for Hispanic and other).

Health

A number of researchers have investigated ethnic group differences in drug-related health issues. Taylor et al. (1986) showed that six percent of all Afro-Caribbean hospital admissions were alcohol related compared with 10 percent of admissions in the British population. Cochrane and Howell (1993) studied drug use among white and African Caribbean men and found that the latter had lower levels of alcohol-related problems than the former. Another study reported that Indian men had higher rates of admission to psychiatric hospitals for alcohol-related problems than men from other countries (Rassool and Kilpatrick, 1998).

Johnson et al. (2003) explored comorbidity (coexisting substance use and psychiatric disorders) among 700 drug users not currently receiving treatment. Nearly two-thirds (64%) were found to have

coexisting substance use and other psychiatric symptoms. The findings indicated that individuals with comorbidity were more likely to
be white, homeless, unemployed, and to have been arrested at some
point.

Darke and Ross (2000) examined fatal heroin overdoses resulting from injecting and noninjecting routes of administration in New
South Wales, Australia, during the period 1992–1996. During this
time, there were 943 deaths involving injecting and 10 involving non-
injecting methods of administration. Sixteen percent of injectors were
born outside of Australia, compared with 40 percent of noninjectors.
The authors concluded that the high rates of deaths from injecting
heroin in Australia reflected the high rates of injecting this drug in
Australia. Conversely, the high rates of deaths from other methods
of administering among users born outside of Australia were likely to
reflect the historical methods of administration of the drug in these
other countries.

Treatment

Research has shown that ethnic minority groups are less likely than
whites to enter drug treatment. Reid et al. (2001) believed that the
underrepresentation of ethnic minority groups in drug treatment was
a product of lower use of these services by these groups rather than a
lower need for treatment. The low rates of entry into drug treatment
by ethnic minority groups have been attributed to many factors including reliance on traditional medicine, cultural dissonance, lower education and literacy, language and communication difficulties, lack of
knowledge about services, and discrimination (Rassool and Kilpatrick,
1998).

Sangster et al. (2002) reported that drug treatment services failed
to meet the needs of minority ethnic communities. They argued that
this failure was, in part, a result of treatment services being focused on
HIV transmission and the needs of white males. Fountain et al. (2003)
summarized this situation as follows:

> the picture that emerges from the literature is that drug service
> development for Black and minority ethnic groups is ad hoc, patchy

and uncoordinated, and the less well-established BME groups are even more marginalised in terms of drug services. (p. 23)

Reid et al. (2001) examined drug treatment services for ethnic communities in Australia. They reviewed the international literature and also conducted interviews and focus groups with key informants. They found that illicit drug use among ethnic communities was often associated with intense shame and loss of face. Hence, there was reluctance among ethnic minorities to make their drug use visible by approaching treatment services. However, even when these services were used, many informants viewed them as insensitive to the cultural differences of ethnic minorities. There were often language barriers that made full communication difficult.

Longshore, Hsieh, and Anglin (1993) examined ethnic group differences in perceived need for treatment among 1,170 drug-using arrestees in Los Angeles. Overall, 37 percent reported a need for treatment. White arrestees (44%) were more likely than African Americans (38%) and Hispanics (31%) to report a need for treatment. This finding could be explained by ethnic minority groups being less likely to have a need for treatment or less likely to seek treatment when they do have a need.

Brewer et al. (1998) conducted a systematic review and meta-analysis of predictors of continued drug use during and after treatment for opiate addiction. Sixty-nine studies were located for inclusion in the analysis. Twenty studies presented findings in terms of white and nonwhite participants. Younger, nonwhite, and unmarried subjects were found to be slightly more likely to continue using than older, white, and married subjects, respectively. Gender and education, however, were found to have no perceptible relationships with continued use.

Hser et al. (2003) examined drug treatment outcomes and predictors among a sample of 511 patients recruited from drug treatment programs across Los Angeles County. Interviews were conducted at baseline and at one-year follow-up. Logistic regression was used to predict abstinence and crime desistence at 12-month follow-up. Among both men and women, ethnic group was not a significant predictor of abstinence. By contrast, ethnic group was a significant predictor of crime desistance. Among men, African Americans were significantly less likely than whites to desist from crime. Among women, African Americans were significantly more likely than whites to desist from crime.

Summary

There have been a number of recent research studies that have investigated ethnic group differences in drug-related issues. Research has shown some variations among ethnic groups in terms of drug preferences, modes of administration, age of onset, health, treatment needs, treatment retention, and treatment effectiveness. However, the number of studies conducted in any single area is small, and it is difficult to draw any overall conclusions. There are also gaps in the literature. Few studies, have examined ethnic group variations in the rate of drug use (i.e., number of days used), quantities used (i.e., doses), or in market experiences (i.e., the prices paid for drugs). There is also little research on ethnic variations in the nature of the drug-crime connection.

In the remainder of this chapter, we examine ethnic group variations in drug use and related problem behaviors using the data collected as part of the NEW-ADAM program. The aim is to provide additional research knowledge in areas that have been investigated by other studies and to provide new research findings in areas not previously investigated.

RESULTS

The Sample

Arrestees interviewed as part of the NEW-ADAM program were asked to define their ethnic group. The majority of arrestees defined themselves as white (79%). The remainder were split across 10 ethnic minority groups. The largest group was black Caribbean (4%), followed by black African (2%), black British (2%), Indian (2%), Pakistani (2%), Bangladeshi (2%), Asian (2%), 'mixed' (2%), Chinese (1%), and 'other' (2%). Given the small number of arrestees in each ethnic minority group, the chapter focuses on comparisons between white arrestees and other ethnic minority groups (henceforth nonwhite arrestees).

Urinalysis

Table 10.1 shows the prevalence of positive tests for selected drug types among white and nonwhite arrestees. The figures show that white arrestees were significantly more likely than nonwhite arrestees to test positive for amphetamines, benzodiazepines, opiates, methadone, and alcohol. White arrestees were also significantly more likely to test positive for two or more drug types. However, there were no significant ethnic group differences in the proportions testing positive for cannabis or cocaine.

Self-Reported Prevalence

The higher prevalence of drug use among white arrestees was also found using the self-report data (see Table 10.2). White arrestees were significantly more likely than nonwhite arrestees to report having used alcohol, amphetamines, ecstasy, heroin, crack, and cocaine in the last 12 months. By contrast, there was little difference in the proportions of white and nonwhite arrestees reported using cannabis in the last year (68% and 65%, respectively). Overall, white arrestees were significantly more likely than nonwhite arrestees to report having used at least one (of 19) illicit drug types in the last 12 months (80% compared with 71%). They were also significantly more likely to have used multiple drug types (64% compared with 41%).

The analysis also showed that there were significant ethnic group differences in the number of different drug types used in the last 12 months. Approximately twice as many white arrestees as nonwhite arrestees reported using five or more drug types in the last year (35% compared with 12%).

High-Rate Drug Use

Table 10.3 shows the prevalence of high-rate drug use among white and nonwhite arrestees. White arrestees were significantly more likely than nonwhite arrestees to be high-rate users of alcohol (30% compared with 23%). Overall, white arrestees were significantly more likely

TABLE 10.1. *Proportion of white and nonwhite arrestees testing positive for selected drug types*

Drug type	White arrestees, % (n)	Nonwhite arrestees, % (n)	All arrestees, % (n)	Sig. of difference
Cannabis	47 (1,063)	51 (289)	48 (1,352)	ns
Amphetamines	7 (161)	1 (8)	6 (169)	***
Benzodiazepines	17 (393)	7 (39)	15 (432)	***
Opiates (including heroin)	36 (814)	19 (107)	33 (921)	***
Cocaine (including crack)	25 (569)	29 (163)	26 (732)	ns
Methadone	7 (168)	3 (19)	7 (187)	**
Alcohol	25 (574)	13 (73)	23 (647)	***
Opiates or cocaine	43 (965)	34 (189)	41 (1,154)	***
Any drug[a]	70 (1,581)	67 (377)	69 (1,958)	ns
Multiple drugs (two or more)[a]	42 (953)	29 (163)	39 (1,116)	***
All arrestees	100 (2,269)	100 (563)	100 (2,832)	

Notes: Among arrestees who provided urine specimens ($n = 2,833$). One missing case.

[a]Excluding alcohol.

Chi-square test: *** $p < .001$, ** $p < .01$, ns = not significant.

TABLE 10.2. *Proportion of white and nonwhite arrestees reporting use of selected drug types in the last 12 months*

Drug type	White arrestees, % (n)	Nonwhite arrestees, % (n)	All arrestees, % (n)	Sig. of difference
Alcohol	89 (2,195)	79 (519)	87 (2,714)	***
Cannabis	68 (1,686)	65 (426)	67 (2,112)	ns
Amphetamines	23 (565)	6 (38)	19 (603)	***
Ecstasy	31 (773)	13 (85)	27 (858)	***
Heroin	36 (889)	19 (127)	32 (1,016)	***
Crack	32 (796)	25 (161)	31 (957)	***
Cocaine	28 (704)	16 (105)	26 (809)	***
Any drug[a]	80 (1,977)	71 (465)	78 (2,442)	***
Multiple drugs (two or more)[a]	64 (1,588)	41 (265)	59 (1,853)	***

Note. Includes all arrestees (n = 3,135).
Chi-square test: *** p < .001; ns = not significant.
[a]Excluding alcohol.

TABLE 10.3. *Proportion of white and nonwhite arrestees reporting high-rate drug use in the last 30 days*

Drug type	White arrestees, % (n)	Nonwhite arrestees, % (n)	All arrestees, % (n)	Sig. of difference
Alcohol	30 (578)	23 (101)	29 (679)	**
Cannabis	55 (795)	57 (221)	55 (1,016)	ns
Amphetamines	17 (44)	21 (3)	17 (47)	ns
Ecstasy	6 (21)	2 (1)	5 (22)	ns
Heroin	81 (637)	76 (80)	81 (717)	ns
Crack	46 (267)	53 (70)	47 (337)	ns
Cocaine	11 (39)	15 (8)	12 (47)	ns
Any drug[a]	74 (1,346)	68 (291)	73 (1,637)	**

Note: Includes only those arrestees who reported use of the specified drug type in the last 30 days. High-rate drug use refers to drug use on at least 15 of the last 30 days. Chi-square test: ** $p < .01$; ns = not significant.
[a]Excluding alcohol.

than nonwhite arrestees to be high-rate users of any drug type (74% compared with 68%).

Injecting Drug Use
There were also some ethnic group differences in the prevalence of injecting. Among heroin and crack users, significantly more white than nonwhite arrestees had injected these drugs in the last 12 months. However, there were no significant ethnic group differences in the prevalence of injecting among amphetamine, ecstasy, or cocaine users. Overall, white arrestees were nearly four times more likely than non-white arrestees to report having injected a drug in the last 12 months (30% compared with 8%).

Dependence
The prevalence of dependence on any illicit drug was significantly higher among white than nonwhite arrestees (47% compared with 34%). With regard to individual drug types, white arrestees were significantly more likely than nonwhites to report current dependence on alcohol. Nonwhite arrestees, however, were significantly more likely than white arrestees to report being currently dependent on crack cocaine (30% compared with 18%). There were no

significant ethnic group differences in terms of dependence on cannabis, amphetamines, ecstasy, heroin, or cocaine.

Treatment

Among arrestees who had used drugs in the last 12 months, a higher proportion of whites than nonwhites reported that they were currently receiving treatment (see Table 10.4). A further 31 percent of white arrestees and 22 percent of nonwhite arrestees reported that they would like to receive treatment (this difference was statistically significant). Overall, more than one-third of white arrestees (37%) and more than one-quarter (27%) of nonwhite arrestees reported that they had a current need for treatment.

Self-Reported Offending

Ethnic group differences were also found in the prevalence of offending among drug-misusing arrestees. Overall, white arrestees were significantly more likely than nonwhite arrestees to report having committed income-generating offenses in the last 12 months (54% compared with 42%). White arrestees were significantly more likely than nonwhite arrestees to report having committed 8 of the 10 offense types (theft of a vehicle, theft from a vehicle, shoplifting, burglary from a dwelling or nondwelling, theft from a person, handling, and drug supply offenses). By contrast, there were no significant differences in the rate of offending (among arrestees who had reported committing offenses in the last year).

Perceived Connection Between Drug Use and Offending

Arrestees who had reported committing crimes and using illicit drugs in the last 12 months were asked about the connection between their drug use and offending. Table 10.5 shows that white arrestees were significantly more likely than nonwhite arrestees to acknowledge a connection between their drug use and offending. Nearly two-thirds of white arrestees (65%) compared with just over half (52%) of nonwhite arrestees reported a drug-crime connection. Similar types of connection were reported by both white and nonwhite arrestees. White arrestees, however, were significantly more likely to describe the

TABLE 10.4. *Proportion of white and nonwhite arrestees who reported a current need for drug treatment*

Drug type	White arrestees, % (n)	Nonwhite arrestees, % (n)	All arrestees, % (n)	Sig. of difference
Currently in drug treatment	9 (176)	6 (27)	8 (203)	*
Would like drug treatment	31 (556)	22 (96)	29 (652)	***
Either in drug treatment or would like drug treatment[a]	37 (732)	27 (123)	35 (855)	***

Note: Includes arrestees who reported using any illicit drug in the last 12 months.

Chi-square test: *** $p < .001$; * $p < .05$.

[a] Excluding alcohol.

TABLE 10.5. *Ethnic group differences in the perceived connection between drug use and crime*

Drug type	White arrestees, % (*n*)	Nonwhite arrestees, % (*n*)	All arrestees, % (*n*)	Sig. of difference
Perceived connection	65 (792)	52 (121)	63 (913)	***
Nature of connection				
Drug use has an affect on judgment	23 (183)	17 (21)	22 (204)	ns
Need for money to buy drugs	86 (684)	74 (89)	85 (773)	**
Proceeds of crime spent on drugs	5 (39)	9 (11)	6 (50)	ns
Other connection	8 (60)	12 (14)	8 (74)	ns

Notes: Includes arrestees who reported using any illicit drug in the last 12 months and who reported commiting one or more income-generating crimes in the last 12 months (excluding prostitution). Multiple responses possible.
Chi-squared test: *** *p* < .001; ** *p* < .01; ns = not significant.

connection in terms of a need for money to buy drugs (86% compared with 74%). This finding might be linked to earlier finding that whites were more likely than nonwhites to use addictive and expensive drugs.

DISCUSSION

The results presented in previous chapter have identified clear ethnic group differences in drug use. Urinalysis results showed that white arrestees were more likely than nonwhite arrestees to test positive for amphetamines, benzodiazepines, opiates, methadone, alcohol, and multiple drug types. However, there was no significant difference between whites and nonwhites in terms of cannabis use and cocaine/crack use. The self-report data yielded similar results. The only drug for which white arrestees were not significantly more likely to report use of was cannabis (there was no difference between the two groups).

In terms of rate of use, there were no clear ethnic group differences for individual drug types, although white arrestees were significantly more likely to report high-rate use of alcohol than nonwhite arrestees. There was also a slightly larger proportion of nonwhite arrestees reporting high-rate use of crack (53% compared with 46%). As reported in the literature, injecting was found to be significantly more prevalent among white arrestees than nonwhites. There was little difference between the two groups in terms of dependence on drugs, although whites were more likely to be dependent on alcohol and nonwhites were more likely to be dependent on crack. These findings support the results of previous research suggesting that people from ethnic minority groups are less likely to have alcohol problems but are more likely to have a problem with crack cocaine (e.g., Borrill et al., 2003; Sangster et al., 2002). As found in previous research, a greater proportion of white than nonwhite arrestees reported that they were currently in treatment and wanted treatment (e.g., Reid et al., 2001). White arrestees were significantly more likely to perceive a connection between their drug use and offending.

Overall, the findings suggest that white arrestees are more heavily involved in drug use and crime than nonwhite arrestees. How can this difference be explained? There are some clear parallels between attempts to explain ethnic differences in drug use and attempts to explain gender differences. The finding that female offenders are more likely than male offenders to be drug users, to use the more serious drug types, and to be higher rate drug users has been explained in the literature in one of three ways: women are worse than men; when women are bad they are very bad; only the worst female offenders are arrested (see Chapter 9 for a discussion; see also Holloway and Bennett, in press). Applying these explanations to ethnic differences would lead to the following hypotheses:

- white arrestees are generally worse (i.e., they are more deviant in the general population) than nonwhite arrestees;
- white arrestees are not generally worse (i.e., they are not more deviant in the general population), but when they are bad they are very bad (i.e., the most deviant group are particularly deviant); and
- only the worst white offenders are arrested (i.e., a kind of chivalry hypothesis applied to white offenders).

The research and policy implications that flow from the analysis of ethnic group differences in drug misuse are similar to those presented in the previous chapter on gender differences. The amount of research conducted on ethnic differences in drug misuse has been limited. Although this situation has changed in recent years, the number of studies conducted on any single issue still remains relatively small, and hence there are few definitive findings. There is therefore a need for more research generally in the broad area of ethnic differences in drug misuse and specifically in relation to those areas that are particularly underresearched.

In terms of policy implications, the findings suggest that some attention needs to be paid to matching more closely treatment need and treatment provision in terms of ethnic group. Attention might also be given to ensure that drug treatment is more widely available and appropriate for users from ethnic minority groups (e.g., access to programs that are culturally sensitive and access to counselors who speak the same language as users). It might also mean that attention should be given to developing treatment programs designed to tackle crack use.

A second policy consideration is the difference in patterns of drug misuse among white and nonwhite arrestees and the implication that this might have for drug and crime prevention. Government strategies designed to reduce drug-related crime might focus more precisely on the differences in the drug-crime connection between various ethnic groups. This might mean ensuring that prevention efforts target both white and nonwhite drug users. It might also mean that policing strategies should ensure that sufficient attention is paid to white drug-misusing offenders.

CHAPTER ELEVEN

Gangs and Gang Members

INTRODUCTION

There is growing debate in the United Kingdom on the number and nature of street gangs and their contribution to crime and violence. However, the discussion is impeded to some extent by a lack of agreement on the definition of what constitutes a gang. Confusion over definitions of gangs is not confined to the United Kingdom. Klein (2001) argued that the concept of gangs in the United States has been shaped by the stereotype of the *West Side Story* gang and the image of gang 'colors'. He argued that both are distortions of reality, and that few American gangs fit this stereotype. He argues instead that gang formations are much more variable and proposes a typology of observable gang structures based on five discrete forms (traditional, neo-traditional, compressed, collective, and specialty). Decker (2001) argued that the concept of the gang has been distorted by the dominance of the view that gangs are well organized and tightly structured. However, an alternative view, supported by his own research, shows that gangs are often disorganized and typically do not have leaders.

It is not necessary to enter into the complexities of this debate in this chapter because it has been discussed at length elsewhere (see Klein et al., 2001, for an overview). However, it is worth noting that the aim of this chapter is to investigate what are typically called 'street gangs' (Klein, 2001) or 'youth gangs' (Sanders, 1994) rather than 'criminal gangs' or 'crime firms' that come together solely to commit a particular criminal act and then disperse. Street gangs are defined by Klein (2001) as groups based on a strong gang identity, moderate

levels of organization, versatile offending patterns (with some excep-
tions), amplification of criminal behavior over time, and a variety of
structures.

Given the level of current interest in the development of street
gangs in the United Kingdom, it is perhaps surprising that so little
attention has been paid by British criminologists to the subject. This
has resulted in important gaps in our knowledge about the number
and distribution of gangs and basic facts about the characteristics of
gang members. There are also important gaps in what is known about
the contribution of street gangs to criminal behavior, including the
extent of gun possession, involvement in violence, drug dealing, drug
misuse, and criminal behavior. However, there is some research on
gangs that provides information on the characteristics and criminal
behavior of gang members.

PREVIOUS RESEARCH

Gangs in the United Kingdom

There are very few studies of early gangs in the United Kingdom.
One possible reason for this is that there were very few early gangs.
Sanders (1994) noted during his discussions with police officers in
London in 1984 that the police were unable to identify any gangs
that matched the US stereotype. However, he concluded from his
interviews with Jimmy Boyle (a famous Glasgow criminal who wrote
a book of his life) that the gangs in Glasgow during Boyle's youth
(during the 1950s) were 'virtually identical' to those currently found
in San Diego. Downes (1966) argued, at the time of writing, that
research on delinquent gangs in England was a fair reflection of their
absence. The only study that he found of relevance was the work of
Scott (1956) based on interviews with boys on remand in London.
He concluded from Scott's work that 'gangs proper' were 'extremely
unusual'. In his own study of delinquent groups in London in the
1960s, he concluded that there were no delinquent gangs in the East
End of London that matched US descriptions. However, there were
small 'cliques' of four of five members who sometimes committed
illegal acts together.

More recent research on gangs has provided some evidence on the number and nature of gangs in the United Kingdom. Bullock and Tilley (2002) obtained information about gangs in Manchester from police databases, interviews with 23 males considered by Greater Manchester Police to be gang members, and a practitioner focus group. They found that there were currently four major South Manchester street gangs with between 26 and 67 gang members. A large majority of gang members was black and male. The gang members were typically heavily involved in criminal behavior and had on average 12 prior arrests and 2.1 convictions. They committed a wide range of offense types, including both serious violent offenses and property offenses. Each gang had a core group of main players and a number of additional and associate members. Weapon carrying was common among members.

Mares (2001) conducted an ethnographic study of gang members in Manchester during 1997 and 1998 and identified the formative stages of two of the four gangs discussed in the Bullock and Tilley (2002) report. He described the heavy involvement of both gangs in drug trading, including heroin, crack, and cocaine. At the time, there were about 90 members in each gang, and the large majority was Afro-Caribbean in origin. The gangs were only loosely organized, and there were no formal leaders. Mares (2001) also identified a number of other gangs operating in the greater Manchester area. These had different structures to those found in the city center area. Gangs in Salford were all white and many had existed for at least 10 years. Most gang members were aged under 25 and some were as young as 10. Gangs in Wythenshawe were much smaller in size with an average of 25 members and were mixed in terms of gender (about a quarter were women) and ethnicity (about 10% were black).

A further source of information about gangs in the United Kingdom is a study by Stelfox (1998) conducted as part of the Home Office Police Award scheme. The research was based on a postal survey of all police forces in the United Kingdom requesting information about the existence of gangs in the police force area. Forty-eight of the fifty-one questionnaires sent out were returned (a response rate of 94%). All command units of those forces that identified gangs (16 of the 48 forces that replied) were sent a second questionnaire

requesting further information about gangs in the area. The command units returned 71 profiles of individual gangs operating in their
areas. The majority of gangs were dominantly adult male in composition. There was one predominantly female gang. The average age
of gang members was in the range 25 to 29. Two-thirds of gangs
were predominantly white, one-quarter was ethnically mixed, and the
remainder were predominantly a single ethnic group. Gang structures
were generally loose with no discernible leader. They typically engaged
in a wide range of offenses, although 17 percent were described as
offense specialists. Three-quarters of gangs were involved in some
form of drug dealing. Most forces reported violence as the main problem associated with gangs. Sixty percent of gangs allegedly possessed
firearms.

Gangs in the United States
Gang research in the United States is much more extensive. Traditionally, US gang research has been based on case studies and, as a
result, more is known about the details of particular gangs than the
characteristics of gangs and gang members more widely (Curry and
Decker, 1998). During the 1990s, this situation changed as interest
grew in monitoring gangs nationally. This resulted in an increase in
new approaches to the study of gangs, including studies based on law
enforcement data and surveys of young people.

The most recent national surveys of gangs based on enforcement
data have been conducted by the National Youth Gang Center (NYGC)
on behalf of the Office of Juvenile Justice and Delinquency Prevention
(OJJDP). The latest published findings concern the national survey
conducted in 1998. The survey was based on a representative sample
of 3,018 police and sheriffs' departments (Moore and Cook, 1999).
Respondents were asked to estimate the number of gangs and gang
members in their areas and to provide basic demographic information
(age, gender, and ethnicity) on them in the form of estimated percentages. Gang activity within each demographic category was analyzed by
geographic region.

The NYGC estimated from these results that there were more than
28,700 gangs and more than 780,000 gang members across the United

States in 1998. They also estimated that 92 percent of all gang members were male and eight percent were female. Female gang members
were least prevalent in large cities (7%) and most prevalent in small
cities (12%). Sixty percent of gang members were aged 18 years or
over (defined by NYGC as adult), and 40 percent were aged under
18 (defined as juveniles). Adult gang members were more prevalent
in larger cities, and juvenile gang members were more prevalent in
rural areas. Forty-six percent of gang members in 1998 were Hispanic and thirty-four percent were African American. The remainder
were white (12%), Asian (6%), and 'other' (2%). The survey also
asked respondents about the proportion of gang members (none,
few, some, most/all) who engaged in six specific offense types (aggravated assault, robbery, burglary, motor vehicle theft, larceny/theft,
and drug sales). The combined results for all jurisdictions showed
that over a quarter of respondents (27%) thought that most/all of
their gang members were involved in drug sales. The next largest
crime category was larceny/theft (17%), followed by burglary (13%),
aggravated assault (12%), motor vehicle theft (11%), and robbery
(3%). More than half of respondents (53%) thought that their gang
members 'often' or 'sometimes' used firearms in assault crimes. The
estimated proportion of gang members who used firearms in assault
crime was highest in large cities and lowest in small cities.

One of the largest self-report surveys of young people in the United
States (which provides details on gang membership) is the National
Evaluation of Gang Resistance Education and Training (GREAT)
based on seventh- and eighth-grade students in public schools across
the United States. Esbensen and Lynskey (2001) used data from 11
cities to investigate the characteristics of self-nominated gang members. The authors acknowledged that their results related only to
juvenile gang members. However, their findings were different in a
number of ways to the national law enforcement findings mentioned
earlier. They found a much higher proportion of female gang members (38%). They also found a much higher percentage (about one-
quarter) of white gang members. The survey results also showed that
the majority of gang members had sold drugs, been involved in a
gang fight, attacked someone, and carried a weapon. Less than half
of respondents from the law enforcement agencies estimated that the

majority of gang members were involved in these kinds of offenses. Over a quarter of gang members said that they had shot at someone.

The difference in the findings of law enforcement data and self-report data are in part a product of the different data collection methods used. It has been argued that police enforcement strategies tend to target individuals who fit the stereotype of the gang member (e.g., dominantly young, black males; Esbensen and Lynskey, 2001). Hence, police descriptions of arrested or known gang members tend to reflect the selection bias of arrest strategies. School surveys may also present a distorted image of the characteristics of gang members because of the restricted age distribution of respondents (Esbensen and Lynskey, 2001).

METHODS

Questions about gang membership were asked as part of the New English and Welsh Arrestee Drug Abuse Monitoring (NEW-ADAM) surveys in 14 of the 16 research locations. The omission of two sites was a result of including this question after the initial surveys had begun. The question included a preamble that explained the meaning of the question and provided a broad indication of what was meant by the term 'gang'. They were then asked whether they were currently a member of a gang or had ever been a member of a gang. The precise wording of the question is as follows:

> In some areas, there are local gangs that sometimes have names or other means of identification and cover a particular geographic area or territory.
>
> *Do you belong to, or have you ever belonged to, a local gang of this kind?*

The preamble included the main elements of a definition of a street gang proposed by Klein and colleagues (2001). The question also allowed respondents flexibility in interpretation. It has been argued that a certain amount of self-definition is perhaps the best method of overcoming the problem of accurately defining gang membership (Thornberry and Porter, 2001). Their responses were recorded to show whether they were current members, past members, or non–gang members.

RESULTS

The following results are divided into the main sections discussed earlier and cover: (1) prevalence of gang membership, (2) characteristics of gang members, and (3) problem behaviors and gang membership.

Prevalence of Gang Membership

The results show (Table 11.1) that 15 percent of arrestees had either current or past experience as a gang member. Four percent of arrestees interviewed said that they were currently members of a gang and eleven percent said that they had been members of a gang in the past.

It is not possible to extrapolate these findings directly to the arrestee or the offender population because the sample is not nationally representative. However, it is possible to produce a conditional estimate of the population of gang members among arrestees in England and Wales based on a few assumptions. The main assumption is that the proportion of gang members among arrestees in England and Wales is the same as the proportion identified in the 14 sites studied.

During the financial year 2001–2, Home Office arrest data showed that 953,800 persons aged 18 and over were arrested (Ayres et al., 2002). This total refers to persons arrested (or arrest events) rather than unique individuals. In other words, it includes people who had been arrested more than once. To estimate the proportion of gang members, it is necessary to calculate the total number of unique individuals arrested. The Home Office data do not provide information on numbers of arrests per individual per year. However, it is possible to estimate this (very roughly) from the NEW-ADAM surveys (accepting that arrestees interviewed in the locations covered by the surveys do not necessarily represent all arrestees). On average, NEW-ADAM respondents reported a median of two arrests (including the current arrest) per individual arrestee in the last 12 months.

Hence, assuming that all persons arrested in the financial year 2000–1 had been arrested on at least one previous occasion, it could be estimated that there were about 20,000 active gang members aged 18 and over among arrestees in England and Wales ($0.04 \times 953,800 \div 2 = 19,076$). It should be stressed that the estimate includes only gang

TABLE 11.1. *Percentage of self-reported gang members among arrestees in 14 research locations in England and Wales*

Force	Current gang member	Past gang member[a]	Non–gang member	Total *n*
Liverpool	2	16	82	210
Plymouth	3	11	86	203
Bolton	3	11	86	208
Nottingham	3	8	88	207
London (Colindale)	4	6	90	175
London (Brixton)	5	14	81	154
Sunderland	3	9	87	207
Norwich	2	11	87	210
Newport	4	16	80	199
Southampton	5	9	87	176
Wolverhampton	3	9	88	207
Bournemouth	4	17	79	206
London (Bethnal Green)	8	9	83	180
London (Hammersmith)	0	11	89	124
TOTAL%	4	11	85	100
TOTAL*n*	92	300	2,274	2,666[b]

[a]Excludes those who are current gang members.

[b]The total excludes 59 missing cases in which the gang question was not answered.

members in the arrestee population and gang members aged 17 years or older. The total number of gang members in England and Wales (including juveniles) would be higher than this.

Characteristics of Gang Members

The vast majority of all gang members were male. (The term 'gang member' refers throughout to both current and past gang members combined, unless otherwise stated.) Only 5 percent of all gang members and four percent of current gang members were female (Table 11.2).

A recent review of the literature by Esbensen and Lynskey (2001) suggests that the proportion of female gang members reported in gang research tends to vary by age of the sample and the methods used. Studies based on case studies and law enforcement data tend to produce lower estimates of female involvement (typically less than 10%). Studies based on self-report surveys tend to show higher levels of female involvement (the authors' own study reported 38% female involvement). They argued that this could be a result of either a selection effect (particularly in relation to the former group of studies) or a maturation effect (whereby female gang members grow out of gang membership at an earlier age). The results of the current survey provide lower estimates of female involvement than either the law enforcement or youth survey research in the United States.

Gang members were also significantly more likely than non–gang members to be aged under 25 (61% compared with 47%). This difference was even greater when just looking at current gang members (77% aged under 25). Overall, the median age was 19 for current gang members, 24 for past gang members, and 25 for non–gang members. The difference between current and past gang members in terms of age might be a product of maturation. Past members might have been the same age as current gang members when they were gang members and then grew out of gang membership. The US research is unclear about the length of gang membership. Thornberry (1998) argued that gang membership is typically short (i.e., a year or two). Decker and van Winkle (1996) argued that the length of gang membership depends of the level of violence of the gang (older members were more

TABLE 11.2. *Characteristics of gang and non–gang members aggregated across 14 research locations in England and Wales (percentages)*

	Current gang member	Past gang member[a]	All gang members[b]	Non-gang member	Significance a[c]	Significance b[c]
Sex						
Male ($n = 2,288$)	96	94	95	84	***	**
Female ($n = 378$)	4	6	5	16		
Age						
17–24 ($n = 1,298$)	77	55	61	47	***	***
25+ ($n = 1,368$)	23	45	39	53		
Race						
White ($n = 2,081$)	66	77	75	79	ns	**
Ethnic minority ($n = 584$)	34	23	25	21		
Marital status						
Single ($n = 1,820$)	80	67	70	68	ns	*
Other ($n = 846$)	20	33	30	32		
Employment status						
Unemployed ($n = 1,194$)	46	53	51	44	**	ns
Other ($n = 1,464$)	54	47	49	56		
FT education						
Left FT education ($n = 2,448$)	89	98	96	94	ns	[*]
Still in FT education ($n = 155$)	11	2	4	6		

Legal income					
Under £5,000 (n = 1,642)	72	69	70	62	** [*]
£5,000+ (n = 961)	28	31	30	38	
Living status in last 30 days					
Parent/guardian (n = 780)	49	29	33	29	[*] ***
Other (n = 1,886)	51	71	67	72	
TOTAL n	92	300	392	2,274	

[a]Excludes those who are current gang members.

[b]Current and past gang members combined.

[c]a = Gang members (current and past) compared with non–gang members. b = Current gang members compared with non–gang members.

*** $p < .001$, ** $p < .01$, * $p < .05$, [*] = significant at a lower level of probability ($p < .06$ to $p < .07$).

likely to remain in gangs with low violence). Curry and Decker (1998) noted that as the gang phenomenon in the United States matured, the number of older gang members would grow. However, past gang members might be older than current members as a result (in addition to maturation) of gang membership recruitment occurring at an earlier age.

Gang members were predominantly white. The remainder described themselves as being a member of an ethnic minority group. Gang members (both groups combined) were no more likely than non–gang members to report being from an ethnic minority (25% compared with 21%; not statistically significant). There was some variation across sites. In two locations (Bethnal Green and Plymouth), gang members were significantly more likely than non–gang members to be from an ethnic minority group. In the remaining 12 locations, there was no significant difference between gang and non–gang members in terms of ethnic minority status.

The question on ethnicity used in the questionnaire was divided into 13 subcategories. Respondents were asked to select the group that best described them. Forty-two percent of ethnic minority current gang members were self-assessed as falling into one of the three categories describing 'black' respondents. These included black Caribbean (26%), black African (3%), and black British (13%). Thirty-five percent of ethnic minority current gang members nominated two of the categories describing 'Asian' respondents. These included Bangladeshi (32%) and Pakistani (3%). The remaining ethnic minority current gang members described themselves as of 'mixed' ethnicity (13%) or 'other' (10%).

There are some differences in the ethnicity of gang members in the current research and those reported in the US studies. The US surveys found that the majority of gang members were from ethnic minority groups, whereas the current study shows that the majority of gang members are white. This finding is likely to reflect broader differences in the ethnic composition of the two populations. However, it may also reflect other differences in those factors associated with the formation of gangs discussed in criminological theory. These include the nature and distribution of social disorganization and the characteristics of criminal and youth group subcultures.

There are also some differences across countries in the involvement of particular ethnic groups in gang membership. The US studies showed that the major ethnic minority groups were African American and Hispanic, whereas the current study shows that the major ethnic minority groups were Caribbean and Bangladeshi. It is also likely that these differences reflect the different histories and the particular ethnic minority composition in the United States and the United Kingdom. However, they might also reflect other differences among the groups in their level of involvement in the local street culture, access to weapons, and attitudes to violence.

Gang members generally were no more likely than non–gang members to be single. However, current gang members were significantly more likely than past gang members and non–gang members to be unmarried. Gang members were slightly more likely than non–gang members to be living with their parents or guardians (33% compared with 29%; significant at a reduced level of $p < .06$). Current and past gang members were more likely than non–gang members to be unemployed (51% compared with 44%; $p < .01$). However, current gang members were less likely to be unemployed than past gang members (46% compared with 53%). Gang members generally had lower levels of legal income than non–gang members.

In summary, the results show that current gang members were measurably different from other arrestees. They were significantly more likely than non–gang members to be male, younger (aged under 25 years), still in full-time education, have lower legal incomes, and live with their parents or guardians.

Problem Behaviors and Gang Membership

Gang members are of particular interest to criminologists because they are commonly involved in various kinds of illegal or deviant behavior. In particular, gang research shows that gang members often commit violent crimes (including homicide), carry guns, commit a broad spectrum of offense types, supply drugs, consume drugs, commit criminal damage (including gang graffiti), and engage in general disorder (some of which leads to fear of gangs among residents).

The NEW-ADAM program collected a wide range of information on the criminal behavior of arrestees, and it is possible to test some of the assumptions mentioned using the sample of UK gang members. Details of the criminal behavior of both gang and non–gang members are shown in Table 11.3.

Gang members (current and past) were more likely than non–gang members to report committing one or more of each of the property crimes shown in the table in the last 12 months. However, current gang members were different from non–gang members only in relation to the offenses of theft of a vehicle and handling stolen goods. Over one-fifth of gang members said that they had stolen a vehicle in the last 12 months, and almost half (45%) said that they had handled stolen goods. The connection with youth gangs and vehicle theft is consistent with ethnographic research in the United States, which shows the importance of vehicles in the 'street culture' of gangs. Jacobs, Topalli, and Wright (2003) found that carjackers interviewed in St. Louis, Missouri, said that they sometimes used cars for joyriding and for showing off to their friends. Decker and van Winkle (1996) reported that cruising in cars was a common pursuit among gang members and cited car theft as one of the most common crimes committed by gang members.

Gang members were significantly more likely than non–gang members to have committed robbery. The highest robbery rates were among current gang members. Again, the link with robbery and gang membership is consistent with the US research. There was no connection with gang membership and theft from a person. Gang members were also much more likely than non–gang members to be involved in drug supply offenses ($p < .001$). Almost one-third (30%) of current gang members said that they had committed drug supply offenses in the last 12 months.

The North American research literature suggests that gang members are typically involved in a wide range of criminal behavior. This generalist approach to crime has sometimes been referred to as 'cafeteria style' offending (Klein, 2001). The current findings show that gang members were more likely than non–gang members to be generalists in terms of offending with over a fifth of current gang members and just under a quarter of past gang members reporting committing three or more of the ten offense types. This compares with just over 10 percent of non–gang members. Gang members (current and

TABLE 11.3. *Criminal behaviour in the last 12 months among gang and non-gang members aggregated across 14 research locations in England and Wales (percentages)*

	Current gang member	Past gang member[a]	All gang members	Non-gang member	Significance a[b]	Significance b[b]
Property crime						
Theft of a motor vehicle	21	14	16	6	***	***
Theft from a motor vehicle	12	16	15	7	***	[*][c]
Shoplifting	24	35	32	27	*	ns
Burglary dwelling	1	8	7	4	*	ns
Burglary nondwelling	5	10	9	4	**	ns
Fraud	15	15	15	9	***	[*]
Handling	45	38	39	21	***	***
Violent crime						
Robbery	7	5	6	2	***	*
Theft person	1	4	3	2	ns	ns
Drug-related crime						
Drug supply	30	22	24	10	***	***
Number of offense types[d]						
One or more	80	68	71	48	***	***
Two or more	49	42	44	23	***	***
Three or more	21	24	23	11	***	**
Number of offenses						
Mean number	958	311	463	177	**[e]	***

(continued)

225

TABLE 11.3 *(continued)*

	Current gang member	Past gang member[a]	All gang members	Non-gang member	Significance a[b]	b[b]
Weapons[f]						
Ever possessed weapon during an offense	63	44	49	20	***	***
Ever possessed a gun	59	47	50	21	***	***
Ever mixed with people who possessed a gun	78	75	76	34	***	***
Ever possessed a gun during an offense	33	31	32	14	***	*
Ever fired a gun	67	71	70	44	***	*
TOTAL n	92	300	392	2,273		

[a]Excludes those who are current gang members.

[b]a = Gang members (current and past) compared with non-gang members. b = Current gang members compared with non-gang members.

[c]*** $p < .001$, ** $p < .01$, * $p < .05$, [*] = significant at a lower level of probability ($p < .66$ to $< .07$).

[d]The total number of 10 offense types was included in the calculation.

[e]Analysis of variance.

[f]These questions were put to half the respondents using a randomized procedure. The number of respondents asked the questions were 51 current gang members, 141 past gang members, and 1,156 non-gang members (total 1,348).

past) also committed a greater total number of offenses over the last 12 months. Current gang members committed over five times the number of offenses committed by non–gang members.

US surveys of gang and non–gang members also show that gang members commit a disproportionate share of all offenses. Thornberry (1998) reported that gang members comprised about one-third of all youths sampled in the Rochester Youth Development Study. However, they were responsible for 86 percent of acts of serious delinquency, 68 percent of violent acts, and 70 percent of drug sales. The current research shows that gang members (current and past) comprised 15 percent of the total sample of arrestees. However, they were responsible for 31 percent of all offenses reported. This included 89 percent of all robberies, 49 percent of burglaries in a dwelling, 41 percent of thefts of a motor vehicle, 38 percent of burglaries in nondwellings, 36 percent of drug supply offenses, 35 percent of thefts from a vehicle, 28 percent of handling offenses, 26 percent of frauds, and 21 percent of shoplifting offenses.

Gang members were also more heavily involved in possession of weapons and guns. All comparisons between gang members and non–gang members were highly significant. About two-thirds of current gang members had taken a weapon to commit an offense. Over half had possessed a gun, and three-quarters said that they had mixed with people who possessed guns. One-third of gang members said that they had taken a gun with them when committing an offense and two-thirds of gang members said that they had fired a gun.

Overall, the findings are consistent with the image of street gangs from research in the United States. Gang members tend to be involved in criminal behavior, generalists in terms of offending pattern, responsible for a notable proportion of all offenses, sometimes violent, involved in drug supply offenses, and have a tendency to carry weapons and guns (and sometimes use them).

The United States research is less clear on the extent to which gang members actually use drugs (as opposed to dealing in drugs). Sanders (1994) argued that previous ethnographic research of gangs has produced mixed findings. A number of studies refer to frequent 'partying' among gang members, which typically involves alcohol and drug misuse (Sanders, 1994). There are also a number of studies showing that some gangs do not permit heroin misuse because their members would be considered unreliable in gang fights (Fagan, 1990). Sanders's own study of gang members in San Diego found that there were no negative sanctions against use of heroin but some sanctions against use of crack, especially when the gang member was supposed to be selling it (Sanders, 1994).

The problem of drug use among gang members is also confounded by the fact that gang members are also young people with their own particular combination of risk and protective factors relating to drug misuse. Fagan (1990) argued that comparisons of gang and non–gang youths from similar social backgrounds are rare. In the absence of such studies, it is difficult to know whether gang members are in any sense different from non–gang members in terms of substance abuse. Fagan's own research aimed specifically at identifying differences in drug use behavior among gang and non–gang members by conducting surveys of school students and school dropouts (Fagan, 1990). He found that gang members had higher prevalence rates and higher incidence rates than non–gang members in relation to 'drug misuse' (a scale based on seven drug types). Gang members were also more likely than non–gang members to be involved in the most serious forms of drug misuse (including use of heroin and cocaine).

The relationship between drug misuse and gang membership in the current research is shown in Table 11.4.

Current gang members were significantly more likely than non–gang members to have used cannabis in the last 12 months (p < .01). However, in relation to most other drug types, they were either no more likely or less likely to have used them. Current gang members were significantly less likely than non–gang members to have used heroin in the last 12 months. They were also slightly less likely (but not significantly so) to have used crack and cocaine. Current gang members were also significantly less likely than non–gang members to report injecting a drug (p < .01). There was no significant difference among gang and non–gang members in dependency on drugs or expenditure on drugs in the last seven days.

TABLE 11.4. *Drug misuse in the last 12 months among gang and non–gang members aggregated across 14 research locations in England and Wales (percentages)*

	Current gang member	Past gang member[a]	All gang members	Non–gang member	Significance b	Significance c
Drug types used						
Cannabis	79	80	80	65	***	**
Amphetamines	26	21	22	19	ns	ns
Ecstasy	36	38	37	26	***	[*][d]
Heroin	15	36	31	30	ns	**
Crack	23	38	35	28	*	ns
Cocaine	22	35	32	25	*	ns
Injected drug						
Injected one or more drug types	8	21	18	17	ns	*
Dependency						
Dependence on one or more drug types	29	41	38	33	ns	ns
Expenditure on drugs[e]						
£100 or over	24	35	32	30	ns	ns
TOTAL *n*	92	300	392	2,274		

[a]Excludes those who are current gang members.

b = Gang members (current and past) compared with non-gang members. c = Current gang members compared with non-gang members.
*** p < .001, ** p < .01, * p < .05, [*] = significant at a lower level of probability (p < .06 to < .07).
[d]*** p < .001, ** p < .01, * p < .05, [*] = significant at a lower level of probability (p < .06 to < .07).
[e]Asked only if one or more drugs ever used (n = 2,258).

These results do not suggest that gang members are more involved in drug misuse than non–gang members. In fact, there is some evidence that they are less likely to be involved in certain kinds of drug misuse and less likely to report some of the more major problems associated with drug misuse, including use of the more serious drug types and the use of injection.

DISCUSSION

The research has shown that about 4 percent of arrestees reported current gang membership and 11 percent reported past gang membership. It was estimated that there were at least 20,000 active gang members in England and Wales at the time of the research among the arrestee population. Taking into account additional membership from the nonarrestee population, the total number of gang members is likely to be well in excess of this figure.

Gang members in the arrestee sample tend to be younger (aged under 25) than non–gang members. They also tend to be male and white. Gang members were more likely than non–gang members to report committing recent property crimes. However, current gang members were different from non–gang members only in relation to theft of a motor vehicle and handling stolen goods. They were more likely than non–gang members to possess a gun and to use it as part of a crime. There was no indication that gang members were more likely than non–gang members to use drugs. In fact, they were significantly less likely to have used heroin and slightly less likely (not significant) to have used crack and cocaine.

There are some differences in the findings of the current research and the findings of research conducted in the United States. Although it is not possible to provide an overall comparison of research in the two countries, it is nevertheless of interest to summarize the broad differences in the results obtained from the NEW-ADAM surveys and from recent surveys of gang membership in the United States.

Ethnic Background
One possible difference in gangs in the United Kingdom and the United States is the ethnic backgrounds of gang members. In the

United States, the research suggests that the majority of gang members are from ethnic minority groups and that the dominant ethnic minority group is African American. The results of the current research suggest that the majority of gang members in the United Kingdom are white and that the dominant ethnic minority groups are black Caribbean and Bangladeshi. Just over one-third of ethnic group gang members were recorded as black (mainly black African and black Caribbean), and just over a third were recorded as Asian (mainly Bangladeshi and Pakistani). Anecdotal reports of Turkish gangs (Thompson, 2001) and Albanian gangs (Hopkins, 2002) in media reports suggest also that the United Kingdom might have a different kind of ethnic mix of gang members.

The role of ethnicity in gang membership has been widely discussed in the United States. The history of youth gangs in the late 19th and early 20th centuries shows that traditionally gangs were formed from within groups of recent immigrants (Curry and Decker, 1998). It is interesting that some of the more recent gangs in the United Kingdom have also emerged from among the more recent immigrant groups (e.g., Turkish and Albanian gangs mentioned earlier). However, generally speaking, gang members in the United Kingdom are predominantly white.

The difference in composition of the ethnic component of gang membership in the United States and United Kingdom might be explained in a number of ways. It might reflect the different ethnic compositions of the population of the two countries. It might also reflect the chronology of different immigration patterns of ethnic groups in the two countries. It is also possible that the findings reflect research method differences. The earlier review of gang surveys in the United States showed some variation across studies depending on the methods used. Unfortunately, it is not possible to provide conclusive answers to these questions until more gang surveys have been conducted in the United Kingdom.

Gender

The current research also suggests there may be proportionately fewer female gang members in the United Kingdom than in the United States. In the United States, the 1998 Youth Gang Survey found that 8 percent of gang members were female. Esbensen and Lynskey (2001) found in their school survey that 38 percent of gang members were female. In comparison, the current research found that just over 4 percent of gang members were female. Estimates of female involvement are likely to vary by survey method and type of location. The current results are closer to the law enforcement survey results than the school survey results, as might be expected. Nevertheless, the reported prevalence rates are still lower than the US estimates.

Drug Misuse
There may also be differences in terms of drug misuse. The relationship between drug misuse and gang membership in the United States is unclear, and even a cursory comparison is difficult to make. Some studies show high levels of involvement in drug misuse among gang members, and some show low levels. However, the results of the current research suggest that gang members are probably no more involved in drug misuse than non–gang members from similar backgrounds. In fact, there is some evidence that in certain respects (especially in relation to use of heroin and injection) they might be less involved in drug misuse.

One reason gang members might be less involved than non–gang members in drug misuse is that drug intoxication can clash with the other objectives of the group. Fagan (1990) referred to a 'new generation' of youth gangs in the United States that are more instrumental in their motives and gave examples of gangs prohibiting drug use among their members. This may be done as a means to ensure the successful completion of acquisitive crimes or drug supply offenses. It may also be done as a means to ensure physical safety at times of conflict with rival gangs. However, in his own surveys of school children and school dropouts, Fagan (1990) found that rates of drug misuse were higher among gang members than non–gang members. He concluded that gangs and gang members probably vary in terms of their level of involvement in drug misuse.

Policy
The study of street gangs is important in terms of fundamental knowledge and in understanding current social developments. However, it

is also important in terms of policy and practice. Research on gangs can help inform policing policy and crime prevention strategies. Gang prevention programs and methods of discouraging gang membership among school children have been adopted in the United States for some time (Curry and Decker, 1998). The existence of gangs in the United Kingdom has only recently been recognized, and there is less of a history of intervention programs designed to prevent them. However, some gang programs have been implemented in the United Kingdom, including Operation Chrome in Manchester based on a problem-oriented policing approach to controlling gun use and violence by gangs (Bullock and Tilley, 2002). It is likely that as knowledge about the prevalence and characteristics of gangs increases, so, too, will the range of programs designed to control them.

CHAPTER TWELVE

Gun Possession and Use

INTRODUCTION

There is a growing concern about the extent of gun possession and use among criminals in the United Kingdom. A recent publication from the National Criminal Intelligence Service (NCIS) reported that criminal possession and use of firearms had increased since 2000 and estimated that that there could be anything from 200,000 to 4 million illegal firearms in circulation. It also noted a concern among the police and the public about possession and use of firearms and the high cost of criminal firearm use for the judicial, prison, health, and police services (NCIS, 2005). There have also been several well-publicized reports of gun crimes in the media including the case of two young women killed in Birmingham who were believed to have been the victims of crossfire between rival gangs (Barker, 2003). Another report concerned a drive-by shooting in which the police estimate that more than a dozen shots were fired (Casciani, 2003).

One problem in assessing the scale of gun possession in the United Kingdom is that there are no routinely collected data on the topic. There are some national data on the use of firearms in recorded crime and some data on seizures relating to firearm offenses and subsequent arrests. However, there are no national statistics on the number of illegal guns in circulation or the number of criminals who possess illegal guns. As a result, little is known about firearm use within the offender population.

There are two main sources of information on the illegal use of firearms in England and Wales. These data focus mainly on offenses rather than offenders. However, they provide some indirect evidence on the criminal use of guns. The first source is government official statistics that cover police recorded crime data, stop-and-search under suspicion of gun possession, and arrest data relating to firearm offenses. The second source is individual research studies that cover firearm possession in specific populations, specific areas, and specific offenses.

Official Statistics

The most detailed source of information on gun involvement in crime is the official police statistics on crimes in which firearms were reported to have been used. The word 'firearms' in this context means real and imitation weapons, and the attribution can be based on the subjective assessment of victims or witnesses. It includes air weapons as well as conventional firearms. The word 'used' in these reports means being fired, used as a blunt instrument, or as a threat. The most recent data cover the period 2004 and 2005 and show that 0.4 percent of all recorded crime involved firearms (including air weapons; Coleman, Hird, and Povey, 2006). This proportion rose to 3.1 percent of all violent offenses (excluding homicide) and to 4.2 percent for all robberies.

The published statistics show that in 2004–5, there were 10,964 recorded crimes involving firearms other than air weapons (a 6% increase over 2003–4; Coleman, Hird, and Povey, 2006). They also show that the number of crimes involving firearms other than air weapons increased year-upon-year over the period 1998–9 to 2004–5. In 1998–9, there were 5,209 offenses involving firearms other than an air gun, compared with 10,964 in 2004–5 (an increase of more than 100%). Similarly, offenses involving air guns (usually regarded as nonlethal weapons) increased over the same period by just over one-third but in the last few years have actually decreased. Hence, it is possible that these recent trends indicate a switch among offenders from nonlethal to lethal weapons. It will be necessary to plot this trend over several more years to determine whether this is in fact the case.

A second source of published official information on gun possession and use is data on the use of firearms in homicide. These data tell us that during the period 1991 to 2000–1, the proportion of male victim homicides involving shooting as the method of killing, remained in a fairly narrow range just above or just below 10 percent. In 2001–2, however, the proportion increased to 16 percent. This represented a 44 percent increase over the previous year and the highest proportion over the last 10 years (Flood-Page and Taylor, 2003). More recently, the statistics show that the proportion of male victim homicides involving shooting decreased back to 11 percent in 2003–4 and 2004–5 (Coleman and Cotton, 2006).

The official reports on homicides provide limited information on the use of firearms as a method of killing. However, some additional data have been published based on further analysis of the Homicide Index database (Brookman and Maguire, 2003). The authors report that more than 40 percent of all homicides involving firearms were undetected (compared with under 10 percent of homicides as a whole). During the period 1995–9, homicides involving firearms were predominantly male on male, and in more than one-quarter of cases both the victim and the offender were black. The authors concluded that young, black males are heavily overrepresented in fatal shootings as both offenders and victims.

A third data source is the official statistics for searches made under Section 1 of the Police and Criminal Evidence Act of 1984 and the arrests that result from them. In 2004–5, 12,800 searches were made in which the reason for the search was suspected firearms (Ayres and Murray, 2005). This represented an increase of 17 percent over the previous year and a 68 percent increase since 1994. In the same period, the number of arrests made in relation to searches for firearms rose by 56 percent over the previous year and by 134 percent since 1994 (Ayres and Murray, 2005).

Official data generate a rough picture of the extent and nature of involvement of guns in crime. The data sources are consistent in suggesting an increase in the use of firearms in crime over the last few years (NCIS, 2005). However, official data are limited and only indirectly address the problem of gun possession and use among the criminal population. Little can be determined from this data about the extent of gun possession and use among offenders or the characteristics of offenders who possess and use them.

Research Studies

Smaller-scale research studies covering specific offender populations, areas, and offenses have the potential to provide more detail on the nature of gun possession and use among offenders.

OFFENDER-BASED SURVEYS

One method of investigating the offender population is through national or large-scale surveys of prisoners. This is a common method used in the United States. The 1991 national survey of state prison inmates based on more than 13,000 inmate interviews found that 43 percent of prisoners had possessed a firearm at some time in their lives, and 34 percent said that they had owned a handgun. Sixteen percent of inmates said that they had a gun with them while committing the offense for which they were incarcerated (Beck et al., 1993). Unfortunately, there have been no similar national surveys of prisoners in the United Kingdom that have included questions on the commission of crime. The first national survey of prisoners in England and Wales conducted in 1991 did not include any questions of gun possession or use among offenders (Dodd and Hunter, 1992).

The offender population can also be investigated through surveys of arrestees. Unfortunately, the only surveys of arrestees conducted in England and Wales that address the issue of gun ownership are those conducted as part of the New English and Welsh Arrestee Drug Abuse Monitoring (NEW-ADAM) program. The largest arrestee surveys outside the United Kingdom that cover gun use have been those conducted as part of the ADAM program in the United States. One of the early publications on this topic conducted in 11 cities in the United States in 1995 showed that 39 percent of arrestees reported ever owning a firearm (Decker and Pennell, 1995). Fifteen percent of the sample reported that they carried a gun all or most of the time. Juvenile arrestees, gang members, and arrestees who reported selling drugs were more likely than other arrestees to report carrying a gun. Interestingly, there was no association between testing positive for illegal drugs and reported possession of a firearm.

AREA-BASED SURVEYS

Some information on gun possession and use among offenders can be found in research studies based in particular locations. One of the most recent research studies describes gun possession and crime in Greater Manchester (Bullock and Tilley, 2002). In those divisions for which there were relevant data, the study showed that 0.8 percent of all recorded crimes involved firearms. This was approximately double the national rate. During the period 1998–2000, the number of crimes involving firearms and the proportion of crimes involving firearms both increased. Some additional information on gun possession and use among offenders was provided from the results of interviews with 15 gang members. According to the report, one-fifth of the gang members interviewed admitted gun carrying, and half of them said that they had friends who did so. Information provided by the police on known shootings estimated that 60 percent of shootings in Manchester involved gang members, as a victim, the offender, or both. Whereas shootings attributable to non–gang members reduced over the study period, shootings attributable to gang members increased.

Another area-based study by Rix, Walker, and Ward (1998) conducted in three rural and three metropolitan police forces investigated incidents known to the police in which a firearm was used. The study was based on 1,373 verified incidents involving firearms. They found that firearm incidents were most common in relation to the offense of robbery (about a quarter of all firearm incidents were associated with robbery or attempted robbery). The most common firearms used in robbery offenses were handguns (49%) and shotguns (26%). Fifteen percent involved replica guns.

OFFENSE-BASED STUDIES

Some additional information about gun possession and use among offenders can be found in research on specific offenses. Smith (2003), for example, in a survey of more than 2,000 personal robberies in seven basic command unit areas and two British Transport Police areas, found that guns were displayed in three percent of personal robberies. This compares with less than half a percent for all offense types.

Morrison and O'Donnell (1994) interviewed 88 armed robbers in Prison Service establishments in England. All of the interviewed robbers were asked about the type of gun they had used in the commission of their first armed robbery. Thirty-seven percent said that they had used a replica gun that was incapable of discharging live rounds, and 23 percent said that they merely intimated that they possessed a gun but produced nothing. The remainder possessed real guns that could discharge live rounds. The most common guns used by armed robbers were sawed-off shotguns (24%) and handguns (17%).

Research Problem

The preceding review of the research literature has shown that there is some official data in England and Wales on the use of firearms in crime and some research data on the use of guns in relation to particular areas and particular offenses. These tend to show that illegal gun use is increasing. However, there remains little information on the possession and use of guns in the offender population. In other words, we know something about guns and offenses, but we know little about guns and offenders. In particular, there is limited information on the proportion of offenders who possess illegal guns, the use of guns in crime, and the characteristics of offenders who possess and use guns.

The issue of gun use among offenders is of policy relevance as it affects both the police and the public and a number of other agencies, including the prison and health services. It is also important because gun crime increases the probability of serious injury of death to the victim, offender, or general public as bystanders. It would aid understanding of how to respond to gun crime if more were known about gun possession and use among offenders. A better knowledge of the level of involvement of offenders in gun crime and the characteristics of these offenders would help in designing targeted intervention strategies.

RESULTS

The main aim of this chapter is to help fill the gap in research knowledge about illegal gun possession among active offenders by drawing on the results of the NEW-ADAM surveys. The findings of the research are presented in this section.

TABLE 12.1. *Prevalence of legal and illegal gun possession among arrestees*

	Ever		In the last 12 months	
	%	n	%	n
Gun possession	23	352	8	127
Illegal gun possession[a]	20	300	8	118
Legal gun possession	3	52	1	9
No gun possession	77	1,176	92	1,400
TOTAL	100	1,528	100	1,527

Note: Some missing values. Maximum $n = 1,570$.
[a] Gun possession is classified as 'illegal' when the stated reasons for possessing the gun included illegal reasons (e.g., for protection, to impress people, use in a criminal activity, and other reasons deemed to be illegal). It includes arrestees who reported both illegal and legal gun possession. Gun possession is classified as 'legal' when the stated reasons for possessing the gun was only for legal use (e.g., hunting, target shooting, or as a legitimate part of their job, such as military use). It excludes arrestees who also reported illegal gun possession.

About one-quarter of arrestees said that they had 'owned or got hold of' (henceforth 'possessed') a gun at some point in their lives and about one-tenth had done so in the last 12 months (see Table 12.1). Gun possession was defined as 'illegal' when the stated reasons for possessing the gun included illegal reasons (e.g., for protection, to impress people, and use in a criminal activity). Gun possession was defined as 'legal' when the stated reasons included only legal uses (e.g., hunting, target shooting, or as part of military training). Using these criteria, the results show that 20 percent of arrestees possessed an illegal gun in their lifetime and 8 percent had done so in the last 12 months.

Type and Number of Guns

All arrestees who reported gun possession at some point in their lives were asked about the type of gun owned. The most common illegal gun possessed was a handgun. This was reported by 60 percent of arrestees who said that they had owned or got hold of a gun for illegal reasons. Thirty percent of arrestees who reported possessing a gun said that they had possessed a shotgun, and one-quarter reported that they had possessed an air gun. Rifles, replica guns, and 'other' guns were cited less frequently (between 6% and 8% of those reporting gun possession).

To get some idea about multiple gun ownership, the responses were aggregated across individuals. On average, arrestees who possessed guns tended to specialize in just one gun type. Nearly three-quarters of respondents reported owning just one gun type. The mean number of gun types possessed across all gun-possessing arrestees was 1.4. A small number of arrestees (about 7% of all those who reported possessing an illegal gun) reported owning three or more gun types.

Reasons for Gun Possession

Arrestees who reported possessing an illegal gun were asked about their reasons for owning one. The most common reason given, reported by more than one-third of arrestees, was protection or self-defense. About one-fifth said that they obtained a gun to use for criminal activity. Others said that they wanted a gun to impress people. Over one-quarter of arrestees who possessed illegal guns gave additional reasons that were coded as 'other'. Other reasons included holding or passing on a gun to others, for fun, to intimidate, and selling on or renting the weapon.

In a supplementary question, the respondents were asked specifically whether their reasons had 'anything to do with drugs'. About one-third of those who said that they possessed an illegal gun said that their reasons for doing so had something to do with drugs. The largest proportion of arrestees (about one-third of those who gave a reason) said that they possessed an illegal gun for protection when dealing drugs. Others said that they obtained a gun to intimidate others when dealing drugs or carried a gun when dealing without specifying whether it was for protection or intimidation. Some arrestees mentioned using a gun to commit crimes relating to drugs. These included robbery for money for drugs and robbery of drug dealers for drugs or cash. Other reasons mentioned were using a gun as currency to trade for drugs and using a gun to take revenge against drug dealers.

Gun Carrying on Offenses

All arrestees who reported possessing an illegal gun were asked if they had ever had a gun with them when they had committed an offense.

TABLE 12.2. *Percentage of arrestees who used an illegal gun on an offense*

	% of arrestees who had taken a gun with them on an offense	
	Ever	Last 12 months
Used on offense[a]	26	23
Not used on an offense	74	77
TOTAL[b]	100	100

[a]The term 'used' refers here to possession of a gun during the commission of a crime.
[b]Some missing values. Includes only arrestees who reported possessing a gun; *n* ever = 300, *n* last 12 months = 118.

Over one-quarter of arrestees (26%) who had ever possessed a gun said that they had carried a gun when offending during this period. A similar proportion (23%) of arrestees who had possessed a gun in the last 12 months said that they carried one on an offense. In total, 5 percent of all arrestees in the study sample said that they had taken a gun with them on an offense at some time in their lives, and 2 percent had done so in the last 12 months (see Table 12.2).

The most common type of gun ever taken on an offense was a handgun (80%) followed by a shotgun (50%). Few arrestees said that they carried an air gun at the time of an offense (13%), and even fewer reported using a replica gun (9%), a rifle (4%), or 'other' types of guns (4%). The type of guns carried on an offense had a similar distribution to the type of guns possessed. However, handguns were slightly overrepresented (60% of all guns possessed and 80% of all guns used on an offense) and air guns were slightly underrepresented (25% of all guns possessed and 13% of all guns used on an offense). Another way of looking at this is to compare the proportion of arrestees who owned a specific gun type with the proportion using it on an offense. About one-third of arrestees who said that they owned a handgun said that they had used it on an offense, compared with 13 percent of arrestees who said that they owned an air gun. Hence, handgun owners are at greater risk of using a gun on an offense than air gun owners. In total, four percent of all arrestees in the study said that they had taken a handgun with them on an offense.

TABLE 12.3. *Prevalence of illegal gun possession among arrestees by demographic characteristics*

	Ever			Last 12 months		
	%	n	p value	%	n	p value
Gender						
Male	21	1,308		8	1,305	
Female	9	220	<.001	5	222	.07
Age						
17–19	23	358		14	356	
20–24	19	400		8	397	
25–29	21	280		7	281	
30 and older	17	490	ns	4	493	<.001
Ethnic group						
White	20	1,228		8	1,207	
Other groups	18	299	ns	8	319	ns
TOTAL	18	1,528		8	1,527	

Notes: Some missing values. % based on valid cases only.
Chi-square test: ns = not significant.

Who Possesses Guns?

As mentioned earlier, there is little official information available on the characteristics of people who possess and use illegal guns. Research conducted in the United States suggests that juveniles, ethnic minorities, and males might be overrepresented in terms of gun possession. However, little evidence of this kind is available in the United Kingdom.

The current research shows that a higher proportion of males than females reported illegal gun possession ever and in the last 12 months. This difference was statistically significant at $p < .001$ for the whole lifetime but fell just short of significance at the .05 level for the last 12 months. However, this difference was significant at the lower probability level of $p = .07$ (see Table 12.3).

There is some evidence from the table that younger arrestees were more likely than older arrestees to possess illegal guns. The relationship between gun possession and age is statistically significant in relation to the 12-month results. The relationship was not significant over the whole lifetime. One explanation for this difference is that there has been an increase in gun possession among young people over time.

The final comparison concerns the relationship between ethnic group status and gun possession. There is no evidence of a statistical association between gun possession and ethnic minority status in either their whole lifetime or in the last 12 months.

Guns, Drugs, and Crime

Studies of gun possession among arrestees in the United States have shown some connection between gun possession and gang membership, violent crime, and involvement in the sale of drugs. However, there is less evidence that there is a connection between use of drugs and gun possession. This final section looks at the links between gun possession, drugs, and crime among the NEW-ADAM arrestees.

The bivariate comparisons show that there is a strong correlation between drug use and gun possession. Six percent of non–drug users reported gun possession, compared with 17 percent of users of drugs other than heroin, crack, and cocaine and 30 percent of users of heroin, crack, and cocaine (see Table 12.4). All differences were statistically significant. There was also a strong correlation between criminal behavior and gun possession. Four percent of self-reported nonoffenders said that they possessed a gun, compared with 14 percent of low-rate offenders and 29 percent of high-rate offenders.

The connection between gun possession and criminal behavior varied slightly by type of offense committed. The highest prevalence of gun possession was among arrestees who reported that they had ever committed robbery (44%) and lowest among arrestees who reported that they had committed shoplifting (21%). These results are similar to those reported in the United States that show an association among gun carrying, violence, and drug supply offenses. The table gives further support to the US findings by showing that gang members were significantly more likely than non–gang members to possess a gun. In fact, half of current gang members reported gun possession (see Bennett and Holloway, 2004).

The relationship was also investigated using multivariate analysis. A number of logistic regression analyses were conducted to determine whether individual factors, criminal behavior, gang membership,

TABLE 12.4. *Prevalence of illegal gun possession ever among arrestees by drug use and crime ever*

Drugs and crime ever	Illegal gun possession ever			
	%	*n*	Sig. [1]	Sig. [2]
Drug Use				
Non–drug users	6	190		
Non-HCC drugs only	17	454	***	
Heroin	25	583	***	**
Crack	26	601	***	**
Cocaine	27	649	***	***
Heroin, crack, and cocaine	30	352	***	***
Criminal behavior				
Nonoffender	4	286		
Low-rate offender	14	480		
High-rate offender	29	759		
Robbery	44	170	***	
Theft person	43	112	***	
Drug supply	39	370	***	
Burglary non-dwelling	36	361	***	
Burglary dwelling	33	340	***	
Theft motor vehicle	33	481	***	
Fraud	32	366	***	
Taking motor vehicle	34	502	***	
Handling	29	699	***	
Shoplifting	21	946	***	
Current gang member [3]	52	48	***	
Past gang member	43	136	***	
Non–gang member	15	1,127		
TOTAL	20	1,528		

Some missing values. % based on valid cases only. Responses are not shown over the last 12 months as the breakdown might result in small cell sizes and potentially misleading results. HCC = heroin, crack, and cocaine. Chi square test corrected for continuity. *** $p < .001$; ** $p < .01$. [1] Significance test comparison based on non–drug users in the 'drug use' section and nonoffenders in the 'criminal behavior' section. [2] Significance test comparison based on non–HCC drug users. [3] Significance test comparison based on non–gang members. The gang question was asked in 14 of the 16 sites included in the survey.

and drug use could independently explain gun possession. The only individual-level variable to predict gun possession was gender. Males were three times as likely as females to report possessing a gun. There was no significant relationship between age or ethnic group status and gun ownership once other factors had been taken into account. The data also show that involvement in criminal behavior independently explained gun possession. Violent offenders were 2.8 times as likely as non-violent offenders to report possessing a gun. Property offenders were also more likely than non-property offenders to admit to illegal gun possession. However, the overall strongest predictor of gun possession was gang membership. Gang members were 5.3 times as likely as non–gang members to report owning a gun.

In line with US research, the current study shows that heroin, crack, and cocaine use (as opposed to supply) was not related to gun possession once other factors had been taken into account. Hence, the bivariate connection between drug use and gun possession discussed earlier is likely to be a product of factors associated with drug use, such as involvement in frequent criminal behavior and lifestyle factors associated with drug dealing.

DISCUSSION

The chapter has argued that there is growing concern about the possible increase in possession and use of illegal guns among criminals. Despite this concern, relatively little is known about gun ownership among offenders. This is because the main official data primarily concern guns and offenses. There are no national statistics on the population of criminals who have access to a gun or who have used a gun on an offense. Independent studies that have investigated gun possession among offenders have been largely confined to specific offenses, offenders, or locations. It is important that more is known about illegal gun possession among offenders to understand the phenomenon and to take effective action against it. In particular, it would be helpful to know more about the possession and use of guns from the offenders' perspective. This includes better information on who carries guns, the types of guns carried, offenders' reasons for carrying guns, and their use of guns in criminal activity.

Some of these questions have been addressed in the current research. The survey showed that about one-quarter of arrestees interviewed said that they had owned or got hold of a gun at some point in their lives, and about one-tenth had done so in the previous

12 months. The most common illegal gun possessed was a handgun, and the most common reason for possessing a gun was protection. One reason for wanting the protection of a gun was during drug dealing or drug purchasing. More than one-third of arrestees who possessed a handgun said that they had used it on an offense. Male arrestees were more likely than female arrestees to possess a firearm, and younger arrestees were more likely than older arrestees to do so. Gun possession was most common among high-rate offenders, violent offenders, those involved in drug supply offenses, and gang members.

Our results are similar to those obtained from ADAM surveys in the United States. These showed that firearm ownership was common among juveniles, gang members, and those who reported selling drugs. These characteristics reflect the broader characteristics of the new forms of youth crime that developed in the United States during the 1980s and 1990s. The main features of this development were an expansion in gang membership, greater gun involvement, an increase in drug misuse, and an increase in youth violence (Zimring, 1998). It has been argued that youth crime in the United Kingdom shares some of the features of youth crime in the United States. Shropshire and McFarquhar(2002), for example, noted the increased incidence of 'turf wars' among rival gangs, 'drive-by shootings', 'rites-of-passage' violence, and 'retaliatory' violence. NCIS have also noted similar elements of violent crime in the United Kingdom such as 'black-on-black firearm crime', use of guns 'to enforce drug debts' and use of guns 'to punish perceived disrespect' (NCIS, 2002).

A growing body of evidence suggests that use of firearms among criminals in the United Kingdom is increasing. To monitor this process and to take effective action, it is important to increase current knowledge about the possession and use of guns among offenders. A number of potential intervention strategies can be used to target gun possession and use of guns in criminal activity, such as education programs, gun amnesties, gang-suppression programs, community organizing, and zero-tolerance policing (Decker and Van Winkel, 1996). However, to implement these programs effectively, it is important to develop a broad knowledge base of the extent, nature, and purpose of gun possession among offenders.

CHAPTER THIRTEEN

Drug Markets

INTRODUCTION

In any particular country, the overall drug market might be thought of as comprising a number of submarkets. Pearson and Hobbs (2001) identified what they refer to as a four-tier classification of drug markets: importers, wholesalers, middle-market brokers, and retail dealers. Dorn and Hunter (1992) suggested a seven-tier typology based on the type of 'firms', or groups of individuals, involved in drug trafficking (trading charities, mutual societies, sideliners, criminal diversifiers, opportunistic irregulars, retail specialists, and state-sponsored traders). Lupton et al. (2002) described two types of drug markets operating in deprived neighborhoods (central place markets and local markets), and Edmunds, Hough, and Urquia (1995) identified two types of market operating at the local level (open and closed). Dorn, Levi, and King (2005) described drug trafficking in terms of individual motives (political, financial, and risk). Hence, researchers to date have tended to use typologies as a means of describing the nature of drug markets.

Although these typologies provide useful descriptive information about different aspects of drug markets, none provides a picture of the drug market as whole. Further, little is known about when these typologies apply and when they do not apply. It is likely that methods of drug trafficking and dealing vary markedly in terms of organization and operation over time and location. In some locations or times, small organized crime groups might cover almost the entire range of operations from importation to street dealing (Brookman, Bennett, and Maguire, 2004). In other locations or times, much more complex chains might exist involving many layers of activity (Pearson and Hobbs, 2001). However, there is little research evidence on the nature of drug markets and the way in which they operate in practice. More research is needed to map out the details of drug markets and to determine the ways in which they might vary.

DRUG MARKETS

Drug markets in the United Kingdom might be usefully conceived as comprising four levels of operation: importers, wholesalers, middle-market brokers, and retail dealers. Whether they operate as such in practice is discussed in the next section.

Importation

Importation concerns the methods by which drugs originating from the producer countries enter the consumer country. According to National Criminal Intelligence Service (NCIS), most heroin enters the United Kingdom through ports in the southeast of England, particularly Dover, Felixstowe, and Harwich (NCIS, 2005). The bulk arrives in freight vehicles, although some is transported by couriers in passenger vehicles or as baggage. The Channel Tunnel is a major route for importing heroin into the United Kingdom. Some heroin also enters the United Kingdom through the main UK airports, particularly those with connections to Turkey or Pakistan (NCIS, 2005). Estimates by Her Majesty's Customs suggest that two-thirds of cocaine destined for the United Kingdom arrives by air, on scheduled flights, concealed in baggage or air cargo (Corkery, 2002). According to NCIS, most cocaine is smuggled into the United Kingdom by couriers hired by organized criminal gangs of Caribbean origin (NCIS, 2005). Ecstasy arrives in the United Kingdom through ferry ports, mainly in the southeast, especially Dover, and the northeast of England. The drugs are often concealed in private and heavy goods vehicles, in freight, or carried by passengers (NCIS, 2005).

The vast majority (more than 90 percent) of all heroin seized in the United Kingdom originates from opium produced in Afghanistan (Corkery, 2002). It is estimated that Afghanistan accounts for around

70 percent of global opium production (NCIS, 2005). Specifically, Afghanistan produces opium for the heroin markets of Europe and South Asia, as well as Africa. However, opium destined for the North American market is usually grown in South America, mainly Colombia. Almost all of the world's cocaine is produced in Colombia, Peru, and Bolivia. In 2002, it was reported that Colombia accounted for the vast majority, although the contribution of Peru was increasing (NCIS, 2005). It is estimated that up to 80 percent of all MDMA (ecstasy) consumed worldwide emanates from laboratories in the Netherlands and Belgium. However, there is some production in Poland, Germany, and in Eastern Europe, including Romania (NCIS, 2005). Corkery (2002) noted that most of the herbal cannabis in the world market originates in South America (e.g., Colombia), Jamaica, and Africa. Morocco is the primary source of cannabis resin for the UK market.

Wholesalers
The first level of distribution in a country is sometimes referred to as upper-level or wholesale distribution. There is widespread agreement in the research that upper-level dealing is mainly organized by criminal gangs. However, there is very little research on gangs of this kind (Pearson and Hobbs, 2001). Nevertheless, it is widely believed that criminal drug gangs are typically based on specific nationalities. For example, it is thought that Turkish criminal groups dominate the European and UK heroin trade. However, gangs of other national groups also play a part in heroin distribution including British Caucasian gangs, Asian gangs, Albanian gangs, and West African gangs (NCIS, 2005). NCIS notes that many of the most significant British Caucasian groups are based in Merseyside, although some are based in Scotland and some in East London. Cocaine distribution into the country appears to be controlled mainly by British Caucasian, West Indian, and Colombian gangs.

Middle-Market Brokers
The next level is usually referred to as middle-level drug distribution. However, there is little agreement about how this should be defined.

Pearson and Hobbs (2001) suggest that the middle-market drug broker is identified as occupying a strategic position that links upper levels (importation and wholesale) and lower levels (retail) of the market. Although at first sight this definition might seem simplistic, it works well in practice in identifying a unique section of the market. There is also little research on middle-market drug distribution. However, there have been one or two recent studies that have helped shed light on this topic. Pearson and Hobbs (2001) described the middle-market dealer as someone who buys in multi-kilo amounts heroin, cocaine, and other substances from the importers and sells in part-kilo amounts or ounces at the retail level. Some middle-market dealers specialize only in recreational drugs. According to Pearson and Hobbs (2001), middle-market drug networks are typically small – just one or two people who control finances and have established contacts and a small team of runners working for them who collect and deliver quantities of drugs. Some runners are employed on a weekly wage basis, and others are paid per transaction (Pearson and Hobbs, 2001).

Retail Dealers
The bottom level of the supply chain is usually referred to as lower-level or retail-level drug distribution. Pearson and Hobbs (2001) suggested that there are three types of retail drug dealer: heroin dealers who sometimes also sell crack cocaine, cannabis dealers who sometimes sell pills, and pill dealers who sometimes sell cannabis. The third type of dealer is closely associated with the clubbing scene. Lupton et al. (2002) conducted a study of retail drug markets in deprived residential areas of England in 2000 and 2001. The authors thought that the markets could be divided into two broad types. The first type was long established and had a widespread reputation. It drew buyers from outside the area and included open as well as closed selling. These were found mainly in inner-city areas, with mixed housing type and mixed ethnicity and tenure. The second type had a less widespread reputation and served a smaller number of buyers mainly from the local area. It had mainly closed selling with established buyer and seller arrangements. These were found outside the city center in areas with stable populations and were almost exclusively white. Most of the

selling took place through a closed system involving mobile phones and personal drug deliveries (Lupton et al., 2002).

RESEARCH

It is widely accepted that the structure and operation of drug markets is an underresearched area. Pearson and Hobbs (2003) described the literature on drug supply as 'comparatively rare' (p. 335). Natarajan and Belanger (1998) referred to the 'void' in research on drug trafficking organizations (p. 1006). Pearson and Hobbs (2001) noted that research on drug dealing in the United Kingdom is 'considerably underdeveloped' (p. 3).

Although the UK research base is generally limited, some studies have been conducted on the nature and organization of drug markets. The bulk of this work is qualitative in nature and small in scale. One of the early pieces of empirical research to explore drug trafficking in the United Kingdom was conducted by Dorn, Murji, and South in the early 1990s. This study was based on interviews with individuals working in enforcement agencies, prisoners convicted of drug trafficking, and users living in the community. The main focus of the research was on the control of drug markets and law enforcement efforts rather than on the operations and dynamics of drug markets. The authors reported that contrary to mythology and media presentation, domestic drug markets were not organized as neat, top-down hierarchies controlled by a "Mr. Big." They found no person or group organizing the market as a whole. Instead, they found a large number of small organizations operating fairly autonomously of each other in a somewhat disorganized manner. They conclude that drug markets are both 'messy' and 'simple' (Dorn et al., 1992, p. 58).

Dorn, Oette, and White (1998) conducted a small-scale, qualitative study focusing mainly on the risks involved in drug importation. Interviews were conducted with 15 persons convicted of serious drug trafficking offenses and 10 informants of Her Majesty's Customs and Excise. The research aimed to explore perceptions of risk and the use of risk-avoidance strategies. The study identified two types of risk: the possibility of seizure of drugs and associated resources (tactical risk) and the possibility of the planner/organizer being observed, arrested, charged, and convicted (strategic risk). They investigated risk in three main areas: (1) how drug dealers became involved in drug dealing and their initial risk assessments, (2) risk appraisals in relation to people inside and outside their own group, and (3) risk appraisals in relation to logistic and practical arrangements of drug dealing. Risk was found to be greatest at the startup stage of operations (i.e., when the organization was being developed). Strategies to reduce risk included employing others to act as 'cut outs' and controlling the flow of information to enforcement agencies. Although the study provides an interesting account of risk management, it provides little descriptive information on how drug markets operate.

By contrast, Pearson and Hobbs (2001) provided some information on the organization and dynamics of drug markets. This research aimed to explore middle-market drug distribution and was based on interviews with offenders imprisoned for drug supply offenses and with police and customs officers. Conflicting definitions of the 'middle market' were reported by interviewees. For the purposes of their study, middle market was defined as something that happened between importation into the country and retail supply to drug consumers on the streets. Pearson and Hobbs (2001) sketched out the structure of markets for different commodities and presented information about the methods of pricing drugs at different levels. The supply chain for heroin, for example, was found to be 'as few as four levels: from 100 kilo upwards bulk shipment at importation; through to 20 to 40 kilo wholesale dealers; to one to ten kilo middle-level drug brokers; to retail level dealers buying in ounces and selling in grams and £20 bags' (p. 24). They also explored the internal organization of drug dealing networks. Family and kinship ties, for example, were found to be most prominent at higher levels of drug trafficking. The role of law enforcement was also examined and imprisonment was found to be 'an extremely important generator of information and contacts for the drug trade' (p. 30). Pearson and Hobbs (2001) concluded that people's perceptions of drug market operations were 'highly fragmented' and that no one has yet been able 'to draw the big picture' (p. 55). They claimed that this is partly a result of the structure of drug markets, which are constantly changing. However, it might also be a result of the lack of in-depth, large-scale research conducted in the area.

Brookman, Bennett, and Maguire (2004) also investigated middle-market drug operations as part of a larger evaluation of a regional drug task force. The research included an investigation into the operations of the force and details of the individuals targeted and apprehended. The research found little use of the term middle market among the police and little agreement over what it might constitute. The organized crime groups investigated tended to have quite variable structures and methods of operation. Some traffickers or dealers handled large amounts of drugs in a single transaction and operated infrequently, whereas others handled relatively small quantities of drugs over many repeated operations. Some operated in a fairly narrow band of the market (e.g., supply to street level dealers), whereas others combined drug trafficking (importation) with street-level dealing. The police were also keen not to stereotype the kinds of people involved in trafficking and dealing. Some were professional and powerful operators, whereas others were described as 'Del Boys' who would turn their hand to anything to make money ('from stolen washing machines to drugs'). The challenge of future research is to identify the proportion of drug markets that are made up of groups of these kinds and the role that they play in shaping the market as a whole.

Lupton et al. (2002) reported the findings of a study of drug markets in deprived neighborhoods in the United Kingdom. The study aimed to identify the extent of drug market activity in these neighborhoods, to draw out any associations between areas and types of market, to understand the impact of drug markets on disadvantaged neighborhoods, and to explore local approaches to tackling drug markets. Whereas Pearson and Hobbs (2001) focused research attention on the middle market, Lupton et al. (2002) focused their research on what they called the retail level (i.e., the point at which drugs are purchased by consumers). All of the eight markets examined were found to be very active. Heroin was easily available in all markets, and crack was available in six of them. Costs were found to be consistent across markets, although they were found to fluctuate depending on whether the buyer was a 'regular' and the quantities that were purchased. Overall, the research provides some important information on the nature of local drug markets. However, it is limited in that it focuses only on sales to end users.

The studies described provide the baseline of knowledge about drug markets and dealing in the United Kingdom. Although some progress has been made in some areas (especially at the level of the end user), there is very little substantive knowledge about the supply chain as a whole. As Pearson and Hobbs (2001) pointed out, no one has yet been able to describe the 'bigger picture'.

The aim of this chapter is to add to this knowledge base by drawing on the findings of the New English and Welsh Arrestee Drug Abuse Monitoring (NEW-ADAM) program.

RESULTS

Questions relating to drug purchases and drug markets where included in the NEW-ADAM program surveys. Arrestees interviewed were randomly allocated to complete either a follow-up questionnaire exploring weapons and guns or a follow-up questionnaire exploring heroin, crack, and cocaine drug markets. The remainder of this chapter is concerned with the subsample of 1,555 arrestees who had been allocated to complete the questionnaire on drug markets. As only some arrestees had experience of drug markets in the last 12 months, the total number of responses is less than this. In total, 270 arrestees provided information about cocaine markets, 92 arrestees answered questions about crack markets, and 421 about heroin markets. Arrestees with experience of both cocaine and crack markets were asked to focus their answers on the drug type that they had used most frequently. It is possible, therefore, to compare statistically responses relating to cocaine and crack markets as arrestees with experience of these drugs were independent of each other. It is not possible, however, to compare statistically the cocaine or crack markets with heroin markets because arrestees may have answered questions relating to both and the samples would not be independent. However, the percentage differences are presented for descriptive purposes.

Table 13.1 provides information about the type of people involved in cocaine, crack, and heroin markets. The figures show that users of all three markets tended to be male, white, and from a low social class. Crack and heroin buyers, however, were more likely than cocaine

TABLE 13.1. *Characteristics of users of cocaine, crack, and heroin markets*

	Cocaine, % (n = 92)	Crack, % (n = 270)	Sig.[a]	Heroin, % (n = 421)
Gender				
Male	91	80		82
Female	9	20	*	18
Age				
17–24	53	38		40
25 and older	47	62	*	60
Ethnic group				
White	91	83		88
Nonwhite	9	17	ns	12
Social class				
Higher	29	6		4
Lower	71	94	***	93

Notes: This question was included on the follow-up questionnaire, which was answered by half of the sample (n = 1,555). Not all of these arrestees had been involved in drug buying or selling. In total, 92 arrestees answered questions relating to cocaine markets, 270 arrestees answered questions relating to crack markets, and 421 arrestees answered questions relating to heroin markets. Social class was calculated using five variables: higher social class = social security benefits (no), tenure (own home), employment (not unemployed), age left education (17+), and legal income (£10 k+). Arrestees who answered yes to three or more of the five variables were deemed to be in the higher social class. All remaining arrestees were deemed to be in a lower social class. Fourteen arrestees did not provide responses to all five questions and were therefore excluded from the analysis.
[a]Significance of difference between cocaine markets and crack markets. Some missing cases. $*p < .05$, $***p < .001$, ns = not significant.

buyers to be female (20% and 18% compared with 9%) and to be aged 25 or older (62% and 60% compared with 47%). Users of cocaine markets, however, were significantly more likely than users of crack and more likely than users of heroin markets to be from a higher social class (29% compared with 6% and 4%). This finding lends support to the idea that powder cocaine tends to be associated with the higher social classes, whereas crack cocaine and heroin tends to be associated with the lower social classes (Spear and Mott, 2001).

One of the distinguishing features of a drug market is drug availability. If there are few drugs available in a local area, then at least some of the potential purchasers of these drugs will be unable to obtain them. The same argument applies to the ease of making the purchase. If it is difficult to make a purchase locally because the drugs are sold through closed markets, then some of the potential purchasers of these drugs will be unable to obtain them. There are a number of ways to measure local availability and ease of obtaining drugs. Tables 13.2 and 13.3 list some of the factors that characterize retail drug markets.

Table 13.2 shows that, at the time of the survey, more than three-quarters of arrestees were able to obtain cocaine in their local neighborhoods. Similarly, over 80 percent were able to obtain crack or heroin in their local neighborhoods. In other words, it was not necessary for them to travel beyond their local neighborhood to obtain their drugs. Nevertheless, some arrestees did travel outside of their local area. Arrestees who had purchased cocaine said more frequently than those who purchased crack that they had bought their drugs outside of their local neighborhood (22% compared with 17%). However, this difference was not statistically significant.

Another important factor is the way in which contact with dealers is initiated. The literature is unclear about methods of contact and whether users typically make the first contact indirectly by mobile phone or directly by personal contact. The current research shows that the vast majority of arrestees who had purchased crack and heroin made contact with dealers indirectly by phone or by pager (72% in each market). In contrast, cocaine users more frequently made their initial contact in person (50%). The difference in mode of contact between cocaine and crack markets was statistically significant.

The next stage in the process of making a drug purchase is physically to obtain the drugs. Just under three-quarters of arrestees in each of the three markets reported that they went somewhere to collect their drugs. The remainder said that they had the drugs delivered to their door. Those arrestees who went somewhere to collect their drugs were asked about the main methods that they used to collect their drugs (multiple responses were possible). Users of cocaine markets were significantly more likely than users of crack markets to collect their drugs from inside someone's house (52% compared with 33%) or from pubs or clubs (32% compared with 14%). However, users of crack markets were significantly more likely than users of cocaine markets to obtain their drugs on the street (74% compared with 39%). Overall, users of heroin markets and crack markets reported collecting drugs from similar locations.

TABLE 13.2. *Location of cocaine, crack, and heroin markets used in the last 12 months*

	Cocaine, % (n)	Crack, % (n)	Sig.[a]	Heroin, % (n)
Do you usually buy in your local neighborhood?				
Yes	78 (72)	83 (224)		88 (371)
No	22 (20)	17 (46)		12 (50)
TOTAL	100 (92)	100 (270)	ns	100 (421)
How do you usually initiate contact?				
Phone/pager	50 (46)	72 (194)		72 (303)
Personal contact	50 (46)	28 (76)		28 (118)
TOTAL	100 (92)	100 (270)	***	100 (421)
How do you usually obtain the purchase?				
Delivered to door	28 (26)	29 (77)		27 (113)
Go somewhere to collect	72 (66)	72 (193)		73 (308)
TOTAL	100 (92)	100 (270)	ns	100 (421)
If go somewhere, where?[b]				
Inside someone's house	52 (34)	33 (64)	*	34 (104)
At the door or window	12 (8)	14 (26)	ns	11 (35)
In an abandoned building	6 (4)	8 (15)	ns	9 (27)
Pubs or clubs	32 (21)	14 (27)	**	13 (39)
On the street	39 (26)	74 (142)	***	75 (231)
Other	6 (4)	7 (13)	ns	5 (16)
TOTAL	100 (66)	100 (193)		100 (308)

If go somewhere, what area[b]

			Significance[a]	
Residential areas	70 (46)	60 (116)	ns	61 (189)
City-center areas	36 (24)	37 (72)	ns	36 (110)
Backstreet areas	20 (13)	45 (86)	**	42 (128)
Other	3 (2)	2 (4)	ns	2 (7)
TOTAL	100 (66)	100 (193)	ns	100 (308)

Notes: This question was included on the follow-up questionnaire, which was answered by half of the sample ($n = 1,555$). Not all of these arrestees had been involved in drug buying or selling. In total, 92 arrestees answered questions relating to cocaine markets, 270 arrestees answered questions relating to crack markets, and 421 arrestees answered questions relating to heroin markets.

[a]Significance of difference between cocaine markets and crack markets. * $p < .05$, ** $p < .01$, *** $p < .001$, ns = not significant.

[b]Multiple responses possible. Some missing cases.

259

TABLE 13.3. *Characteristics of cocaine, crack, and heroin markets used in the last 12 months*

	Cocaine, % ($n = 92$)	Crack, % ($n = 270$)	Sig.[a]	Heroin, % ($n = 421$)
How many buyers does your main supplier have?				
Many buyers	73 (60)	84 (220)		87 (364)
A few buyers	15 (12)	13 (35)		9 (37)
One or two	11 (9)	2 (4)		1 (3)
Just you	1 (1)	1 (2)	**	1 (4)
How many people can you currently buy from?				
Mean number	12.68	18.60		22.75
Median number	6.00	10.00	ns	10.50
How easy has it been to obtain the drug in the last 12 months?				
Very easy	69 (63)	77 (206)		82 (346)
Fairly easy	22 (20)	15 (40)		9 (39)
Neither easy nor difficult	4 (4)	3 (8)		3 (13)
Fairly difficult	4 (4)	5 (12)		4 (18)
Very difficult	1 (1)	1 (1)	ns	1 (4)
How good was the quality of the drug purchased in the last 12 months?				
Very good	39 (35)	23 (62)		23 (98)
Fairly good	34 (31)	43 (114)		40 (168)
Neither good nor bad	13 (12)	15 (39)		21 (86)
Fairly bad	10 (9)	12 (33)		11 (46)
Very bad	4 (4)	8 (20)	ns	5 (22)

Notes: This question was included on the follow-up questionnaire, which was answered by half of the sample ($n = 1,555$). Not all of these arrestees had been involved in drug buying or selling. In total, 92 arrestees answered questions relating to cocaine markets, 270 arrestees answered questions relating to crack markets, and 421 arrestees answered questions relating to heroin markets.
[a]Significance of difference between cocaine markets and crack markets. Some missing cases. **$p < .01$, ns = not significant.

There was also variation in terms of the type of area in which drugs were obtained. Sixty percent of heroin and crack users compared with 70 percent of cocaine users reported obtaining their drugs in residential areas, and just over one-third of arrestees in each market reported collecting their drugs from city-center areas. However, crack users were significantly more likely than cocaine users to go to backstreet areas to collect their drugs (45% compared with 20%).

These findings indicate that there are marked variations in drug markets depending on the type of drug sold. Heroin and crack markets appear to operate fairly similarly, and it is plausible that they might, in fact, be part of the same market. Cocaine markets, however, appear to operate quite differently. This difference might reflect the fact that cocaine tends to be used on a more recreational and social basis. As a result, it is more likely to be purchased through personal contact in pubs or clubs. It is also likely that powder cocaine is more socially acceptable as a result of its association with the wealthy and famous and might, therefore, have become 'normalized' in UK society as an acceptable social activity (Parker et al., 2001). Conversely, heroin and crack tend to be used on a more habitual and dependent basis. Use of these drugs might be viewed as a more desperate activity by people compelled to obtain and consume them. This might mean that they are more likely to be purchased in a more clandestine manner using phones or pagers and collected from hidden backstreet areas.

One of the most important characteristics of a retail drug market is whether it is an 'open' or a 'closed' market. One measure of this is the number of buyers in the market. The smaller the number of buyers, the more appropriate it is to view it as a closed market, and the greater the number of buyers the more appropriate it is to view it as an open market. These are important concepts in the study of drug markets, and it is believed that the two types of market are substantially different in terms of personnel and methods of operation.

Table 13.3 provides information on the size of markets and the quality of drugs sold within them. The table shows that there is a significant difference between cocaine and crack markets in terms of the number of buyers within the market. Sixteen percent of arrestees who had bought crack in the last 12 months compared with twenty-seven percent of arrestees who had bought cocaine reported that their main supplier had a small number of buyers. Hence, cocaine market users were significantly more likely than crack market users to be 'closed' markets.

Arrestees were also asked to approximate the number of people that they could currently buy drugs from. Although the mean difference was not statistically significant, the figures again point to variations between the markets. Arrestees who had bought cocaine reported that they could buy from a mean of 13 dealers, whereas arrestees who had bought crack reported being able to buy from 19 dealers; arrestees who had bought heroin said they could buy from 23 dealers.

Perhaps as a result of this, most arrestees found that it was either 'very easy' or 'fairly easy' to obtain cocaine, crack, and heroin in the last 12 months. The quality of the drugs purchased varied somewhat across the markets. The quality of cocaine was reported to be either 'very good' or 'fairly good' by 73 percent of arrestees, whereas the quality of crack was described as 'very good' or 'fairly good' by 66 percent of arrestees, and the quality of heroin was described in this way by 63 percent of arrestees. This finding might suggest that the quality of drugs is better in closed markets where there are fewer buyers and sellers who might often be personally known to each other than in open markets where buyers and sellers might more frequently be strangers.

Given the variations in market structure and operations just described, it might be expected that drug markets also differ in terms of the prices charged by dealers and the amounts of money spent by users. In fact, there was no significant difference in typical daily expenditure (£50 per day among both cocaine and crack users and £55 per day among heroin users). However, cocaine users reported spending more in their last purchase (average of £138) compared with crack users (average £77) or heroin users (average £35). To determine whether there were changes in price of drugs over time, they were each asked whether drug prices had risen, fallen, or stayed the same over the last 12 months. The majority of arrestees in each of the three markets reported that the cost of drugs was either the same or less expensive than it had been 12 months before. Only a small proportion (approximately 10%) of arrestees felt that the cost of drugs had increased in the last year.

Table 13.4 presents information on the characteristics of open and closed markets. It should be noted that the small number of closed markets makes statistical comparisons between the two markets difficult. Nevertheless, some significant findings did emerge. Within cocaine markets, arrestees buying drugs within open markets were significantly more likely than buyers in closed markets to find it easy to purchase drugs (97% compared with 82%). They also reported paying significantly less for their drugs than buyers in closed markets (£44 compared with £50). Buyers in open markets were also significantly more likely (at the reduced level of $p = .051$) than

TABLE 13.4. *Characteristics of open and closed cocaine and heroin markets used in the last 12 months*

	Cocaine, %			Crack, %			Heroin, %		
	Closed (n = 22)	Open (n = 60)	Sig.[a]	Closed (n = 41)	Open (n = 220)	Sig.[a]	Closed (n = 44)	Open (n = 364)	Sig.[a]
Method of contact									
Phone/pager	32	52		85	71		77	72	
In person	68	48	ns	15	30	ns	23	28	ns
Location									
Local	68	82		78	84		93	88	
Nonlocal	32	18	ns	22	16	ns	7	12	ns
Quality of drugs									
Very/fairly good	73	76		54	69		57	65	
Not good	27	24	ns	46	31	ns	43	35	ns
Method of collection									
Delivered home	27	28	ns	22	31	ns	25	28	ns
Go somewhere	73	72	ns	78	69	ns	75	72	ns
House[b]	56	56	ns	38	33	ns	30	35	ns
Pubs or clubs	44	26	ns	22	13	ns	21	11	ns
On street	13	44	.051	56	77	*	67	75	ns
Building	6	5	ns	9	7	ns	12	8	ns

(continued)

TABLE 13.4 (continued)

	Cocaine, %			Crack, %			Heroin, %		
	Closed (n = 22)	Open (n = 60)	Sig.[a]	Closed (n = 41)	Open (n = 220)	Sig.[a]	Closed (n = 44)	Open (n = 364)	Sig.[a]
Place of collection									
Residential[b]	56	79	ns	69	58	ns	61	61	ns
City center	38	35	ns	31	38	ns	39	34	ns
Backstreet	13	23	ns	34	47	ns	49	40	ns
Ease obtaining drugs									
Very/fairly easy	82	97	*	83	95	*	86	94	ns
Not easy	18	3		17	6		14	6	
Average price[c]									
Mean	£49.74	£43.68	*	£20.27	£20.43	ns	£42.97	£46.39	
Median	£50	£45		£20	£20		£40.00	£45.00	ns

Notes: These questions were included on the follow-up questionnaire, which was answered by half of the sample (n = 1,555). Not all of these arrestees had been involved in drug buying or selling. In total, 92 arrestees answered questions relating to cocaine markets, 270 arrestees answered questions relating to crack markets, and 421 arrestees answered questions relating to heroin markets.

[a]Significance of difference between open and closed markets. * p < .05, ns = not significant.

[b]Among arrestees who went somewhere to collect their drugs.

[c]Crack = price per rock (0.2g). Heroin = price per gram. Excludes cocaine markets. Some missing cases.

buyers in closed markets to purchase cocaine on the street. A similar pattern of results was found for crack markets. Buyers in open crack markets were significantly more likely than buyers in closed crack markets to buy drugs on the street (77% compared with 56%). They were also significantly more likely than buyers in closed markets to find it easy to purchase crack (95% compared with 83%). No significant differences were found between open and closed heroin markets.

The results shown in Table 13.4 also highlight differences between the three types (i.e., cocaine, crack, and heroin) of closed and open market. In the main, the characteristics of open and closed heroin and crack markets were very similar. One exception, however, was in respect of the location in which drugs were purchased in closed markets. Just 7 percent of heroin buyers in closed markets reported buying drugs from outside of their local neighborhood compared with more than one-fifth (22%) of crack buyers.

Buyers in closed cocaine markets appear to be quite different from buyers in closed crack and heroin markets. In closed cocaine markets, buyers were more likely to make contact with dealers in person (68% compared with 15% and 23% respectively). They were also more likely to purchase drugs outside of their local area (32% compared with 22% and 7%) and to buy drugs that were of a very or fairly good quality (73% compared with 54% and 57%). Buyers in closed cocaine markets were also more likely to purchase their drugs in clubs or pubs (44% compared with 22% and 21%) and were less likely to buy drugs on the street (13% compared with 56% and 67%).

Differences between open cocaine markets and open crack and heroin markets were also apparent. One difference was in the method by which contact was made with dealers. Nearly half (48%) of all buyers in open cocaine markets reported making contact with dealers in person compared with approximately 30 percent of arrestees in open crack and heroin markets. The quality of drugs purchased was also slightly better in open cocaine markets (76% described the drugs as very or fairly good compared with 69% and 65%), and the method of collection also differed with more arrestees in open cocaine markets buying drugs in pubs and clubs than on the street.

DISCUSSION

The first part of this chapter reviewed the literature on drug markets in the United Kingdom and concluded that there is little substantive knowledge about the supply chain as a whole. However, progress had been made in some areas, particularly at the level of the end user. The aim of this chapter was to add to this knowledge base and provide further information about the characteristics and operation of drug markets at the lower end of the supply chain.

Arrestees who had purchased cocaine, crack, or heroin in the last 30 days were asked to provide information about the way in which they purchased these drugs and details about where they purchased them from. The results have identified some useful information about the way in which these markets operate.

Heroin and crack markets were found to be similar in many ways, including the sociodemographic characteristics and the offending behavior of buyers, the location in which buyers bought their drugs, and the method by which buyers made contact with dealers (i.e., by phone). The use of mobile phones to initiate contact with heroin and crack dealers was also reported by Lupton et al. (2002). In the current study, the heroin and crack markets were also similar in terms of the place from which buyers collected their drugs and the number of buyers and sellers operating in each market. The similarities between the crack and heroin markets identified here suggest that the two markets might, in fact, be the same. In an earlier piece of research on drug markets in the United Kingdom, Pearson and Hobbs (2001) identified three types of retail drug dealer. One of these was described as a heroin dealer who sometimes also sold crack cocaine. Lupton et al. (2002) also found that heroin and crack were both available and very easy to obtain in the majority of the markets examined.

Although heroin and crack markets were very similar, clear differences were found between cocaine markets and crack and heroin markets. In cocaine markets, buyers were significantly more likely to be male, to be in the younger age group, and to be from a higher social class. Differences were also found in the way in which contact was made with dealers and the places at which drugs were collected. Cocaine buyers were more likely to contact dealers in person and were more likely to collect their drugs from inside someone's house or from pubs and clubs. They were less likely to collect drugs on the street. This difference may reflect the fact that cocaine buyers are more recreational drug users than crack and heroin buyers. As a result, cocaine sales are more likely to be conducted in social situations, such as in pubs and clubs.

The markets were also found to differ in terms of whether they were open or closed. Cocaine markets were more likely to be closed (with few buyers), whereas crack and heroin markets were more likely to be open (with many buyers). These results contrast with those of Lupton et al. (2002) who found that heroin and crack markets in deprived neighborhoods were mostly closed. However, in some areas, they were a mixture of open and closed.

The analysis also revealed differences between open and closed markets. Buyers in open cocaine markets were more likely than buyers in closed markets to purchase drugs on the street and were more likely to find it 'very' or 'fairly easy' to buy drugs. The price of drugs was also lower in open cocaine markets. A similar pattern of findings was found between open and closed crack markets, although there was no significant variation in price. The ease with which drug users reported being able to purchase drugs in each of the three markets has important implications for drug policy. It could be argued that drug prevention policy should vary by type of market. There are notable differences between crack and cocaine markets in the way in which they operate. Drug prevention strategies might be tailored to the characteristics of each market.

CHAPTER FOURTEEN

Assisted Desistance and Treatment Needs

INTRODUCTION

This chapter discusses treatment needs of arrestees and treatment methods provided for drug misuse. In particular, it looks at treatment offered by traditional programs aimed at drug users who voluntarily present themselves and treatment offered through court orders or other criminal justice processes whereby treatment for drug misuse as part of the disposal. The former is sometimes referred to as 'voluntary' treatment in that they are based on self-referral. The latter is sometimes described as 'coercive treatment' in that they are based on referral to treatment by the criminal justice system.

One of the central platforms of the government's drug strategy is to tackle drug misuse and drug-related crime through treatment provision. To be effective, the strategy needs to encourage users who have not sought treatment to enter into treatment. It also needs to satisfy the demand for treatment of users who have sought treatment. It is also important that drug users enter into treatment programs that have been shown in the past to reduce drug misuse or drug-related crime. This chapter reviews the literature on the type of treatment services available and user demand for these services. It then looks at the level of demand for treatment among drug-using arrestees and the extent to which this demand is met.

TREATMENT PROGRAMS AVAILABLE

Treatment programs for drug-misusing offenders comprise a combination of traditional treatment methods and criminal justice programs.

Traditional Treatment Methods

Traditional treatment methods refer here to the various types of medical, social, or psychological programs for drug users. These are typically provided by doctors or other trained professionals working in settings specific for the treatment of drug misuse. Users are typically referred to these settings through self-referral or other medical or professional referral with the primary aim of treating their drug misuse. However, they can also be referred through criminal justice processes.

Treatment programs for drug users can be divided into four main categories: 'methadone treatment', 'heroin treatment', 'therapeutic communities', and 'psychosocial approaches'.

Methadone Treatment is based on replacing illegal opiates with prescribed methadone. Methadone is a synthetic opiate and produces similar effects to heroin and other opium-based products. However, it is manufactured rather than natural. It is regarded by the medical profession as a preferred alternative to heroin in that it is longer lasting and can be taken orally. It can be used for purposes of withdrawal or maintenance. The most common form of methadone treatment is maintenance prescribing whereby users are prescribed methadone as an alternative to heroin over extended periods of time. The aim of this method of treatment is to stabilize users and allow them to lead normal lives while drug dependent.

Heroin Treatment is similar to methadone treatment in that an opiate is prescribed by a doctor usually over extended periods of time to stabilize drug dependence. However, in this case, the drug user's drug of choice is used rather than an alternative. It has been argued that heroin taken over long periods of time under controlled and sterile conditions is safe and is also preferred among drug users (Metrebian et al., 2001). However, heroin treatment is generally not preferred among doctors, and relatively few heroin treatment programs exist.

Therapeutic Communities for substance abuse were first established in the late 1950s as a self-help alternative to existing treatments, particularly for heroin addicts (Nemes, Wish, and Messina, 1999). They are now one of the most common residential treatment methods for substance misusers. Therapeutic communities are usually drug-free residential programs based on peer influence and group processes. The aim of the program is to encourage individuals to assimilate the norms of the group and to learn effective social skills to tackle their drug use problems. The main agent of change is the community in which the individual lives and includes the treatment staff as well as other drug users at various stages in their recovery. Members of the community interact in various ways to influence attitudes, perceptions, and behavior associated with drug use. The programs are also based on the principle of self-help in that the individual is seen as an important contributor to the change process.

Psychosocial Approaches typically cover a range of programs that use psychological, social, or behavioral approaches in the treatment of drug misuse. The programs can be quite wide ranging and include psychotherapy, counseling, cognitive-behavioral approaches, and family therapy. One of the most common psychosocial approaches is cognitive-behaviorism. These are approaches based on psychological theories of learning and behavior. They tend to stress the role of the external environment in shaping an individual's actions. They also give importance to the individual's thought processes, such as reasoning, memory and problem solving. Programs drawing on social learning theory stress the role of learning and social interaction. All of these approaches are based on the principles that drug users lack certain psychological or social skills that can be improved with suitable interventions.

Criminal Justice Programs

In this chapter, we use the term 'criminal justice programs' to refer to court orders and sentences that (among other things) aim to reduce drug-related crime. Criminal justice interventions of these kinds sometimes involve traditional treatment programs (e.g., offenders who receive drug rehabilitation orders are sometimes referred to standard detoxification programs) and sometimes to specialist criminal justice programs (e.g., pre-conviction drug testing of arrestees).

Since the mid 1990s, the criminal justice process has been used to channel drug users into treatment. Diversion into treatment is now possible at almost every stage of the criminal justice process.

Offenders can be referred into treatment upon arrest (through arrest referral schemes), at the point of bail (through restriction on bail programs), at the point of being cautioned (through conditional cautioning schemes), at the point of sentencing (through Drug Rehabilitation Requirements), and during prison and following release (through the Counselling Assessment Referral Advice and Throughcare scheme).

Criminal justice programs for drug misusing offenders can be subdivided into three categories: 'drug testing', 'drug courts', and 'probation and aftercare'.

Drug Testing provides a scientific measure of drug use and a means of identifying patterns of drug use. It is believed to be a deterrent to future drug use and criminal activity (Haapanen and Britton, 2002). Drug testing or drug monitoring is a common component of community penalties used to control drug use among known offenders. *Drug Treatment and Testing Orders* (DTTO) were introduced in the United Kingdom as a new community sentence under the *Crime and Disorder Act 1998*. Other court orders involving drug testing introduced about the same time included *Drug Abstinence Orders* (DAO) and *Drug Abstinence Requirements* (DAR). Under the Criminal Justice Act 2003, DTTOs, DAOs, and DARs were replaced by Drug Rehabilitation Requirements (DRRs), which are attached to generic Community Orders or Suspended Sentence Orders. DRRs can last for up to three years and involve regular drug testing in addition to other treatment programs such as counseling or substitute prescribing. In the United Kingdom, offenders can also be tested for drugs before they have been convicted or sentenced. In fact under recent legislation offenders can now be tested for drugs before they have even been charged with an offense. Under the Drugs Act 2005, offenders who have been arrested under suspicion of committing certain 'trigger offenses' must now be tested for opiates and cocaine.

Drug Courts are specialist courts that provide judicially monitored treatment, drug testing, and other services to drug-involved offenders. Diversionary drug courts usually enroll offenders into treatment shortly after arrest and determine outcomes on the basis of their graduation from the program. In contrast, postadjudication drug courts intervene after defendants have been convicted and offer deferred or suspended sentences to those who complete treatment programs. Some courts employ a combination of these approaches. The first drug court was established in the United States (Florida) in 1989 (Gottfredson and Exum, 2002).

Probation and Parole Supervision interventions cover a wide range of court orders and judicial processes. In some states in the United States, entering drug treatment can be a condition of parole. Similarly, a provision of probation supervision might be that the offender remains drug free. Drug-involved probationers might also be given some kind of intensive supervision that would involve surveillance and monitoring their drug use.

PREVIOUS RESEARCH

Research on Treatment Needs

A number of studies have examined perceived treatment needs among samples of arrestees. Schulte, Mouzos, and Makkai (2005), for example, investigated treatment experiences of arrestees in Australia as part of the Drug Use Monitoring in Australia (DUMA) program. They found that 1 in 10 arrestees who had used illegal drugs in the last 12 months had been turned away from treatment because of a lack of places. Lo (2004) explored the treatment needs and experiences of a sample of 296 female and 503 male arrestees interviewed as part of the United States Arrestee Drug Abuse Monitoring (US-ADAM) program. Few significant gender differences were identified in terms of perceived treatment needs. However, significantly more female arrestees than males said that they could use treatment for their cocaine habit (31% compared with 23%). Kim and Fendrich (2002) explored treatment needs among juvenile arrestees in the United States. Overall, about 6 percent of boys and girls stated that they could use treatment for any one of seven drug types. Of those who reported a need for treatment, more girls than boys reported a need for treatment for use of cocaine, crack, heroin, and amphetamines. In contrast, significantly more boys reported a need for treatment for cannabis use. Parry et al. (2004) used data from the South Africa 3-Metros study to explore the perceived need for treatment among various types of drug users. The results showed that across the three sites, between 27 and 34 percent of those who reported cannabis use indicated that they could use treatment. Perceived treatment needs were also found to be high among arrestees who had used harder drugs such as mandrax and cocaine. In Cape Town, for example, only 8 percent of mandrax users reported having previously received treatment for mandrax-related problems, but 33 percent of users indicated that they could benefit from treatment.

Perceived treatment needs have also been explored among samples of prisoners. For example, Borrill et al. (2003) conducted research exploring the differential substance misuse treatment needs of women, ethnic minorities, and young offenders in prison in the United Kingdom. The results showed that 87 percent of drug-dependent women reported that they would have liked some help with drugs in the 12 months before prison. This proportion was the same for white and black/mixed race women. In terms of treatment needs, 41 percent of drug dependent women reported wanting to receive counseling. In addition, more than one-third (35%) of drug-dependent women said that they wanted help in cutting down their drug use, and a further 35 percent said that they wanted help giving up drugs. Detoxification was reported as a treatment need by 27 percent of women.

Research on the Effectiveness

What evidence is there that treatment approaches are effective in reducing drug use or criminal behavior? To answer this question, we look at the research evidence relating to a selection of traditional treatment methods and criminal justice programs. This is not intended to be a thorough review of the effectiveness literature, which is beyond the scope of the current chapter. Instead, it is designed to give a flavor of the types of research that has been done. In the following section, we summarize just two evaluations and the results of our own systematic review of the literature on treatment effectiveness for each treatment approach.

TRADITIONAL TREATMENT METHODS

Methadone Treatment

The majority of evaluations of methadone maintenance have been conducted in the US. French and Zarkin (1992), for example, used data from a longitudinal survey of 2,420 drug abusers to investigate the effects of drug abuse treatment on legal and illegal earnings. Subjects undertaking outpatient methadone treatment were compared with subjects who were outpatient drug free. Illegal earnings among the methadone group decreased from $9,324 in the year before treatment to $3,383 in the year after treatment (a 64% decrease). Among the drug-free group, illegal earnings decreased from $8,179 before treatment to $3,792 after treatment (a 54% decrease). The authors concluded that, on average, clients in all three groups experienced large changes in real illegal earnings from the year entering treatment to the year after leaving treatment (p. 108).

Few evaluations of methadone treatment have been conducted in the United Kingdom. One of the more recent studies by Gossop et al. (2003) investigated the effects of methadone using data from the UK National Treatment Outcome Research Study (NTORS). The results showed that methadone treatment was more effective than residential care in reducing the mean number of drug crimes committed by patients over a five-year period since treatment. However, residential care was more effective than methadone treatment in reducing the mean number of all crimes committed. Overall, the differences between the treatment types were small, and both treatment options were associated with a reduction in crime.

Our own systematic review of the effectiveness of treatment programs conducted for the UK Home Office showed that six of seven studies that met the criteria for inclusion in the review found that methadone treatment was more effective than at least one other comparison program in reducing criminal behavior (Holloway, Bennett, and Farrington, 2005). Overall, the review concluded that methadone treatment was effective in reducing criminal behavior.

Heroin Treatment

Few studies have been undertaken in either the United States or the United Kingdom to assess the effectiveness of heroin prescribing. One of the most frequently cited UK studies was by Hartnoll et al. (1980), who investigated the effect of heroin treatment on 96 confirmed heroin addicts. The addicts were randomly allocated to treatment with injectable heroin or oral methadone. Those offered heroin maintenance were less likely than those offered oral methadone to be arrested during the follow-up period (8% of the former compared with 19% of the latter). A similar result was found for the proportion spending time in prison during the follow-up period. During the first year, 19 percent of the heroin maintenance group spent some time in prison compared with 32 percent of the oral methadone group. The heroin treatment group who were imprisoned in the follow-up period spent less time in prison than the methadone treatment group who were imprisoned.

In Switzerland, Perneger et al. (1998) conducted an evaluation of an experimental heroin maintenance program. Twenty-seven subjects who received intravenous heroin treatment were compared with 24 control subjects who received other forms of drug treatment. The results showed that heroin maintenance was more effective than conventional treatments in reducing crime. The proportion of subjects in the heroin group who reported committing drug dealing offenses decreased from 26 percent in the six-month period before treatment to 0 percent during the six-month follow-up period (a 100% decrease). The proportion of subjects in the conventional drug treatment group who reported committing drug dealing offenses increased from 5 percent to 10 percent over the same period (a 50% increase). A similar pattern of results was found for other offenses with the heroin group reporting decreases and the conventional drug treatment group reporting increases. The authors concluded that heroin maintenance was better than conventional drug treatment in reducing criminal behavior.

The systematic review conducted for the Home Office found that each of the three studies that met our inclusion criteria showed that heroin was more effective than the comparison forms of treatment in reducing criminal behavior among drug users (Holloway et al., 2005). Hence, we concluded that, on the basis of the evidence, heroin was effective in reducing offending.

Therapeutic Communities

Most evaluations of therapeutic communities have been conducted in the United States. Wexler et al. (1999) evaluated the effectiveness of an in-prison therapeutic community in which 715 inmates were randomly assigned to either the prison therapeutic community group or to a no-treatment control group. The results showed a greater reduction in criminal behavior among prisoners offered therapeutic community treatment than those on the normal prison routine. At the 24-month follow-up, 14 percent of subjects who had completed therapeutic community treatment and aftercare had been reincarcerated, compared with 67 percent of subjects in the no-treatment group. The authors concluded that therapeutic communities in prison can be effective in reducing reincarceration rates among inmates treated for substance abuse.

Hser et al. (2001) conducted an evaluation of drug treatments for adolescents in four cities in the United States. More than 1,000 adolescents aged 11 to 18 were interviewed in the year before commencing treatment and again in the year after treatment. Subjects were divided into three groups on the basis of the type of treatment they received: (1) residential treatment programs (including therapeutic communities), (2) outpatient drug-free programs, and (3) short-term inpatient programs. The proportion of residential subjects that reported committing any illegal act decreased from 79 percent in the year before treatment to 50 percent in the year after treatment (a decrease of 37 percent). Comparable figures for the outpatient drug-free subjects were 66 percent in the year before treatment and 51 percent in the year after (a decrease of 23 percent). The proportion of subjects reporting any arrests decreased by more than 50 percent among the residential subjects but increased by 7 percent among the outpatient drug-free subjects. The authors concluded that therapeutic communities can produce greater reductions in criminal behavior than outpatient drug-free programs.

The Home Office review mentioned earlier showed that 9 of 10 studies that investigated therapeutic communities found they reduced criminal behavior by a greater amount than the comparison group (Holloway et al., 2005).

Psychosocial Approaches

Most evaluations of psychosocial approaches have been conducted in the United States. Henggeler et al. (1991), for example, presented findings from two independent evaluations of the efficacy of multisystemic therapy (MST) in treating antisocial behavior among serious juvenile offenders in Missouri. The results of the Missouri Delinquency Project (MDP) showed some evidence of success in reducing criminal behavior among drug users. The participants in the MDP were 200 adolescents who had been referred to the project by juvenile court after a recent arrest. The offenders were randomly assigned to receive either MST or individual counseling (IC) and were interviewed four years later. At the time of the follow-up interview, 4 percent of subjects who received MST had been arrested for a substance-related offense compared with 16 percent of those who received IC.

Woody et al. (1987) evaluated the effectiveness of psychotherapy among 93 male veterans who were addicted to opiates and were receiving methadone maintenance treatment. The subjects were randomly assigned to one of three conditions: (1) drug counseling (DC) alone, (2) counseling plus supportive-expressive (SE) psychotherapy, or (3) counseling plus cognitive-behavioral psychotherapy. Interviews were conducted with the subjects at intake and 12 months later. Among SE subjects, the mean number of days spent committing crimes in the 30 days before interview, decreased from five at baseline to three at 12-month follow-up. Among the DC subjects, the mean number of days spent committing crimes increased from two to four. SE subjects also performed better than DC subjects in terms of changes in overall criminality score. The mean score decreased from 219 to 117 among SE subjects, but increased from 81 to 142 among DC subjects. The authors concluded that the psychotherapy groups showed more improvements than the drug counseling group over a wider range of outcome measures, including criminal behavior.

The Home Office review mentioned earlier included four studies that evaluated psychosocial approaches (Holloway et al., 2005). The review showed that all four studies found that the psychosocial approaches investigated were more effective than the comparison interventions in reducing criminal behavior.

CRIMINAL JUSTICE PROGRAMS

Drug Testing

The effectiveness of drug testing has been investigated in the United States at the pretrial stage and the postrelease stage. Britt et al. (1992) conducted an experiment that explored the effects of drug testing on defendants on pretrial release. Subjects were randomly allocated into either a drug-testing group or a no-testing control group. In Pima County (Arizona), 2 percent of subjects in the drug-testing group were arrested in the pretrial period compared with 4 percent of subjects in the no-testing group. In Maricopa County (Arizona), a larger proportion of subjects in the testing groups than in the no-testing groups were rearrested. The authors concluded that there is no evidence from the research that monitoring the drug use of defendants on pretrial release has a statistically significant effect in reducing pretrial misconduct.

There have also been evaluations of drug testing at the postrelease stage. Haapanen and Britton (2002) conducted an experimental study examining the parole outcomes and arrests for 1,958 parolees in the United States. Subjects were randomly assigned to various levels of routine drug testing ranging from no-testing to two tests per month. The results indicate that frequent drug testing was less effective than no-testing in reducing criminal behavior. At 42 months after treatment, the mean number of arrests for the drug testing group was 3.8 compared with 3.0 for the no-testing group. Similarly the mean arrest rates for property crimes and drug crimes were also higher among the drug testing group than the no-testing group. The results do not indicate, therefore, that drug testing was more effective than the comparison.

Our own review of the literature found that four of six studies with sufficiently rigorous research designs showed evidence that drug testing was more effective than the comparison method. However, only 4 of the 13 findings drawn from these studies showed that drug testing worked. The review concluded that the findings were mixed (Holloway et al., 2005).

Drug Courts

All of the currently available evaluations of drug courts have been conducted in the United States. Turner et al. (1999), for example, compared the efficacy of drug courts with the efficacy of drug testing. Five-hundred-and-six subjects were randomly allocated into either the drug testing group or the drug court group. At 36 months, a smaller proportion of subjects in the drug court group than in the drug testing group were found to have been arrested for any offense (33% compared with 44%) and for property offenses (10% compared with 15%). The drug court group was also associated with a smaller mean number of arrests (0.6 compared with 0.8). The authors conclude that drug courts were effective in reducing criminal behavior.

Gottfredson et al. (2003) evaluated the outcome of the Baltimore Drug Treatment Court. Two hundred and thirty-five subjects were randomly allocated into the drug court group or a treatment as usual group. The results showed that at the follow-up interviews there were fewer mean arrests and convictions among the drug court group than among the treatment as usual group. The proportion of subjects who were reconvicted in the follow-up period was also lower among the drug court group than among the treatment as usual group (49% compared with 53%). The authors concluded that drug court subjects who participated in treatment were significantly less likely to recidivate than were untreated drug court subjects and control subjects.

Our own study included just the two studies just described in the quantitative review and concluded that drug courts were effective in reducing offending among drug users (Holloway et al., 2005).

Probation and Parole Supervision

There have been few evaluations of probation and parole supervision, and the small number that have been conducted have been based in the United States. Turner et al. (1992), for example, reported the results of a randomized experiment that tested the effects of intensive supervision under probation and parole (ISP) for drug-involved offenders in five sites across the United States. Subjects were randomly allocated into either the ISP group or a routine supervision control group. The results were in the reverse direction to those hypothesized. At one-year follow-up, 28 percent of subjects under routine supervision had been jailed compared with 39 percent of subjects under intensive supervision. Similarly, 10 percent of subjects under routine supervision had been imprisoned, compared with 13 percent of subjects under intensive supervision. The authors explained that the result was likely because ISP programs are often surveillance-oriented, and this tends to increase the number of violations of the sanction imposed by the courts. They concluded that their results lend 'serious doubt' to the belief that increased supervision will reduce recidivism.

Farabee et al. (2001) examined criminal activity among 1,167 adolescents who participated in a community-based substance abuse treatment study (Drug Abuse Treatment Outcome Study). As part of the study, the authors explored the effect of criminal justice supervision on treatment outcome. Those subjects who were under criminal justice supervision at the time of treatment were compared with subjects who were not under such supervision. The proportion of subjects with arrests for any crime decreased by a larger amount among the supervised group than among the nonsupervised group. However, with respect to drug dealing, the proportion of arrests increased among the nonsupervised group.

The Home Office review found that three of the four studies that met the eligibility criteria (the earlier study by Turner et al. 1992 being the exception) showed probation and parole supervision can be effective in reducing criminal behavior (Holloway et al., 2005).

RESULTS

The previous review has looked at both the demand for treatment and the effectiveness of treatment. To be effective, government drug strategies need to respond to both. In other words, they need to ensure that users are encouraged into treatment and that the programs they are encouraged into are capable of reducing drug use and ultimately crime.

Demand for Treatment

There is little research on the extent to which drug users want treatment or are able to obtain it. The New English and Welsh Arrestee Drug Abuse Monitoring (NEW-ADAM) surveys included several questions that aimed to examine the correspondence between the demand for treatment and the supply of treatment services. Arrestees were asked whether they had ever been in treatment or were currently receiving treatment for drug-related problems. If not, they were asked whether they wanted treatment. Arrestees were also asked whether they had ever been in treatment for problems with alcohol. More

TABLE 14.1. *Percentage and frequency of arrestees who have ever received or who are currently receiving drug treatment*

	Proportion and frequency of arrestees	
	%	n
Treatment received in the past	28	682
Treatment not received in the past	72	1,755
TOTAL	100	2,437
Treatment currently received	8	204
Treatment currently not received	92	2,233
TOTAL	100	2,437
Treatment currently not received but wanted[a]	29	652
Treatment currently not received but not wanted[a]	71	1,581
TOTAL	100	2,233

Notes: Includes all arrestees who reported having used one or more illicit drugs in the last 12 months ($n = 2,443$).

[a] Among arrestees not currently receiving treatment ($n = 2233$). Some missing cases.

than one-fifth (22%) of all interviewed arrestees said that they had received treatment for drug misuse at some point in their lives. Six percent of arrestees said that they had received treatment for alcohol problems.

To explore treatment needs, it is most useful to focus on those arrestees who have actually used illicit drugs. Hence, the figures in the rest of this chapter focus on those arrestees who had used one or more of 19 illicit drug types in the last 12 months.

The results presented in Table 14.1 show that just over one-quarter (28%) said that they had received treatment for drug misuse at some point in their life. Less than one-tenth (8%) of arrestees said that they were currently receiving treatment for drug misuse. Of those arrestees who said that they were not currently receiving treatment, 29 percent reported that they would like to receive drug treatment. Hence, more than one-quarter of drug-using arrestees had a current unmet need for treatment.

Those arrestees who reported that they were currently receiving treatment were asked about the process by which they had entered their treatment program. Nearly two-thirds (63%) reported that they had referred themselves into treatment. A further 10 percent said

that they had been referred into treatment by a court and 9 percent
by a general practitioner; 6 percent had entered treatment via arrest
referral schemes, and the remaining 12 percent had been referred
into treatment by some 'other' method. Most of the arrestees currently
receiving treatment described it as being either very helpful (48%)
or fairly helpful (30%). More than three-quarters (78%) explained
that the treatment had helped them to reduce their drug use, and
more than half felt that it had helped them to reduce their criminal
behavior (57%) or improve their health (52%).

Type of Treatment Wanted

One of the key components of the success of the government's treatment strategy is provision of the kinds of treatment that arrestees
want. Tables 14.2 and 14.3 show the nature and source of treatment
services used by arrestees in the past and wanted in the future. The
most common types of treatment ever received were fairly evenly split
between detoxification/withdrawal programs (49% of arrestees who
had received treatment in the past) and maintenance/stabilization
programs (46%). The most common sources of treatment in the

TABLE 14.2. *Kinds of treatment received and wanted for drug misuse*

	Among arrestees who had ever had drug treatment, % (*n*)	Among arrestees currently receiving drug treatment, % (*n*)	Among arrestees not receiving treatment but who want drug treatment, % (*n*)
Detoxification/ withdrawal	49 (331)	24 (48)	68 (444)
Maintenance/ stabilization	46 (313)	57 (117)	40 (263)
Counseling	34 (234)	26 (53)	48 (310)
Therapy individual	11 (75)	6 (12)	36 (234)
Therapy group	13 (85)	5 (11)	28 (180)
Self-help	8 (53)	4 (8)	26 (167)
Other treatment	11 (77)	14 (29)	11 (69)
TOTAL	682	204	652

Note: Figures do not add up to 100% because multiple responses were possible.

TABLE 14.3. *Sources of treatment received and wanted for drug misuse*

	Among arrestees who had ever had drug treatment, % (*n*)	Among arrestees currently receiving drug treatment, % (*n*)	Among arrestees not receiving treatment but who want drug treatment, % (*n*)
Drug clinic	44 (300)	51 (103)	47 (308)
General practitioner	28 (191)	39 (80)	35 (228)
Private practitioner	2 (10)	1 (2)	22 (141)
Hospital inpatient	7 (45)	3 (7)	36 (232)
Other residential	17 (118)	7 (15)	49 (322)
Other	18 (123)	10 (20)	9 (56)
TOTAL	652	204	652

Note: Figures do not add up to 100% because multiple responses were possible.

past were drugs clinics (44%) and general practitioners (28%). A similar pattern emerges in relation to the source of current treatment received but not for the nature of current treatment. More than twice as many arrestees reported currently receiving maintenance/stabilization treatment (57%) than detoxification/withdrawal (24%).

Perhaps the most important findings in Tables 14.2 and 14.3 relate to those arrestees who reported having an unmet need for treatment. The most common kind of treatment wanted among this group was detoxification/withdrawal, mentioned by 68 percent of arrestees not currently receiving treatment but who wanted treatment. Forty-eight percent said that they wanted individual counseling in relation to drug misuse, and 40 percent said that they wanted maintenance prescribing. The most commonly mentioned source of treatment wanted was from a residential source (49%) followed by a drug clinic (47%).

The results suggest that there is a substantial unmet need for treatment services among drug-misusing arrestees. Their treatment needs are fairly mixed, combining programs that will get them off drugs with programs that will make their drug misuse safer and better controlled. The preferred source of drug treatment is also fairly mixed, with the strongest preference for residential sources and drug

TABLE 14.4. *Percentage of arrestees reporting receiving treatment ever and currently by demographic characteristics*

	Treatment ever, % (*n*)	Treatment current, % (*n*)	Treatment wanted,[a] % (*n*)
Male	26 (542)	8 (166)	27 (527)
Female	42 (140)	12 (38)	43 (125)
Sig. of difference	***	*	***
17–19	11 (63)	3 (18)	15 (88)
20–24	26 (178)	7 (47)	30 (195)
25–29	41 (195)	12 (57)	43 (178)
30+	36 (246)	12 (82)	32 (191)
Sig. of difference	***	***	***
White	31 (604)	9 (176)	31 (556)
Nonwhite	17 (77)	6 (27)	22 (96)
Sig. of difference	***	*	***
TOTAL	2,437	2,437	2,233

Notes: Includes all arrestees who reported having used one or more illicit drugs in the last 12 months (*n* = 2,443).
Chi-square test: * *p* < .05; *** *p* < .001; ns = not significant.
[a]Among arrestees not currently receiving treatment (*n* = 2,233). Some missing cases.

clinics. However, other sources of treatment are also mentioned. Hence, the results suggest that for the treatment arm of the drugs strategy to be effective, it is necessary not only to provide additional treatment services, but also to provide the kinds of treatment services that are wanted and will be used.

Variations in the Need for Treatment

Variations by Demographic Factors. The figures in Table 14.4 show significant demographic variations in treatment experiences and needs. Female drug-using arrestees were significantly more likely than males to report having ever received drug treatment (42% compared with 26%) and to report that they were currently receiving drug treatment (12% compared with 8%). Among those arrestees not currently receiving treatment, women were significantly more likely than men to report wanting drug treatment (43% compared with 27%). Significant differences were also found among arrestees of different ages. Those aged 25 or older were more likely than younger arrestees (aged 17–24)

TABLE 14.5. *Percentage of arrestees currently receiving treatment and wanting treatment by types of drug used in the last 12 months*

	Treatment current, % (n)			Treatment wanted,[a] % (n)		
	Yes	No	Sig.	Yes	No	Sig.
Cannabis	8 (165)	12 (39)	*	28 (537)	40 (115)	***
Ecstasy	6 (50)	10 (154)	**	25 (199)	32 (453)	***
Amphetamines	8 (47)	9 (157)	ns	31 (172)	29 (480)	ns
Heroin	18 (181)	2 (23)	***	67 (560)	7 (92)	***
Crack	16 (155)	3 (49)	***	62 (494)	11 (158)	***
Cocaine	9 (70)	8 (134)	ns	34 (250)	27 (402)	**
Methadone	29 (139)	3 (65)	***	75 (253)	21 (399)	***
Multiple drugs	11 (199)	1 (5)	***	38 (629)	4 (23)	***

Notes: Includes all arrestees who reported having used one or more illicit drugs in the last 12 months ($n = 2,443$).

Chi-squared test: * $p < .05$; ** $p < .01$; *** $p < .001$; ns = not significant.

[a] Among arrestees not currently receiving treatment ($n = 2,233$). Some missing cases.

to report ever having received treatment or to be currently receiving treatment. Older arrestees were also more likely than younger arrestees to report that they wanted treatment. Ethnic group differences can also be seen in Table 14.4. White arrestees were significantly more likely than nonwhite arrestees to have ever had treatment (31% compared with 17%) and to be currently receiving treatment (9% compared with 6%). White arrestees were also significantly more likely to report that they wanted treatment (31% compared with 22%).

Variations by Drug Types. Table 14.5 shows the proportion of arrestees currently receiving treatment and wanting treatment by the type of drugs used in the last 12 months. The figures show that arrestees who had used cannabis or ecstasy in the last 12 months were significantly less likely than arrestees who had not used these drug types (but had used other drug types) to report that they were currently receiving drug treatment. By contrast, users of heroin, crack, and methadone were significantly more likely than users of other drug types to say that they were currently receiving drug treatment. There was no significant difference between users of amphetamines and users of other drug types or between users of cocaine and users of other drug types.

TABLE 14.6. *Percentage of arrestees reporting receiving treatment ever and currently by types of crime committed in the last 12 months*

	Treatment current, % (n)			Treatment wanted,[a] % (n)		
	Yes	No	Sig.	Yes	No	Sig.
Theft of a motor vehicle	4 (9)	12 (153)	**	36 (73)	42 (477)	ns
Theft from a motor vehicle	10 (24)	11 (138)	ns	47 (104)	40 (446)	ns
Shoplifting	14 (122)	6 (40)	***	58 (424)	21 (126)	***
Burglary dwelling	7 (9)	11 (153)	ns	50 (61)	40 (489)	*
Burglary nondwelling	8 (13)	11 (149)	ns	43 (64)	41 (486)	ns
Robbery	9 (7)	11 (155)	ns	41 (31)	41 (519)	ns
Theft from a person	15 (13)	11 (149)	ns	51 (37)	41 (513)	ns
Fraud/ deception	9 (26)	11 (136)	ns	41 (104)	41 (446)	ns
Handling	8 (55)	13 (107)	**	36 (225)	46 (325)	***
Drug supply	10 (36)	11 (126)	ns	39 (131)	42 (419)	ns

Notes: Includes all arrestees who reported having used one or more illicit drugs in the last 12 months and having committed one or more offense types in the last 12 months ($n = 1,495$).

Chi-square test: * $p < .05$; ** $p < .01$; *** $p < .001$; ns = not significant.

[a]Among arrestees not currently receiving treatment ($n = 1,333$). Some missing cases.

Table 14.5 also presents information about unmet treatment needs among arrestees not currently receiving treatment. As before, users of cannabis and ecstasy were significantly less likely than users of other drug types to say that they wanted drug treatment. Users of heroin, crack, cocaine, and methadone, however, were more likely than users of other drug types to say that they wanted treatment. There was no statistical difference between amphetamine users and users of other drug types in terms of unmet treatment needs. Overall, these findings suggest that users of what might be referred to as recreational drug types were less likely than users of harder drugs to be receiving treatment and to have unmet treatment needs.

Variations by Crime Types. Table 14.6 focuses on arrestees who have committed one or more income-generating crime (excluding prostitution) in the last 12 months. It presents information about current treatment and treatment needs among different types of offender. The figures show that arrestees who had committed shoplifting in the last 12 months were significantly more likely than arrestees who had committed other offenses to say that they were currently receiving drug treatment (14% compared with 6%). The reverse was true for arrestees who had committed theft of a motor vehicle (4% compared with 12%) or handling offenses (8% compared with 13%). In terms of unmet treatment needs among arrestees not currently receiving treatment, arrestees who had committed shoplifting and burglary from a dwelling were significantly more likely than other offenders to report that they wanted treatment. Arrestees who had committed handling offenses, however, were less likely than other offenders to report an unmet treatment need (36% compared with 46%). Overall, these results show that certain types of offenders are more likely than other types of offenders to be currently receiving treatment and to have unmet treatment needs.

Variations by Drug and Crime. Table 14.7 shows the history of treatment for drug misuse among drug misusing repeat offenders (DMROs), drug-using offenders, and drug-using nonoffenders. The figures show that DMROs were more likely than other drug-using offenders and drug-using nonoffenders to report having received treatment for drug misuse at some point in their lives (59% compared with 23% and 15%, respectively). DMROs were also more likely than other arrestees to report that they were currently receiving drug treatment (16% compared with 8% and 5%). Of the 463 DMROs not currently receiving drug treatment, the majority (79%) reported a current unmet need for treatment (i.e., they wanted treatment but were not currently receiving it). By contrast, approximately one-fifth of drug-using offenders and one-tenth of drug-using nonoffenders reported a current unmet need for treatment. The difference between the three groups was statistically significant.

DISCUSSION

The results presented in this chapter show that only a small minority of drug-using arrestees have ever received treatment for drug misuse

TABLE 14.7. *Percentage of arrestees reporting ever having or currently receiving treatment for drug misuse*

	Drug-misusing repeat offenders, % (n)	Drug-misusing offenders, % (n)	Drug-misusing nonoffenders, % (n)	All drug-using arrestees, % (n)
Ever received drug treatment				
Yes	59 (326)	23 (218)	15 (137)	28 (681)
No	41 (225)	77 (724)	85 (804)	72 (1,753)
Sig. of difference	***			
Currently receiving drug treatment				
Yes	16 (88)	8 (73)	5 (42)	8 (203)
No	84 (463)	92 (869)	96 (899)	92 (2,231)
Sig. of difference	***			
TOTAL[a]	23 (551)	39 (943)	39 (945)	(100) 2,439
Current unmet demand for drug treatment				
Yes	79 (365)	21 (185)	11 (102)	29 (652)
No	21 (98)	79 (684)	89 (797)	71 (1,579)
Sig. of difference	***			
TOTAL[b]	100 (463)	100 (869)	100 (899)	100 (2,231)

[a]Includes arrestees who reported having used one or more illicit drug types in the last 12 months ($n = 2,443$). Some missing cases.
[b]Includes arrestees who reported having used one or more illicit drug types in the last 12 months and who said that they were not currently receiving treatment ($n = 2,233$).
Chi-square test: *** $p < .001$.

(28%). An even smaller proportion (less than 1 in 10) said that they were currently receiving treatment. Of those not currently receiving treatment, more than one-quarter (29%) said that they wanted treatment. Schulte et al. (2005) also found a high level of unmet treatment need among arrestees in Australia. These authors found that 1 in 10 drug-using arrestees had actually been turned away from treatment due to a lack of places.

Demographic differences in experiences of and need for drug treatment were also reported in this chapter. Women were found to be more likely than men to report that they were currently receiving treatment and that they wanted treatment. Lo (2004) found few gender differences in treatment experiences and needs among arrestees in the United States. She did find, however, that men were more likely than women to report having received treatment for amphetamines, sedatives, PCP, and hallucinogens. By contrast, women were more likely than men to report a need for treatment for cocaine use. In terms of age and ethnicity, older arrestees and white arrestees were more likely than their counterparts to report receiving treatment and to have an unmet need for it.

In terms of perceived effectiveness, more than three-quarters of arrestees currently receiving treatment said that it had been helpful in some way. More specifically, 78 percent said that it had helped them reduce their use of illicit drugs, and 57 percent said that it had helped them to reduce their offending behavior.

This chapter has also shown that certain types and sources of treatment are more popular than others. Hence, it is important that specific types of treatment programs are developed and made available. Most arrestees with an unmet treatment need reported that they would like to receive assistance with detoxification and withdrawal (68% of arrestees wanting treatment). Individual counseling and maintenance prescribing were also popular and were requested by 48 percent and 40 percent of arrestees, respectively. Most arrestees wanted to receive treatment through a drug clinic (47%) or in a residential setting (49%). Previous research in this area has also found that counseling is a particularly popular form of treatment. Borrill et al. (2003), for example, found that 41 percent of drug dependent female prisoners reported a need for counseling.

The relationship between particular types of drug use and treatment experiences was also investigated. The results show that arrestees who had used hard drug types (such as heroin, crack, and methadone) were more likely than users of other drug types to be currently receiving treatment. Harder drug users who were not currently receiving treatment were also more likely than other drug users to report that they wanted to receive treatment. These findings suggest that certain types of drugs (i.e., the more addictive or harder drug types) are more closely connected with a need for treatment than other types.

Similarly, certain types of offenders were also more likely to report treatment needs than other types. Arrestees who had committed shoplifting in the last 12 months were more likely than other offenders to express a need for treatment (58% compared with 21%). Arrestees who had committed burglary from a dwelling were also more likely than other offenders to say that they wanted treatment (50% compared with 40%). By contrast, arrestees who had committed handling offenses were significantly less likely than other offenders to report a need for treatment (36% compared with 46%).

The relationship between drug use and crime has been discussed in detail in earlier chapters. Analyses have shown that certain types of drug use are associated with particular types of crime (e.g., heroin and shoplifting). Hence, the relationships between treatment and offending and between treatment and drug use are likely to be interconnected. The results showed that drug-misusing repeat offenders were significantly more likely than other drug users to have ever received treatment, to be currently receiving treatment, and to have a current unmet need for treatment. Arrestees who had used drugs but had committed no crimes in the last 12 months were the least likely to report a need for treatment.

CHAPTER FIFTEEN

International Comparisons

INTRODUCTION

Since 1997, the United Nations Office on Drugs and Crime (UNODC) has published estimates of the extent of drug misuse in the world. The most recent figures were presented in the World Drug Report 2005 (UNODC, 2005). It was estimated that about 200 million people, comprising 5 percent of the world's population aged 15 to 64, had used drugs at least once in the last 12 months. Cannabis was found to have been consumed by approximately 160 million people or (4% of the population aged 15 to 64). At the global level the main hard drugs reported were opiates and cocaine.

In addition to providing global estimates of drug misuse, the World Drug Report 2005 also published estimates for individual countries. The results show wide variation in the prevalence of drug use across countries. Opiate use in the last 12 months, for example, was found to range from a low of 0.01 percent in Brunei, Saudi Arabia, and Kuwait to a high of 2.8 percent in Iran. Estimates of cocaine use in the last 12 months ranged from 0.001 percent in Hong Kong to 3 percent in the United States. Cannabis use was estimated to be particularly high in some African and Caribbean countries with an estimate of 21.5 percent in Ghana and 16.1 percent in Haiti. By contrast, cannabis use was estimated to be just 0.02 percent in Brunei.

The figures presented in the World Drug Report 2005 suggest that there are marked variations in the prevalence of drug misuse in different countries. The reason for these variations may, in part, be explained by trade routes and the availability of certain drug types.

Australia, for example, is not on a direct cocaine trafficking route, and the subsequent lack of availability may explain why cocaine use is comparatively rare there. Variations might also be explained by religious differences. For example, in Muslim countries such as Brunei and Saudi Arabia, Islam prohibits alcohol and drug use, hence use of these substances is less common than in other non-Islamic societies. The strictness of the law and the type of punishment imposed on users might also influence the prevalence of drug use. In Singapore, for example, the death penalty is mandatory for those convicted of trafficking, manufacturing, importing, or exporting more than 15 g of heroin, 30 g of cocaine, or 500 g of cannabis. Possession of these quantities is deemed as prima facie evidence of trafficking and punishable by the death penalty. Hence, it is perhaps not surprising that drug use in Singapore is particularly low (0.1% opiates, 0.01% cocaine, and 0.03% cannabis).

International variations in the type of drug used are relevant to understanding the drug-crime connection. It is obviously the case that if a certain drug type is not consumed at all, then it cannot be associated with crime. To explore cross-country variations in the drug-crime connection, it is necessary to use sources of data that provide information about both drug use and offending behavior. The World Drug Report 2005 does not help in this respect because it focuses on the extent of drug use only. The International Arrestee Drug Abuse Monitoring program (I-ADAM), however, provides data on drug use and offending behavior among samples of arrestees across various countries. I-ADAM data can be used, therefore, to explore national variations in the drug-crime connection.

I-ADAM PROGRAM

The I-ADAM program developed out of the Arrestee Drug Abuse Monitoring (ADAM) program in the United States. When it was first launched, I-ADAM was described as an informal network of researchers from different countries who adhered to similar research protocols for collecting drug use data from arrestees (Taylor et al., 2003). It was described as an international partnership of government-sponsored research organizations. The main aim of the program was to inform national and international drug policy (Taylor et al., 2003). It was argued that evidence of a rapid increase in a certain kind of substance abuse in a particular country could indicate a shift in international drug trafficking. It was hoped that the I-ADAM data could be used to plan prevention efforts and to coordinate international responses.

There were some attempts to replicate US-ADAM data collection methods before the launch of I-ADAM. In 1996, for example, both the United Kingdom (as part of the developmental stage of the New English and Welsh Arrestee Drug Abuse Monitoring (NEW-ADAM) program) and Chile began interviewing and collecting urine specimens from arrestees. However, I-ADAM was formally launched in April 1998. The National Institute of Justice (NIJ) sponsored an international conference in Miami that included representatives from eight nations (Australia, Chile, England, the Netherlands, Panama, Scotland, South Africa, and Uruguay). The conference was also attended by representatives from the Organization of American States and the United Nations International Drug Control Program, experts in the field of drug surveillance systems, NIJ staff, and other US federal representatives.

In April 1999, a second I-ADAM meeting was held in Chicago. This conference was attended by representatives of the countries attending the first meeting and representatives of two new countries: Malaysia and Taiwan. In the same year, NIJ published the report *Comparing Drug Use Rates of Detained Arrestees in the United States and England*, which represented the first comparative analysis of arrestee drug use using data from countries participating in the I-ADAM Program (Taylor and Bennett, 1999). In September 2000, the third annual I-ADAM conference was held in Washington, D.C. This was the largest I-ADAM conference and included representatives from 11 countries (Australia, Chile, England, Malaysia, Russia, Scotland, South Africa, Taiwan, Thailand, Ukraine, and the United States). The fourth, and most recent, I-ADAM conference was held in London in September 2001.

There are several benefits to using I-ADAM arrestee data to compare differences in drug use and crime across countries. The main problems of international comparison using government statistics or the results of national or local surveys are that the methods of data collection and the definitions of drug use and crime can vary across countries. I-ADAM data, however, were collected using similar techniques including similar methods of drug testing and similar self-report survey questionnaires. Hence, the I-ADAM program provides an opportunity for researchers to explore variations in drug use and related offending behavior across a number of countries.

The aim of this chapter is to investigate cross-country variations in the relationship between drug use and crime by reviewing the results of comparisons that have been made using I-ADAM data. The main sources of the data for the chapter are three collaborative publications: the first is a broad comparison of the prevalence of drug misuse in four countries (Taylor et al., 2003), the second is a comparison of a larger number of I-ADAM countries (Taylor, 2002), and the third is a more detailed comparison of the characteristics of drug using arrestees in two countries (Taylor and Bennett, 1999). Each of the three publications included data collected by the NEW-ADAM program.

RESULTS

The following compares the results of the NEW-ADAM program with those of other countries involved in I-ADAM. The main source of the data was the analysis conducted in three collaborative publications, each including NEW-ADAM data. The first of these was called, "Monitoring the use of illicit drugs in four countries through the International Arrestee Drug Abuse Monitoring (I-ADAM) program" and was published in *Criminal Justice: An International Journal of Policy and Practice* in 2003 (Taylor et al., 2003). This was largely a comparison of prevalence rates of drug use among arrestees in the four countries broken down by drug type and crime type. The second was called *I-ADAM in Eight Countries: Approaches and Challenges,* which was published as an NIJ report (Taylor, 2002). This was described as a compendium and summarized progress to date in eight I-ADAM countries and included some early findings. This publication provides prevalence data from countries not included in the above study. The third was called *Comparing Drug Use Rates of Detained Arrestees in the United States and England* and was published by NIJ as a research report in 1999 (Taylor and

Bennett, 1999). This publication provided a more detailed breakdown of drug use and crime by arrestee characteristics.

MONITORING THE USE OF ILLICIT DRUGS IN FOUR
COUNTRIES THROUGH THE INTERNATIONAL ARRESTEE
DRUG ABUSE MONITORING (I-ADAM) PROGRAM

The first publication was based on an analysis of ADAM-type data
from four countries (Australia, England, South Africa, and the United
States). The Australian data were collected as part of the Drug Use
Monitoring in Australia (DUMA) program, the English and Welsh
data derived from the NEW-ADAM program, the South African data
came from the 3-Metros study, and the US data were collected as
part of the ADAM program. The surveys were conducted in each site
on a rolling basis with data collection conducted at different times.
However, all countries collected some data in the year 2000. In this
year, the Australian program collected data from four sites, NEW-
ADAM collected data from eight sites, the South African program
collected data from three sites, and the United States collected data
from 28 sites. In total, the number of arrestees included in the survey
ranged from 1,410 in England and Wales to 22,729 in the United
States.

Prevalence of Drug Misuse Among Arrestees

The prevalence of drug misuse was measured using the percentage of
positive urine tests and self-reported drug misuse in the last 12 months.
Table 15.1 shows that marijuana was the most commonly used drug
among the four drugs measured. The median percentage of positive
tests ranged from 56 percent in Australia to 41 percent in the United
States. It is interesting to note that the United States, a country commonly associated with drug misuse, had the lowest prevalence rates
of the four countries. The United States also had the second lowest
prevalence of positive tests for amphetamines next to South Africa with
a median percentage of two percent. The highest rate was Australia
with a median proportion of positive tests of 16 percent. A similar
spread of results was also found for opiate use (including heroin).
The United States also had the second lowest percentage of positive

TABLE 15.1. *Percentage of positive tests among male arrestees*

	Australia	England	South Africa	United States
Marijuana	56	48	48	41
Cocaine	2	17	2	31
Opiates	33	33	2	7
Amphetamines	16	3	<1	2

Source: Taylor, B., Brownstein, H., Parry, C. D. H., Plüddemann, A., Makkai, T., Bennett, T., and Holloway, K. (2003). Monitoring the use of illicit drugs in four countries through the International Arrestee Drug Abuse Monitoring (I-ADAM) program. *Criminal Justice: An International Journal of Policy and Practice* 3(3):269–279.
Notes: Data collected for 2000. The proportions presented are median values.

tests for opiates (again next to South Africa) with a median percentage of 7 percent. Australia and England and Wales both had the highest rates of 33 percent. However, the results change substantially when looking at cocaine use. In this case, the United States had the highest rates (31%) of positive tests for cocaine (including both powder and crack cocaine), whereas Australia had the lowest rates (2%). This low rate of cocaine use may reflect the fact that Australia does not feature in any of the main cocaine trafficking routes. Overall, the results of these four comparisons show that the United States and South Africa have the lowest prevalence rates of three of the four drug types. The only drug for which the United States had the highest rate was cocaine. Because the questionnaires of the four countries were very similar, it was also possible to provide a comparison of self-reported drug use over the last 12 months. The results of the urinalysis and self-reported drug use covered different periods (approximately three days in the case of urinalysis and 12 months in the case of self-reports).

In all four countries, marijuana was the drug most frequently reported. The highest self-report rate was 70 percent in England and Wales, and the lowest rate was 28 percent in South Africa (see Table 15.2). The low rate of cannabis use in South Africa may be explained by the preference for mandrax (methaqualone), which is usually crushed and mixed with dagga (cannabis) and smoked. These results are slightly different to the urinalysis results in that Australia has the second highest rate rather than the highest, and the United States has the second lowest rate rather than the lowest. Nevertheless,

TABLE 15.2. *Percentage of male arrestees reporting drug use in the last 12 months*

	Australia	England	South Africa	United States
Marijuana	66	70	28	53
Cocaine	19	47	4	25
Heroin	36	30	<1	6
Amphetamines	37	22	<1	5

Source: Taylor, B., Brownstein, H., Parry, C. D. H., Plüddemann, A., Makkai, T., Bennett, T., and Holloway, K. (2003). Monitoring the use of illicit drugs in four countries through the International Arrestee Drug Abuse Monitoring (I-ADAM) program. *Criminal Justice: An International Journal of Policy and Practice* 3(3):269–279.

Notes: Data collected for the year 2000. The proportions presented are median values.

the broad pattern showing Australia and England and Wales in the top half and the United States and South Africa in the bottom half are similar. The pattern of results for self-reported amphetamine use was identical to the urinalysis findings. The highest prevalence rate was found in Australia (37%), whereas the United States had the second lowest rate next to South Africa (5% and <1% respectively). This pattern of results was maintained for self-reported heroin use. The highest prevalence rates were found in Australia (36%) and the lowest in the United States (6%) and South Africa (<1%). The results were slightly different in relation to cocaine. In this case, the highest median self-reported rates were found in England and Wales (47%). The United States had the second highest rates at 25 percent and South Africa had the lowest rates at 4 percent.

Prevalence of Drug Misuse by Offense Types

The urinalysis and self-report analysis were repeated with the results broken down by the offense for which the arrestee was held or charged. A comparison was then made among arrestees held or charged with property offenses or violent offenses. Arrestees held or charged for other offenses were excluded from the analysis.

Looking first at the urinalysis results shows that there is some variation across countries in terms of type of drug and type of offense (Table 15.3). In Australia, the highest prevalence of positive tests for all drug types was among property offenders. Almost twice as many

TABLE 15.3. *Percentage of positive tests among male arrestees by offense type*

	Australia	England	South Africa	United States
Marijuana				
Violent offenses	51	42	42	39
Property offenses	59	48	53	37
Cocaine				
Violent offenses	1	6	0	22
Property offenses	3	22	4	35
Opiates				
Violent offenses	21	10	3	4
Property offenses	46	52	2	2
Amphetamines				
Violent offenses	10	4	1	2
Property offenses	20	2	1	2

Source: Taylor, B., Brownstein, H., Parry, C. D. H., Plüddemann, A., Makkai, T., Bennett, T., and Holloway, K. (2003). Monitoring the use of illicit drugs in four countries through the International Arrestee Drug Abuse Monitoring (I-ADAM) program. *Criminal Justice: An International Journal of Policy and Practice* 3(3):269–279.
Notes: Data collected for 2000. The proportions presented are median values.

arrestees held or charged for property offenses tested positive for opiates (46%) compared with those held for violent offenses (21%). A similar pattern exists in relation to the results for England and Wales. In this case, the highest prevalence of positive tests for three of the four drug types was among property offenders, and five times as many arrestees charged with property offenses tested positive for opiates (52%) than those held for violent offenses (10%). The lower rate of violent offending than property offending among opiate users is not counterintuitive. Opiates have a depressant effect on the body, and because users tend to become relaxed, they may be less likely to commit acts of violence. This distinction by type of offense was less pronounced in the United States and South Africa. In the United States, the proportion of positive tests was higher among property offenders for one of the four drug types (cocaine) and was higher among violent offenders for two of the four drug types (marijuana and opiates). In South Africa, the proportion of positive tests was higher among property offenders for two drug types (marijuana and cocaine) and marginally higher among violent offenders for one drug type (opiates).

TABLE 15.4. *Percentage of male arrestee reporting drug use by offense type*

	Australia	England	South Africa	United States
Marijuana				
Violent offenses	58	54	25	45
Property offenses	72	78	25	52
Cocaine				
Violent offenses	15	27	3	20
Property offenses	22	52	3	36
Heroin				
Violent offenses	24	13	0	2
Property offenses	54	51	0	11
Amphetamines				
Violent offenses	35	10	0	4
Property offenses	47	22	0	6

Source: Taylor, B., Brownstein, H., Parry, C. D. H., Plüddemann, A., Makkai, T., Bennett, T., and Holloway, K. (2003). Monitoring the use of illicit drugs in four countries through the International Arrestee Drug Abuse Monitoring (I-ADAM) program. *Criminal Justice: An International Journal of Policy and Practice* 3(3):269–279.
Notes: Data collected for 2000. The proportions presented are median values.

The analysis was also conducted using self-reported drug-use data over the last 12 months. The general direction of results was reinforced for Australia and England and Wales showing that self-reported drug use was higher for all drug types among property offenders. The results relating to the United States also fell in line with this general pattern. In relation to all drug types (marijuana, cocaine, heroin, and amphetamines), a higher proportion of arrestees held or charged with property offenses than violent offenses reported drug use in the last 12 months. However, this pattern was not evident in relation to South Africa, which showed no difference in the proportion reporting any type of drug misuse in terms of the offense for which they were held or charged.

Discussion

There are several findings that can be summarized from this analysis. The first is that there were some important differences in drug misuse among arrestees across the four countries. These differences are most pronounced when looking at opiates (including heroin) and cocaine (including crack). In Australia and in England and Wales, arrestees tested positive for opiates more frequently than for cocaine. In the

United States, arrestees tested positive for cocaine more frequently than for opiates. The reason for these cross-country variations might reflect trafficking routes and drug availability in each country.

A second important finding is the relatively low prevalence of drug misuse among arrestees in the United States. The United States is commonly regarded as a major drug consumer with high levels of drug consumption in the criminal population. However, the results of the urinalysis show that the United States had the lowest prevalence rates of positive tests for marijuana use and the second lowest rates of amphetamine use and opiate use. It was only in relation to cocaine use that the urinalysis prevalence rates exceeded all other countries. Nevertheless, in relation to self-reported use of cocaine in the last 12 months, the United States fell into second place next to England and Wales.

The third general finding is that drug use prevalence rates are higher among arrestees held or charged with property offenses than violent offenses. However, there were some variations across countries in relation to the urinalysis results. In Australia and England and Wales arrestees held or charged with property offenses were more likely to test positive for all or most drug types. In the United States, this was so for cocaine use, but was not the case for marijuana and opiates. The use of these drugs was more common among those held or charged with violent offenses.

I-ADAM IN EIGHT COUNTRIES: APPROACHES AND CHALLENGES

The second publication is described in its introduction as primarily a progress report on the implementation of the I-ADAM program in eight countries. The special feature of the publication is the fact that it includes information on drug use among arrestees across a large number of locations. The countries included in the report were Australia, Chile, England, Malaysia, The Netherlands, Scotland, South Africa, and the United States. The main aim of the report was to describe the experiences of the countries in implementing ADAM-type procedures. However, the report also contained early findings for each of the countries (with the exception of Malaysia) covering the percentage of positive tests for various drug types.

In many respects, the methods of data collection and urinalysis were the same. All sites used trained interviewers who were not law enforcement officials to conduct individual interviews with arrestees and to collect urine specimens. Each country used similar eligibility criteria for selecting study participants. Site staff interviewed both male and female arrestees, and most were interviewed before they had been charged. Typically, the site surveys took about two to three weeks to complete. Most sites collected data from about 200 adult arrestees in each survey.

In other respects the surveys were slightly different – for example, the package of drugs to be tested varied across countries. However, all countries included urinalysis tests for marijuana, cocaine, opiates, amphetamines, methadone, and benzodiazepines, which meant that comparisons could still be made. The interview schedules also varied as they were designed to meet the needs of the particular countries. However, there were several common questions included in the interview schedule that could be compared across sites. There were also differences in the methods used across countries. Some sites included juveniles, whereas others interviewed only adult arrestees. Furthermore, in England and Scotland, the surveys sought to interview the entire population of eligible arrestees during the selected time period, whereas other countries used a system of proportionate sampling.

Prevalence of Drug Misuse Among Arrestees

The prevalence of drug misuse was calculated for each country included in the report using urinalysis. The results are included for each country separately in the section of the report allocated to that country. To show more clearly variations across countries the results have been consolidated into a single table (Table 15.5). The results all relate to surveys conducted in the period 1999 to 2000. At the time of the report, Malaysia had not completed its data collection and has been excluded from the analysis. Hence, the results relate to the seven countries that had collected urinalysis data.

TABLE 15.5. *Percentage of positive tests among male arrestees in eight countries*

	Australia[a]	Chile[b]	England[c]	Malaysia[d]	The Netherlands[e]	Scotland[f]	South Africa[g]	United States[h]
Marijuana	61	31	49	—	41	52	48	41
Opiates	39	0	29	—	17	31	2	7
Cocaine	1	27	20	—	32	3	4	31
Amphetamines	12	1	12	—	—	8	<1	2
Benzodiazepines	—	2	12	—	16	33	3	—
Methadone	—	0	8	—	8	12	3	—
Any drug	74	43	69	—	61	71	49	64
Multiple drugs	27	12	36	—	—	—	—	21

Source: Taylor, B., editor. *I-ADAM in Eight Countries: Approaches and Challenges* (National Institute of Justice Research Report Series, NCJ 189768). Washington, DC: Government Printing Office.

[a]Year of data collection is 1999. Median percentage (measured as the third highest percentage of four locations). Any drug = one or more of four drugs (cannabis, opiates, cocaine, or amphetamines).

[b]Year of data collection is 1999. Mean percentages. Any drug = one or more of 10 drugs (marijuana, cocaine, benzodiazepines, amphetamines, barbiturates, methadone, methaqualone, opiates, PCP, and propoxyphene).

[c]Year of data collection is 1998–9. Mean percentages. Any drug = one or more of six drugs (cannabis, opiates, cocaine, amphetamines, benzodiazepines, and methadone).

[d]No data were collected at the time of the report.

[e]Year of data collection is 1999. Mean percentages. Any drug = one or more of seven drugs (alcohol, cannabis, opiates, cocaine, ecstasy, benzodiazepines, and methadone).

[f]Year of data collection is 1999. Mean percentages. Any drug is one or more of six drugs (cannabis, opiates, cocaine, amphetamines, benzodiazepines, and methadone).

[g]Year of data collection is 2000. Mean percentages read from bar chart (some errors possible). Any drug = one or more of seven drugs (cannabis, opiates, cocaine, amphetamines, benzodiazepines, mandrax, and LSD).

[h]The median percentage positive tests for each drug type were not presented in the current report. The results shown are taken from the 2000 ADAM report to enable comparison. Any drug = one or more of five drugs (marijuana, cocaine, opiates, methamphetamines, and PCP).

In all seven countries, the drug most frequently detected was marijuana. The percentage testing positive ranged from 31 percent in Chile to 61 percent in Australia. The remaining countries fell in the fairly narrow range of 41 percent to 52 percent.

It is interesting to note the difference in detection of opiates (including heroin) and cocaine (including crack) across the countries. In three countries (Australia, England and Wales, and Scotland) opiates were more prevalent than cocaine. Sometimes the difference between the two was quite large. In Australia and Scotland, about one-third of arrestees tested positive for opiates, whereas hardly any (1% and 3%, respectively) tested positive for cocaine. In Chile and the United States, about one-third of arrestees tested positive for cocaine, whereas very few (0% and 7%, respectively) tested positive for opiates. It is noteworthy that Chile and the United States lie closest to the main distributor countries of cocaine, whereas Australia and Scotland lie on the trade routes of the main distributor countries of opiates. In comparison, England and Wales and the Netherlands show notable prevalence rates for both opiates and cocaine.

The percentage of positive tests for the remaining two recreational drugs shown in the table (amphetamines and benzodiazepines) varied across countries, with one exception, in the narrow range of 0 to 16 percent. However, the prevalence of positive tests for benzodiazepines was 33 percent in Scotland. It is possible that benzodiazepine use in Scotland is linked to opiate use because heroin users often take benzodiazepines as an opiate substitute. The fact that Scotland had the second highest rate of opiate use provides some support for this view.

Discussion

Overall, the results show some themes and variations across countries. The prevalence of positive tests for any drug varied from 43 percent (Chile) to 74 percent (Australia) and the prevalence of multiple drugs varied from 12 percent (Chile) to 36 percent (England and Wales). It could be argued that the variations across countries on these two measures are quite small. In other words, the data could be interpreted to show that arrestees tend to be current consumers of illegal drugs and that a notable proportion of them are consumers of multiple drugs. However, there are some clear differences. The absence of evidence of opiate use among arrestees in Chile and the fact that the results show hardly any cocaine use among arrestees in Australia is quite striking. Conversely, more than a third of arrestees in Australia tested positive for opiates, and just under a third of arrestees in the United States tested positive for cocaine.

Hence, the results have identified patterns of drug misuse that might be used as a baseline in monitoring international drug trends. The original aim of I-ADAM was to monitor stability and change in drug misuse across countries with the view of developing national and international drug strategies.

COMPARING DRUG USE RATES OF DETAINED ARRESTEES IN THE UNITED STATES AND ENGLAND

The third publication comprises an analysis of comparable data from the United States and England and Wales. The US data derive from the ADAM program, and the UK data derive from the second developmental stage of the NEW-ADAM program. Overall, the matching procedure of the survey sites was more rigorous in this publication than in the previous publications. Whereas in the previous study all selected US and UK sites were used for 2000, in the current study, five matched sites from each country were compared for 1996. The sites were matched on population density, and the subjects were matched on selection criteria and sample weighting. The five sites selected in the United States were New York, New York; Fort Lauderdale, Florida; Miami, Florida; Washington, DC; and Birmingham, Alabama. The five sites selected in England and Wales were London, Manchester, Nottingham, Sunderland, and Cambridge. An important difference between the analysis for this publication and the analysis for the previous publication is that this one included a more detailed breakdown of the results.

Prevalence of Drug Misuse Among Arrestees

The prevalence of positive tests for six drug types for the five US and five UK sites for male arrestees is shown in Table 15.6. The

TABLE 15.6. *Percentage of positive tests among male arrestees in the United States and England and Wales*

	United States	England and Wales
Marijuana	44	49
Opiates	8	17
Cocaine	40	8
Amphetamines	<1	5
Benzodiazepines	8	8
Methadone	3	6

Source: Taylor, B., and Bennett, T. H. (1999). *Comparing Drug Use Rates of Detained Arrestees in the United States and England.* Washington, DC: National Institute of Justice, US Department of Justice.
Note: Data collected for the year 1996.

urinalysis results generally support the findings of the previous analysis in showing higher rates of most drug types among UK arrestees than US arrestees. The proportion of positive tests in England and Wales was higher than the United States in relation to marijuana (49% compared with 44%), opiates (17% compared with 8%), amphetamines (5% compared with <1%), and methadone (6% compared with 3%). The rates were identical for benzodiazepines (8% for each), and only in relation to cocaine was the rate higher in the United States than in the UK (40% compared with 8%). These percentages are different to those shown in the previous publication as a result of differences in the year the data were collected, differences in the sites selected, and differences in the method of analysis. Nevertheless, the broad direction of the findings is similar in both studies.

Prevalence of Drug Misuse by Arrestee Characteristics

One important advantage of the matched comparison was that data from both countries could be combined into a single data set. It was possible, therefore, to conduct a detailed breakdown of drug use and individual characteristics.

Gender. In both countries, female arrestees were more likely than male arrestees to test positive for opiates, cocaine, methadone, and amphetamines (see Chapter 9 for a discussion of gender issues).

Similarly, in both countries males were more likely than females to test positive for marijuana. The only difference between countries in terms of single drug type use was in relation to benzodiazepines. In the United States, females were more likely than males to test positive for these drugs (15% compared with 8%; $p < .001$), and in England and Wales males were more likely than females to test positive (8% compared with 7%; not significant). There was no difference between the United States and England and Wales in relation to use of any of the six drugs, with both showing higher proportions among males. This result is likely to reflect the higher proportion of males in both countries who use marijuana. However, there was a country difference in the detection of multiple drug use. In the United States, males were more likely than females to have multiple positive tests (28% compared with 24%; not significant), and in England and Wales females were more likely than males to have multiple positive tests (30% compared with 21%; not significant).

Age. In the United States and England and Wales, older arrestees (aged 21 or older) were more likely than younger ones (aged 20 or younger) to test positive for opiates, cocaine, methadone, and amphetamines. In both countries, younger arrestees were more likely than older arrestees to test positive for marijuana. The only difference between countries occurred in relation to benzodiazepines. In the United States, a higher proportion of younger than older arrestees tested positive for this drug (11% compared with 9%; not significant) and in England and Wales a higher proportion of older than younger arrestees tested positive (11% compared with 2%; not significant). In neither country was there a statistically significant difference in the proportion of younger and older arrestees testing positive for any drug or multiple drugs.

Race. In both the United States and England and Wales, white arrestees were more likely than nonwhite arrestees to test positive for opiates, amphetamines, benzodiazepines, and methadone. Similarly, in both countries nonwhites were more likely than whites to test positive for marijuana. The only difference between the two countries was in relation to cocaine. In the United States, a slightly greater proportion of white than nonwhite arrestees tested positive (41% compared with 40%; not significant) and in England and Wales slightly more nonwhite than white arrestees tested positive (15% compared with 8%; not significant). However, these differences are slight and not significant, which suggest no underlying difference between the two countries. The percentage of positive tests for any drug and multiple drugs was very similar across countries and across ethnic groups (no differences were statistically significant).

Prevalence of Drug Misuse by Offense Types

Type of Crime. The offense for which arrestees were charged were categorized as personal crimes, property crimes, alcohol and drug offenses, public disorder offenses, and other offenses. The results discussed here concern only the difference between the United States and England and Wales in terms of personal crimes and property crimes. In almost all comparisons, property offenders were more likely than those held or charged with personal crimes to test positive for one or more of the six drug types. The only exception was in relation to amphetamines. In the United States, a slightly higher proportion of property offenders than those who committed offenses against the person tested positive for amphetamines, whereas in England and Wales, a slightly higher percentage of arrestees held or charged with personal crimes than property crimes tested positive. In neither case, was the difference statistically significant.

Discussion

The main conclusions from the matched comparison of arrestees from the United States and England and Wales are that there are some differences between the two countries in terms of drug use. The main differences concern the generally lower prevalence rates of positive tests for drug misuse in the United States compared with England and Wales. The main exception to this was in relation to cocaine.

However, there are also some similarities between the two countries. In both the United States and England and Wales, arrestees held or charged with property offenses were more likely than those held or charged with offenses against the person to test positive for most drug types. This similarity was not so evident in the previous

TABLE 15.7. *Percentage of positive tests among male arrestees in the United States and England and Wales by demographic characteristics*

	Gender		Age						Race	
	Male	Female	15–20	21+	21–25	26–30	31–35	36+	Nonwhite	White
Marijuana										
United States	44	22	65	35	44	39	32	19	44	40
England	49	27	56	43	54	36	54	22	59	44
Opiates										
United States	8	10	1	10	4	14	16	12	6	9
England	17	28	10	21	17	34	27	9	16	18
Cocaine										
United States	40	43	23	45	35	49	65	46	40	41
England	8	14	3	11	10	17	13	3	15	8
Amphetamines										
United States	<1	2	0	1	<1	0	2	1	<1	1
England	5	10	3	7	4	11	8	4	0	6
Benzodiazepines										
United States	8	15	11	9	5	9	17	9	2	10
England	8	7	2	11	9	15	11	10	6	9
Methadone										
United States	3	4	0	4	1	3	6	7	2	3
England	6	13	2	8	6	14	8	5	2	7

Any of six drug types

United States	69	64	71	68	65	69	85	63	68	68
England	60	52	62	59	65	62	66	35	66	57

Multiple drugs

United States	28	25	25	28	20	36	41	23	23	28
England	21	30	12	26	22	36	34	14	22	22

Source: Taylor, B., and Bennett, T. H. (1999). *Comparing Drug Use Rates of Detained Arrestees in the United States and England*. Washington, DC: National Institute of Justice, US Department of Justice.

Note: Data collected for the year 1996.

TABLE 15.8. *Percentage of positive tests among male arrestees in the United States and England and Wales by offense type*

	Type of crime	
	Personal	Property
Marijuana		
United States	39	40
England	48	51
Opiates		
United States	4	10
England	17	22
Cocaine		
United States	26	44
England	4	12
Amphetamines		
United States	<1	1
England	5	4
Benzodiazepines		
United States	7	9
England	7	11
Methadone		
United States	2	4
England	2	9
Any of six drug types		
United States	55	71
England	59	64
Multiple drugs		
United States	18	28
England	17	28

Source: Taylor, B., and Bennett, T. H. (1999). *Comparing Drug Use Rates of Detained Arrestees in the United States and England.* Washington, DC: National Institute of Justice, US Department of Justice.
Note: Data collected for the year 1996.

publication, which compared four countries including the United States and England and Wales. However, it is possible that some of the differences between the two publications are a result of the fact that the samples in the current publication were matched. The current publication also showed some important similarities in terms of the association between arrestee characteristics, such as gender, age, and race, and the likelihood of testing positive for the six drug types.

DISCUSSION

The analysis of ADAM-type data from three publications has shown that there are some similarities and differences across countries in terms of illegal drug misuse among arrestees.

The first publication based on a comparison of four countries showed that country differences were most pronounced when looking at opiates (including heroin) and cocaine (including crack). In Australia and England and Wales, arrestees tested positive for opiates more frequently than for cocaine. In the United States, arrestees tested positive for cocaine more frequently than for opiates. The publication showed that, with the exception of cocaine use, the United States did not have a particularly high prevalence rate of drug misuse among arrestees compared with other countries. It was noted that the United States is commonly regarded as a major drug consumer with high levels of drug consumption. However, the results of the urinalysis show that the United States had one of the lowest prevalence rates of positive tests for marijuana, amphetamine, and opiate use.

The second publication expanded the analysis to include eight countries (seven of which provided urinalysis results). The results showed that arrestees across many countries were current consumers of illegal drugs. In particular, they showed that the prevalence of positive tests for any drug varied only slightly across countries. As in the first publication, the main differences between countries were in relation to opiates (including heroin) and cocaine (including crack). For example, there was no opiate use among arrestees in Chile, whereas more than one-third of arrestees in Australia tested positive for these drugs.

The third publication provided a more detailed breakdown of drug misuse by arrestee characteristics. The main conclusions of the matched comparison of arrestees from the United States and England and Wales was that there were generally lower prevalence rates of positive tests for drug misuse in the United States compared with England and Wales. However, there were some similarities in terms of arrestee characteristics. In both the United States and England and Wales, arrestees held or charged with property offenses were more likely than those held or charged with personal offenses to test

positive for most drug types. The publication also showed some similarities among arrestees in terms of gender, age, and race, and the
likelihood of testing positive for certain drug types.

There are a number of advantages in using arrestee data to compare differences in drug use and crime across countries. I-ADAM data
were collected using similar techniques, including similar methods of
drug testing and similar self-report survey questionnaires. Hence, any
differences between the countries are more likely to be the result of
real differences in drug use among arrestees rather than differences
in methods of data collection. It is also of benefit to know something
about international variations in the type of drug used among arrestees
as it can aid understanding of the drug-crime connection. It was mentioned earlier that it is obviously the case that if a certain drug type
is not consumed at all in a country, then it cannot be associated with
crime. Conversely, drug types consumed by a large proportion of the
arrestee population are more likely to be implicated in the drug-crime
connection.

PART FIVE

CONCLUSIONS

CHAPTER SIXTEEN

Conclusions

INTRODUCTION

In this final chapter of the book, we reflect on what has been found from the results of the New English and Welsh Arrestee Drug Abuse Monitoring (NEW-ADAM) program as a whole. We briefly review the main findings from each chapter and consider the themes that have emerged. We also discuss what has happened to the NEW-ADAM program in the United Kingdom and the Arrestee Drug Abuse Monitoring (ADAM) program in the United States since their demise. Finally, we consider some of the policy and research implications of the study.

SUMMARY

In Chapter 2, we discussed the research methods used in the NEW-ADAM program and described the method of urine collection and the personal interview. Arrestees were selected by a system of two-stage sampling with the first stage based on purposive rather than random sampling. We noted some of the limitations of the research including the considerable difficulties of interviewing arrestees in the chaotic conditions of police custody suites. Arrestees were often highly agitated, and some were potentially violent having been free on the streets just hours before interview. Despite these barriers, the research team succeeded in interviewing more than 4,500 arrestees during the research period and collected urine samples from almost all of them.

Chapter 3 examined the prevalence and incidence of drug misuse among arrestees. The results presented in the chapter provide evidence for the first time in the United Kingdom of the high levels of involvement of arrestees in drug misuse. It was found that drug use among arrestees was many times greater than among the general population. It showed that almost 90 percent of arrestees said that they had consumed at least one illicit drug in their lifetime, and more than half had consumed heroin, crack, or cocaine powder. In other words, arrestees were at much higher risk of drug misuse than the general population. Hence, the chapter provided prima facia evidence of a statistical association between drug misuse and crime.

In Chapter 4, we discussed the health problems of drug-misusing arrestees. It is widely known that drug use is associated with a range of personal, economic, and social problems. However, it was not known the extent to which arrestees generally have health problems. The results showed that arrestees were more likely to have health problems than the general population. More than one-quarter of all arrestees had visited a doctor in the three days before interview, and one-tenth had bought over-the-counter drugs. In addition, one-third of all arrestees were dependent on one or more drugs, and approximately one-quarter had injected an illegal drug at some time in their lives. A small proportion (1%) of all arrestees said that they were HIV positive. However, this increased to 2 percent of heroin users and 3 percent of injectors.

Chapter 5 considered the statistical association between drug misuse and crime by looking at aggregate level data. Some information was disaggregated to provide specific breakdowns. The chapter examined the nature of the relationship by looking at the association between various combinations of prevalence and incidence of drug use and prevalence and incidence of criminal behavior. The results showed that drug users were more likely than non–drug users to commit crimes and to commit crimes at a high rate, and that high-rate drug users were more likely than low-rate drug users to commit crimes and to commit them at a high rate. In other words, drug use and crime were strongly connected in terms of both prevalence and incidence.

Chapter 6 investigated the statistical association between drug use and crime using disaggregated data. In particular, it aimed to investigate whether specific types of drug use were associated with specific types of crime. In relation to the prevalence of offending, drug use was associated with a general increase in the likelihood of offending across a range of offense types. However, in relation to the incidence of offending, there were few associations between drug use and rate of offending. The only significant connections found were between heroin and shoplifting and crack use and fraud, handling stolen goods, and drug supply offenses. Overall, the results suggest that the relationship between drug use and crime is general when talking about prevalence of offending and specific when talking about incidence of offending.

Chapter 7 explored the relationship between multiple drug use (i.e., use of two or more drug types) and crime. The results showed that multiple drug users were significantly more likely than users of just one drug type to report offending in the last 12 months. Multiple drug users reported committing twice as many offenses as users of just one drug type. The rate of offending was found to increase as the number of drug types used increased. The rate of offending also varied in terms of the types of drugs used. For example, multiple drug users, who included heroin, crack, or cocaine in their drug combinations, committed a greater number of offenses than multiple drug users who used only recreational drugs. The chapter concluded that the drug-crime connection varied by the number of drug types consumed.

Chapter 8 investigated users' explanations of the link between drug misuse and crime. Most drug-misusing offenders reported that their drug use and crime were connected. The most common reasons given were economic need, judgment impairment, and the fact that drugs just happened to be purchased from the proceeds of crime. The research also identified variations in the characteristics of drug users and the types of explanation given. Users who stated that they committed crimes for money for drugs were more likely to be white females and older than those who mentioned other reasons. They were also more likely to be users of hard drugs such as heroin, crack, and methadone. Users who mentioned judgment impairment as an explanation were more likely to be male and to use only recreational drugs.

Chapter 9 looked at gender differences in drug use and associated problem behaviors. The results showed that female arrestees were significantly more likely than males to have used heroin and crack, whereas male arrestees were significantly more likely than females to have used cannabis, ecstasy, and cocaine powder. In addition, female arrestees who used heroin and crack also used them at a higher rate than male arrestees and were more likely to be in treatment or to want treatment. Overall, the results suggest that female arrestees were more problematic than males in their drug use and associated behaviors.

Chapter 10 investigated ethnic group differences in drug misuse and problem behaviors. The results showed that white arrestees were more likely than nonwhite arrestees to be drug users in relation to most drug types. The only drug for which white arrestees were not significantly more likely to use was cannabis. There were no significant differences in terms of rate of use among reported drug users. However, white arrestees were significantly more likely to report high-rate use of alcohol than nonwhite alcohol users. Injecting was found to be significantly more prevalent among whites than nonwhites. A greater proportion of white than nonwhite arrestees reported that they were currently in treatment and wanted treatment.

Chapter 11 examined the relationship between gang membership and drug misuse and criminal behavior. The results showed that about 4 percent of arrestees were current gang members and 11 percent had been members in the past. Gang members were generally younger (aged under 25) than non–gang members and were more likely to be male and white. Gang members were also more likely than non–gang members to report committing recent property crimes. Gang members were more likely than non–gang members to possess a gun and to use it as part of a crime. They were less likely to consume drugs but were more likely to sell drugs.

Chapter 12 discussed weapons and guns among arrestees in the United Kingdom. About one-quarter of arrestees interviewed reported having owned or got hold of a gun at some point in their lives, and about one-tenth said they had done so in the previous 12 months. The most common illegal gun possessed was a handgun, and the most common reason for possessing a gun was protection. One reason for wanting the protection of a gun was during drug dealing and drug purchasing. More than one-third of arrestees who possessed a handgun said that they had used it on an offense. Gun possession was most common among high-rate offenders, violent offenders, those involved in drug supply offenses, and gang members.

Chapter 13 looked at drug markets. Heroin and crack markets were found to be similar in many ways, including the sociodemographic characteristics and the offending behavior of buyers, the location in which buyers bought their drugs, and the method by which they made contact with dealers (e.g., by personal contact or by phone). The similarities between the crack and heroin markets identified suggest that the two markets may, in fact, be the same. However, cocaine markets were quite different. In cocaine markets, buyers were significantly more likely to be male, to be young, and to be from a higher social class. There were also differences in the way in which contact was made with dealers and the places at which drugs were collected. Cocaine sales were more likely to be conducted in social situations, such as in pubs and clubs, and were more likely to be closed markets (i.e., few buyers).

In Chapter 14, drug treatments were investigated. Only a small minority (28%) of drug-using arrestees had ever received treatment for drug misuse, and less than 1 in 10 were currently receiving treatment. Women, older arrestees, and white arrestees were more likely to report that they were receiving treatment. Certain types of treatment were more sought after than others. Detoxification and help with withdrawal were particularly popular. Arrestees who used hard drug types (such as heroin, crack, and methadone) were more likely than users of other drug types to be currently receiving treatment.

Chapter 15 compared findings from the NEW-ADAM surveys with arrestee surveys conducted in other countries. The chapter was based on the results of three published documents. The first publication found that arrestees in Australia and England tested positive for opiates more frequently than for cocaine, whereas arrestees in the United States more frequently tested positive for cocaine than for opiates. The second publication expanded the analysis to include eight countries. As before, the main differences between countries were in relation to opiates and cocaine. There was no opiate use among arrestees in Chile, whereas more than one-third of arrestees in Australia tested positive for these drugs. The third publication provided a more detailed breakdown of drug misuse by arrestee characteristics. The main conclusion was that there were generally lower prevalence rates of positive tests for drug misuse in the United States compared with England.

THEMES AND VARIATIONS

There are several overall conclusions that can be drawn from the NEW-ADAM research about drug-crime connections.

The first conclusion concerns the extent to which the drug-crime connection is general and pervasive, affecting all drugs and all crimes. In practice, it has been taken as understood that neither the strong version of this argument (every drug is connected to every crime) nor the weak version (no drugs are connected to any crimes) accurately reflect the nature of the relationship. Having said this, there is little agreement about where in the middle of these two extremes the truth lies. Overall, the results of the NEW-ADAM surveys suggest that the relationship between drug use and crime appears to be general only when talking about prevalence of offending. In other words, there appears to be a generally high level of involvement in a wide range of offenses among a wide range of drug users. However, when looking at rate of involvement in crime (the total number of offenses committed), this general relationship disappears. In relation to the number of offenses committed, it does not appear that the drug-crime connection is general and pervasive.

The second conclusion continues the foregoing argument. It appears that the drug-crime connection (when looking at rate of offending) is highly specific in terms of particular drug types and particular crimes. The disaggregated analysis discussed in Chapter 6 showed that there was hardly any connection between drug use and rate of crime among recreational drug users. The only relationship that could be found was among hard drug use. However, even among this group of drug users, there were only a few specific connections. These were mainly to do with the connection between heroin and shoplifting and crack and fraud, handling, and drug supply offenses. It is possible, in the case of crack, that fraud and handling are offenses linked to shoplifting (i.e., using false credit cards and selling stolen goods). Hence, it could be argued that the crime problems generated by drug misuse, at least in the United Kingdom, focus mainly on crimes against shops. In this sense, the concept of a drug-crime connection (suggesting that most drugs cause most crimes) is a misnomer.

The third general conclusion is that the relationship between drug use and crime is not fixed but variable, both between and within offenders. Chapter 8 showed variation in users' accounts of the causal connection between drug use and crime. The most common reasons concerned economic need. However, there were other connections including judgment impairment and purchasing drugs for pleasure from the proceeds of crime. The research also has shown variations in the drug-crime connection by user characteristics. Chapter 9 looked at gender differences in drug use and crime, and Chapter 10 investigated ethnic differences. Overall, females were more likely than males and whites were more likely than nonwhites to be involved in hard drug use. Hence, the results suggest that there are a small number of highly specific connections between drug use and crime and that these might vary from user to user.

THE DECLINE OF ARRESTEE MONITORING

In recent years, the number of countries conducting arrestee surveys has reduced considerably. It was mentioned in the introduction that between the end of the 1990s and the beginning of the 2000s, nine countries were collecting arrestee monitoring data: the United States, Australia, Chile, England, Malaysia, The Netherlands, Scotland, South Africa, and Taiwan. At the time of writing, it is believed that only two countries are currently conducting ADAM type research (the Drug Use Monitoring in Australia [DUMA] program in Australia and the new version of the NEW-ADAM program in the United Kingdom).

Arrestee Monitoring in the United Kingdom

In 2002, the NEW-ADAM program ceased data collection. The program was initially funded on a three-year basis. However, the research was designed in a way that the program could have continued to collect data subject to future funding. However, the end point of the first stage of the research coincided with some important policy developments that led to its termination.

The main development was the increasing concern that the targets set for the Key Objectives of the government strategy were unlikely to be met in the time available. Some argued that they were impossible to achieve over any reasonable period of time. The whole issue of performance assessment was investigated by a Select Committee on Home Affairs, which was set up to consider the viability of the government's drug strategy. The Committee reported back in a report titled *The Government's Drugs Policy: Is it Working?* The report concluded, 'We believe it is unwise, not to say self-defeating, to set targets which have no earthly chance of success. We recommend . . . that the Government distinguishes explicitly between aspirational targets and measurable targets' (Home Affairs Select Committee, 2001). Reports from witnesses summoned by the Committee indicated that they were not impressed by the early outcomes. Representatives from the Association of Chief Police Officers reported that there was no evidence that any of the desired results were being achieved. One retired chief constable reported to the committee that, in his view, all four major indicators of drug misuse and drug-related crime had moved in the opposite direction to that proposed in the strategy documents. There is some support for this view in the trend results of the NEW-ADAM program. which investigated drug misuse among arrestees during the period 1999–2002 (the period immediately following the implementation of the strategy; Holloway, Bennett, and Lower, 2004). The report found that during this early period, the proportion of arrestees testing positive for opiates or cocaine actually increased across the eight sites investigated.

At about that time, the UK Drugs Coordinator was fired, and a revised drug strategy was developed with new performance targets. The new focus of attention of measuring the effectiveness of the government's drug strategy led to a reappraisal of the ability of the NEW-ADAM program to deliver appropriate measures of drug misuse. The program was reviewed, and it was thought that the methods used and the outputs obtained were not sufficiently focused on the policy needs of the time, which were to measure the effectiveness of the drug strategy.

It should be noted that the original aim of the program was to generate a system of arrestee monitoring in the United Kingdom close to that of the ADAM program in the United States and to have similar aims. In other words, it was hoped to generate a surveillance and monitoring system that could provide a platform for both research and policy. The design of the NEW-ADAM program was outlined in the Home Office specification for the research and the broad aims of the research and the methods for surveying arrestees were determined by the Home Office. Hence, there was a disparity between the aims and methods of the research as outlined in the mid-1990s when the research was first established and in the early 2000s when the issue of performance target measurement came to the fore.

The main reason why the NEW-ADAM program was no longer suitable for the government's needs were the following: (1) that the original method of selecting 16 sites based on purposive sampling could not generate reliable national indicators of change in drug misuse in the arrestee population and (2) the original aims of the research to include data on research as well as policy interest generated an unnecessary cost that was unrelated to the new purpose of the research. Hence, the Home Office began the process of generating a new research specification that would enable probability sampling at both sampling stages and would, therefore, generate valid national estimates. They also sought to focus the drug testing methods and interview questions closely on issues of performance measurement.

In 2002, the Home Office commissioned a study to explore the feasibility of conducting a new arrestee survey using different research methods. The results of this study showed that computer-assisted, self-completed questionnaires, and saliva drug tests could be conducted successfully on arrestees in custody suites. It also showed that it was possible to select police custody suites using probability sampling and to increase the number of sites covered in order to reduce sampling error.

A second tender was circulated by the Home Office to commission a new Arrestee Survey that would incorporate these revised design features. The tender was won by the National Center for Social Research and the new Arrestee Survey was launched in September 2003.

The Arrestee Survey is based on 60 randomly selected custody suites in England and Wales. It is estimated that more than 9,000 adult arrestees (17 years or older) will be interviewed and drug tested each year. The interviews are being conducted using three different methods: Computer-Assisted Personal Interviewing (CAPI), Computer-Assisted Self-Interviewing (CASI), and Audio-Computer

Assisted Self-Interviewing (A-CASI). CASI and A-CASI are used for the majority of the questionnaires (Home Office, 2006).

The questionnaire covers several of the issues covered in the NEW-ADAM questionnaire, including demographics, previous contact with the CJS, offending behavior, use of weapons and guns, drug use and injecting behavior, expenditure on drugs, drug markets, the drug-crime connection, drug dependence, and treatment experiences. Unlike NEW-ADAM, however, the drug testing involves the collection of saliva samples not urine samples. A further difference is that the saliva samples are sent off to be tested for opiates and cocaine only and not for any other drug types. In addition, 10 percent of samples are subject to confirmatory tests.

At the moment, the Arrestee Survey is still collecting data and as yet no results have been published. Hence, at the time of writing, the results of the NEW-ADAM program remain the only published source of information on drug misuse among arrestees in the United Kingdom.

ARRESTEE MONITORING IN THE UNITED STATES

It is interesting that about the same time as the demise of the NEW-ADAM program in the United Kingdom, the ADAM program in the United States was terminated. In January 2004, the National Institute of Justice published a press release stating that the ADAM program had ended (cited in Center for Substance Abuse Research [CESAR], 2004). It noted as a reason the significant reduction in congressional funds for the fiscal year 2004 for social science research.

The NIJ Annual Report for 2003 also commented on the decision to terminate the ADAM program (NIJ, 2004).

> In early 2004, NIJ stopped work on the ADAM program data collection effort. This action was taken in response to a significant reduction in the congressional appropriation to NIJ in fiscal year 2004 for social science research. Although the President's budget requested sufficient funds to continue the ADAM program in fiscal year 2004, the appropriations bill that Congress passed did not appropriate the funds the President requested. (p. 7)

The report continued to explain that there was an intention to continue arrestee monitoring in the future, subject to funds being available. However, this would be based on a different research aim and a different research design. Specifically, the revised research aim would be to provide a national estimate of drug use among persons arrested for crimes and the revised research method would be based on a program of 25 core sites.

The newsletter from the CESAR mentioned earlier noted that the ending of the program surprised many experts and ADAM site directors had expressed frustration over the lack of communication regarding the decision (CESAR, 2004).

Kleiman (2004) also expressed concern over the decision in an article in *Issues in Science and Technology*. He argued that the cost of ADAM was not great and that there must have been other reasons, apart from funding, that led to its demise. He thought one of the reasons was scientific respectability, because of its unconventional sampling process. Further, the population of arrestees was not a natural population, but, to some extent, was determined by police arrest and processing practices. However, he thought that these problems were manageable and were not greatly different to the problems faced by many large surveys. The main reason for its termination, he believed, had more to do with cost-effectiveness. The program cost a little too much, and the results were open to a little too much criticism.

Maccoun (2004) responded to Kleiman's article in the same journal and thought that there were other reasons for the demise. He thought that political support for ADAM might have been weakened by the fact that researchers using ADAM data had consistently shown that the drug-crime connection was in part spurious because of the common causes of both criminality and drug use. In other words, ADAM data served to undermine the government's position that drug use caused crime. He also noted that researchers had found that prohibition of drugs helped to escalate drug markets and drug-market violence. However, he thought that a deeper reason might be that government drug policy is not really based on rational evidence but more on what he called 'moral symbolism'.

RESEARCH IMPLICATIONS

The main research implications raised by the NEW-ADAM program relate to (1) fundamental research and obtaining information in areas previously not studied or understudied and (2) monitoring research that can determine trends in drug use and crime over time and provide information on related trends such as gang formation and gun possession.

Fundamental Research

Little research has attempted to disaggregate the findings of research to reveal specific drug-crime connections. The current research has shown that the general drug-crime connection might be a product of a very small number of specific connections. Hence, it is important that more is known about these specific connections and the way in which they vary over time and place. There has also been little research that has examined differences between the prevalence and incidence of offending among drug users. The current research indicated that the drug-crime connection might be largely a product of differences in rate of offending among drug users and non–drug users rather than solely of their involvement in offending. More research should be done on the relationship between level of involvement in drug use and crime.

Empirical research on specific drug-crime connections might also be supplemented by theoretical developments and explanations of the various drug-crime connections. In the past, there has been a tendency to develop general theories that have attempted to explain all drug-crime connections. However, it would appear more appropriate to develop multiple drug-crime theories that address specific types of connection. The heroin-shoplifting link, for example, might be explained by a version of the economic necessity argument. However, other links especially those relating to drugs and violence or those relating to drugs and expressive crimes might require different kinds of explanation.

Another area of research that should be expanded is research that looks at variations in the drug-crime connection among and between offenders and drug users. Many studies have demonstrated variations in relation to particular drug-misusing groups (e.g., studies of

prostitutes and studies of robbers). However, there are far fewer studies that have looked across a wide range of groups in the search for
patterns in the nature of the connection. The NEW-ADAM research
has shown that it is unlikely that the drug-crime connection is the
same for all offenders and it is unlikely that the connection remains
constant over time for any particular offender. This type of investigation would be particularly suited to qualitative research that could
investigate both between and within-subject variations. As mentioned
in Chapter 7, variations between subjects could be studied by selecting across different drug-using groups, combining perhaps samples
drawn from treatment sources and criminal justice sources. Variations
within subjects could be studied by asking respondents about different
time periods in their drug-using career or by investigating different
contexts in which drugs and crime coexisted.

The final research gap worth plugging is the problem of missing
populations. Most research on drugs and crime has been conducted
on mixed samples that have rarely been broken down by offender or
drug user characteristics. As a result, relatively little is known about
gender or ethnic differences in terms of the drug-crime connection.
It was mentioned in Chapter 9 that although the number of studies
on gender and ethnic differences is increasing, the number of studies
conducted on any single issue remains small, resulting in few definitive findings. Hence, there is a need for more research on gender
differences in drug misuse. In particular, more research needs to be
done on differences in types of drugs used, the rate of use, dosages,
and the methods of administration, which to date have produced few
consistent findings. It was also mentioned that more research needs to
be done that could assist in informing treatment policy. In particular,
it is important to determine whether women and men are different
in terms of health-related issues, including dependency, unmet treatment needs, equipment sharing, and whether they are affected by
these problems in different ways.

Monitoring Research

It is worrying that just at a point when arrestee monitoring was reach-
ing its peak in terms of spread and sophistication in the United
States, that the ADAM program was terminated. The NEW-ADAM

program was also terminated just before this. Other countries, such as Scotland and The Netherlands, have also disbanded arrestee monitoring. It would appear that one important monitoring aim is to continue arrestee monitoring. The original justifications for arrestee monitoring still exist. Arrestees represent some of the most problematic members of society and are likely to be the first in terms of trying new drugs or in terms of finding new drug-crime connections. In this sense, they are a vanguard for social problems to come and can provide an early warning that can inform criminal justice and treatment agencies.

Other forms of monitoring arrestee behavior should be developed. It was mentioned earlier that the NEW-ADAM program was one of the first sources of empirical information on the development of gangs in the United Kingdom. It would be useful to continue monitoring gang formations through arrestee and other surveys to determine not only their spread but also possible changes in their organization, structure, and behavior. In particular, it is important, with respect to the drug-crime connection, to know more about the involvement of gangs in drug consumption and supply and their involvement in violence and other forms of street crime.

Similar monitoring research would be useful in the area of gun possession and use in crime. The current research has shown a connection between drug misuse and gun possession. It would be important, therefore, to monitor developments in gun possession, both in terms of its spread and the nature of gun carrying and use in crime. Ideally, there should be regular gun surveys that could monitor possession and use of guns and to determine the relation among guns, drugs, and crime.

POLICY IMPLICATIONS

The main policy implications raised throughout the book concern mainly (1) rehabilitation of those already involved in drugs and crime in the past and (2) prevention of those who might become involved in drugs and crime in the future. In each case, the main policy lessons to be learned concern accurately identifying problems and intervention points and effectively matching responses to problems.

Rehabilitation

The first set of policy implications concerns rehabilitation or treatment of those offenders already involved in drugs and crime. A number of recommendations flow from the findings of the research. In relation to health, the research has shown that arrestees often enter the criminal justice system with a wide range of health problems including drug dependency, infectious diseases, psychiatric problems, and physical ailments. At the moment, the criminal justice system only tackles some of these problems, and arrestees can be released back into the community with a wide range of drug-related health problems. Entry into the criminal justice system can provide an opportunity to tackle these problems.

Little attention has been paid by the government to the problem of multiple drug use. The NEW-ADAM research has shown that there were some differences between users who consume only heroin or crack and users who consume these drugs along with other drugs. Heroin users who also use crack might require a different treatment approach to heroin users who use only heroin. Similarly, heroin users who use many other drug types might require a different treatment approach to those who use just a few.

The chapter on gender and drug use showed that there were different treatment needs for men and women. Almost twice as many female arrestees as male arrestees said that they had an unmet need for treatment. Hence, some attention needs to be paid to matching more closely treatment need and treatment provision in terms of gender. It was also argued that drug treatment is made more widely available for women and to ensure adequate childcare facilities. Overall, it was proposed that more attention should be given to developing 'women-friendly' treatment programs.

Prevention

The second set of policy implications concern prevention of offenders becoming involved in drug use and crime in the future.

The general findings of the research concerning the types of offender involved in drug-related crime and the characteristics of high rate drug-misusing offenders might be useful as a guide to targeting preventative actions. Similarly, the information provided on the specific types of drug-crime connections such as the strong heroin-shoplifting link and the connection between crack and fraud, handling, and drug supply could also be used to target police actions. The relationship between heroin and shoplifting is particularly strong in the United Kingdom, and this information could be used to focus on this particular drug-crime link.

The chapter on users' accounts of the causal connection between drug use and crime also suggests preventative options. The research suggests that preventative efforts might be more effective if they responded differently to the different kinds of drug-misusing offender and the different kinds of connection. Programs designed to reduce crack use among street prostitutes might focus on outreach services, whereas programs that aim to reduce shoplifting among heroin addicts might focus on situational crime prevention. Similarly, programs designed to reduce drug use among street robbers might focus on gang formations and street culture. In other words, a targeted strategy that took into account the different causal connections might be more productive than a general strategy that did not.

The research has also indicated other preventative options that might help tackle the drug-crime connection. Chapter 11 showed that street gangs are often involved in drug-supply offenses and can also be involved in street violence and other offenses. Although antigang programs are very common in the United States, little progress has been made in the United Kingdom to target gangs and youth groups. Chapter 12 also discussed the links among drugs, crime, and gun possession and use. As before, there are many gun suppression programs operating in the United States, but to date there have been few programs designed to prevent use of guns in crime in the United Kingdom. The current research shows a strong connection between gun possession and drug use. Although it is not known whether drug use causes gun possession or gun possession causes drug use, prevention programs designed to tackle guns could have an overall impact on drugs and crime.

CONCLUSION

The NEW-ADAM program was established in 1999 to monitor drug misuse in the arrestee population and to generate data on the drug-crime connection that might inform both research and policy. During its first three years of operation, it generated useful data on the drug-crime connection in relation to over 4,500 arrestees. This concluding chapter has shown that the analysis of this data has generated findings relevant both to fundamental research on the nature of the drug-crime connection and to government policy on ways of tackling drug-related crime. However, more research needs to be done both to help understand the various drug-crime connections and to provide a basis for effective government intervention. Arrestee surveys are a useful part of the overall research endeavor that might help to achieve this.

References

Advisory Council on the Misuse of Drugs. (1998). *Drugs and the Environment.* London: HMSO.

Alterman, A. I., Randall, M., and McLellan, A. T. (2000). Comparison of outcomes by gender and for fee-for-service versus managed care. A study of nine community programs. *Journal of Substance Abuse Treatment* 19: 127–134.

Anglin, M. D., Hser, Y., and Booth, M. W. (1987). Sex differences in addict careers. 4. Treatment. *American Journal of Drug and Alcohol Abuse* 13: 253–280.

Anglin, M. D., Hser, Y., and McGlothlin, W. (1987). Sex differences in addict careers. 2. Becoming addicted. *American Journal of Drug and Alcohol Abuse* 13: 59–71.

Aust, R., and Smith, N. (2003). *Ethnicity and Drug Use: Key Findings from the 2001/2002 British Crime Survey* (Home Office Findings 209). London: Home Office.

Australian Institute of Health and Welfare. (2003). *Statistics on Drug Use in Australia 2002.* Accessed 26 May 2006 from http://www.aihw.gov.au/publications/phe/sdua02/sdua02.pdf.

Ayres, M., and Murray, L. (2005). *Arrests for Recorded Crime (Notifiable Offences) and the Operation of Certain Police Powers under PACE: England and Wales 2004/05* (Home Office Statistical Bulletin 21/05). London: Home Office.

Ayres, M., Perry, D., and Hayward, P. (2002). *Arrests for Notifiable Offences and the Operation of Certain Police Powers under PACE* (Home Office Statistical Bulletin, 12/02, 7 November). London: Home Office.

Baker, O. (1997). *Drug Misuse in Britain.* London: Institute for the Study of Drug Dependence.

Balding, J. (2005). *Young People in 2004.* Exeter: Schools Health Education Unit.

Barker, P. (2003). Break this murderous fashion. *The Guardian*, Tuesday 7 January. Retrieved 10 April 2007 from http://www.guardian.co.uk/comment/story/0,,869917,00.html.

Barnes, G. M., Welte, J. W., and Hoffman, J. H. (2002). Relationship of alcohol use to delinquency and illicit drug use in adolescents: gender, age, and racial/ethnic differences. *Journal of Drug Issues* 32: 153–178.

Baumer, E., Lauritsen, J. L., Rosenfeld, R., and Wright, R. (1998). The influence of crack cocaine on robbery, burglary, and homicide rates: a cross-city longitudinal analysis. *Journal of Research in Crime and Delinquency* 35(3): 316–340.

Beck, A., Gilliard, D., Greenfeld, L., Harlow, C., Hester, T., Jankowski, L., et al. (1993). *Survey of State Prison Inmates, 1991*. Washington, DC: US Department of Justice, Office of Justice Programs, Bureau of Justice Statistics.

Becker, J., and Duffy, C. (2002). *Women Drug Users and Drugs Service Provision: Service-level Responses to Engagement and Retention*. London: Home Office.

Bennett, T., and Holloway, K. (2004). Gang membership, drugs and crime in the UK.. *British Journal of Criminology* 44(3): 305–323.

Bennett, T., and Holloway, K. (2004a). *Drug Use and Offending: Summary Results of the First Two Years of the NEW-ADAM Programme* (Research Findings No. 179, Home Office Research and Statistics Directorate). London: Home Office.

Bennett, T., and Holloway, K. (2004b). Possession and use of illegal guns among offenders in England and Wales. *Howard Journal of Criminal Justice* 43(3): 237–252.

Bennett, T., and Holloway, K. (2005a). Disaggregating the relationship between drug misuse and crime. *Australian and New Zealand Journal of Criminology* 38(1): 102–121.

Bennett, T., and Holloway, K. (2005b). The association between multiple drug misuse and crime. *International Journal of Offender Therapy and Comparative Criminology* 49(1): 63–81.

Bennett, T., and Holloway, K. (2005c). *Understanding Drugs, Alcohol and Crime*. Berkshire: Open University Press/McGraw-Hill.

Bennett, T., and Holloway, K. (2006). Variations in explanations for the link between drug misuse and crime. Paper accepted for publication by the *Journal of Psychoactive Drugs*.

Bennett, T., Holloway, K., and Farrington, D. P. (in press). The statistical association between drug misuse and crime: a meta-analysis. *Journal of Drug Issues*.

Bennett, T., Holloway, K., and Williams, T. (2001). *Drug Use among Arrestees* (Research Findings No. 148). Home Office Research and Statistics Directorate. London: Home Office.

Bennett, T. H. (1998). *Drugs and Crime: The Results of Research on Drug Testing and Interviewing Arrestees* (Home Office Research Study 183). London: Home Office.

Bennett, T. H. (2000). *Drugs and Crime: The Results of the Second Developmental Stage of the NEW-ADAM Programme* (Home Office Research Study 205). London: Home Office.

Best, D., Rawaf, S., Rowley, J., Floyd, K., Manning, V., and Strang, J. (2001a). Ethnic and gender differences in drinking and smoking among London adolescents. *Ethnicity and Health* 6(1): 51–57.

Best, D., Sidwell, C., Gossop, M., Harris, J., and Strang, J. (2001b). Crime and expenditure among polydrug misusers seeking treatment. *British Journal of Criminology* 41: 119–126.

Borrill, J., Maden, A., Martin, A., et al. (2003). Substance misuse among white and black/mixed race female prisoners. In: M. Ramsay, editor. *Prisoners' Drug Use and Treatment: Seven Studies* (Home Office Research Study 267: pp. 49–71). London: Home Office.

Boys, A., Farrell, M., Bebbington, P., et al. (2002). Drug use and initiation in prison: results from a national survey in England and Wales. *Addiction* 97: 1551–1560.

Braithwaite, R. L., Conerly, R. C., Robillard, A. G., Stephens, T. T., and Woodring, T. (2003). Alcohol and other drug use among adolescent detainees. *Journal of Substance Use* 8(2): 126–131.

Bramley-Harker, E. (2001). *Sizing the UK Market for Illicit Drugs* (Research, Development and Statistics Directorate Occasional Paper 74). London: Home Office.

Brewer, D. D., Catalano, R. F., Haggerty, K., Gainey, R. R., and Fleming, C. B. (1998). A meta-analysis of predictors of continued drug use during and after treatment for opiate addiction. *Addiction* 93(1): 73–92.

Britt, C. L., Gottfredson, M. R., and Goldkamp, J. S. (1992). Drug testing and pretrial misconduct: an experiment on the specific deterrent effects of drug monitoring dependents on pretrial release. *Journal of Research in Crime and Delinquency* 29(1): 62–78.

Brochu, S. (2001). *The Relationship between Drugs and Crime.* University of Montreal. Retrieved 10 July 2003 from http://www.parl.gc.ca/37/1/parlbus/commbus/senate/Com-e/ille-e/presentation-e/brochu-e.htm.

Brooke, D., Taylor, C., Gunn, J., and Maden, A. (2000). Substance misuse as a marker of vulnerability among male prisoners on remand. *British Journal of Psychiatry* 177: 248–251.

Brookman, F., and Maguire, M. (2003). *Reducing Homicide: A Review of Possibilities* (Online Report 01/03). London: Home Office. Retrieved 10 April 2007 from http://www.homeoffice.gov.uk/rds/pdfs2/rdsolro103.pdf.

Brookman, F., Bennett, T., and Maguire, M. (2004). *Operation Tarian Regional Task Force: A Pilot Evaluation of a Regional Drugs Strategy* (Home Office Final Report). London: Home Office.

Broom, D., editor. (1994). *Double Bind: Women Affected by Alcohol and Other Drugs.* Allen and Unwin: St. Leonards.

Brownstein, H., and Crossland, C. (2002). *Drugs and Crime Research Forum: Introduction.* Washington, DC: National Institute of Justice, US Department of Justice. Retrieved 1 September 2004 from http://www.ojp.usdoj.gov/nij/drugscrime/Introduction.pdf.

Budd, T., Collier, P., Mhlanga, B., Sharp, C., and Weir, G. (2005a). *Levels of Self-Report Offending and Drug Use among Offenders: Findings from the Criminality Surveys* (Home Office Online Report 18/05). London: Home Office.

Budd, T., Sharp, C., Weir, G., Wilson, D., and Owen, N. (2005b). *Young People and Crime. Findings from the 2004 Offending, Crime and Justice Survey* (Home Office Statistical Bulletin 20/05). London: Home Office.

Bullock, K., and Tilley, N. (2002). *Shootings, Gangs and Violent Incidents in Manchester: Developing a Crime Reduction Strategy* (Crime Reduction Research Series Paper 13). London: Home Office.

Cabinet Office. (1995). *Tackling Drugs Together: A Strategy for England 1995–1998.* London: HMSO.

Cabinet Office. (1998). *Tackling Drugs to Build a Better Britain: The Government's 10-Year Strategy for Tackling Drug Misuse – Guidance Notes.* London: The Stationery Office.

Casciani, D. (2003). Did the gun amnesty work? Wednesday, 30 April, BBC News, UK Edition. Retrieved 10 April 2007 from http://news.bbc.co.uk/1/hi/uk/2988157.stm.

Center for Substance Abuse Research. (2004). NIJ Ending Arrestee Drug Abuse Monitoring Program (ADAM): Experts Agree That Program's Demise Is a 'Huge Loss'. *CESAR FAX* 13(11): 1.

Chaiken, J. M., and Chaiken, M. R. (1990). Drugs and predatory crime. In: M. Tonry and J. Q. Wilson, editors. *Drugs and Crime.* London: University of Chicago Press, pp. 203–239.

Chen, K., and Kandel, D. B. (1995). The natural history of drug use from adolescence to the mid-thirties in a general population sample. *American Journal of Public Health* 85(1): 41–47.

Cochrane, R., and Howell, M. (1993). *A Survey of Drinking Patterns among Afro-Caribbean Men.* Birmingham, UK: University of Birmingham.

Coleman, K., and Cotton, J. (2006). Homicide. In: K. Coleman, C. Hird, and D. Povey, editors. *Violent Crime Overview, Homicide and Gun Crime 2004/2005* (Home Office Statistical Bulletin 02/06: 49–70). London: Home Office.

Coleman, K., Hird, C., and Povey, D. (2006). *Violent Crime Overview, Homicide and Gun Crime 2004/2005* (Home Office Statistical Bulletin 02/06). London: Home Office.

Collins, J., Hubbard, R., and Rachal, J. (1985). Expensive drug use and illegal income: a test of explanatory hypotheses. *Criminology* 23(4): 743–764.

Corkery, J. M. (2002). *Drug Seizure and Offender Statistics, United Kingdom 2000.* London: Home Office.

Cromwell, P. F., Olson, J. N., Avary, D. W., and Marks, A. (1991). How drugs affect decisions by burglars. *International Journal of Offender Therapy and Comparative Criminology* 35(4): 310–321.

Curry, D., and Decker, S. (1998). *Confronting Gangs: Crime and Community.* Los Angeles, CA: Roxbury.

Darke, S., and Hall, W. (1995). Levels and correlates of polydrug use among heroin users and regular amphetamine users. *Drug and Alcohol Dependence* 39(3): 231–235.

Darke, S., and Ross, J. (2000). Fatal heroin overdoses resulting from non-injecting routes of administration, NSW, Australia, 1992–1996. *Addiction* 95(4): 569–573.

Davis, W. R., Johnson, B. D., Randolph, D., and Liberty, H. J. (2005). Gender differences in the distribution of cocaine and heroin in Central Harlem. *Drug and Alcohol Dependence* 77: 115–127.

Decker, S. (2001). The impact of organizational features on gang activities and relationships. In: M. W. Klein, H. J. Kerner, C. L. Maxson, and E. G. M. Weitekamp, editors. *The Eurogang Paradox: Street Gangs and Youth Groups in the U.S. and Europe.* London: Kluwer Academic, pp. 21–40.

Decker, S., and Pennell, S. (1995, September). *Arrestees and Guns: Monitoring the Illegal Firearms Market.* Research Preview. Washington, DC: Office of Justice Programs, National Institute of Justice, US Department of Justice.

Decker, S. H. (1992). *Drug Use Forecasting in St. Louis: A Three Year Report.* St. Louis: Department of Criminology and Criminal Justice, University of Missouri—St. Louis.

Decker, S. H., and Van Winkle, B. (1996). *Life in the Gang: Family, Friends, and Violence.* New York: Cambridge University Press.

Department of Health. (2002a). *Prevalence of HIV and Hepatitis Infections in the United Kingdom: Annual Report of the Unlinked Anonymous Prevalence Monitoring Programme.* London: Department of Health.

Department of Health. (2002b). *Statistics from the Regional Drug Misuse Databases for the Six Months Ending March 2001.* London: Department of Health.

Derzon, J. H., and Lipsey, M. W. (1999). A synthesis of the relationship of marijuana use with delinquent and problem behaviors. *School Psychology International* 20(1): 57–68.

DeWit, D. J., Offord, D. R., and Wong, M. (1997). Patterns of onset and cessation of drug use over the early part of the life course. *Health Education and Behavior* 24(6): 746–758.

DiClemente, C. C. (2003). *Addiction and Change: How Addictions Develop and Addicted People Recover.* New York: Guilford Press.

Dobinson, I., and Ward, P. (1984). *Drugs and Crime: A Survey of NSW Prison Property Offenders.* Sydney: Bureau of Crime Statistics and Research.

Dodd, T., and Hunter, P. (1992). *The National Prison Survey 1991.* London: HMSO.

Dorn, N., Levi, M., and King, L. (2005). *Literature Review on Upper Level Drug Trafficking* (Home Office Online Research Report 22/05). Retrieved 10 April 2007 from http://www.homeoffice.gov.uk/rds/pdfs05/rdsolr2205.pdf. London: Home Office.

Dorn, N., Murji, K., and South, N. (1992). *Traffickers. Drug Markets and Law Enforcement.* London: Routledge.

Dorn, N., Oette, L., and White, S. (1998). Drugs importation and the bifurcation of risk. *British Journal of Criminology* 38(4): 537–560.

Downes, D. (1966). *The Delinquent Solution: A Study in Subcultural Theory.* London: Routledge & Kegan Paul.

DrugScope. (2006). Drug Search. Retrieved 10 February 2006 from http://www.drugscope.org.uk/druginfo/drugsearch/home2.asp.

Eaves, C. S. (2004). Heroin use among female adolescents: the role of partner influence in path of initiation and route of administration. *American Journal of Drug and Alcohol Abuse* 30(1): 21–38.

Edgar, K., & O'Donnell, I. (1998). *Mandatory Drug Testing in Prisons: The Relationship between MDT and the Level and Nature of Drug Misuse* (Home Office Research Study 189). London: Home Office.

Edmunds, M., Hough, M., and Urquia, N. (1995). *Tackling Local Drug Markets* (Crime Detection and Prevention Series Paper 50). London: Home Office.

Elliott, D. S., and Huizinga, D. (1984, April). *The Relationship between Delinquency Behavior and ADM Problems.* Report prepared for the Alcohol, Drug Abuse, and Mental Health Administration/Office of Juvenile Justice and Delinquency Prevention State-of-the-Art Conference on Juvenile Offenders with Serious Drug, Alcohol, and Mental Health Problems.

Erickson, P.G., Butters, J., McGillicuddy, P., and Hallgren, A. (2000). Crack and prostitution: gender, myths and experiences. *Journal of Drug Issues* 304: 767–788.

Esbensen, F. A., and Lynskey, D. P. (2001). Young gang members in a school survey. In: M. W. Klein, H. J. Kerner, C. L. Maxson, and E. G. M. Weitekamp, editors. *The Eurogang Paradox: Street Gangs and Youth Groups in the U.S. and Europe.* London: Kluwer Academic, pp. 93–114.

Fagan, J. (1990). Social processes of delinquency and drug use among urban gangs. In: C. R. Huff, editor. *Gangs in America.* London: Sage, pp. 39–74.

Farabee, D., Joshi, V., and Anglin, D. M. (2001). Addiction careers and criminal specialization. *Crime and Delinquency* 47(2): 196–220.

Farrell, M., Howes, S., Taylor, C., Lewis, G., Jenkins, R., Bebbington, P., Jarvis, M., Brugha, T., Gill, B., and Meltzer, H. (1998). Substance misuse and psychiatric co-morbidity: an overview of the opcs national psychiatric morbidity survey. *Addictive Behaviours* 23(6): 909–918.

Faupel, C. E., and Klockars, C. B. (1987). Drug-crime connections: elaborations from the life histories of hard core heroin addicts. *Social Problems* 34: 54–68.

Fendrich, M., and Yanchun, X. (1994). The validity of drug use reports from juvenile arrestees. *International Journal of the Addictions* 29: 971–1985.

Flood-Page, C., and Taylor, J. (2003). *Crime in England and Wales 2001/2002* (Home Office Statistical Bulletin No. 01/03). London: Home Office.

Fountain, J., Bashford, J., Underwood, S., Khurana, J., Winters, M., Carpentier, C., and Patel, K. (2004). Drug use amongst black and minority ethnic communities in the European Union and Norway. *Probation Journal* 51(4): 362–378.

Fountain, J., Bashford, J., Winters, M., and Patel, K. (2003). *Black and Minority Ethnic Communities in England: A Review of the Literature on Drug Use and Related Service Provision.* London: National Treatment Agency for Substance Misuse.

Fountain, J., Griffiths, P., Farrell, M., Gossop, M., and Strang, J. (1999). Benzodiazepines in polydrug using repertoires: the impact of the decreased availability of temazepam gel-filled capsules. *Drugs: Education, Prevention and Policy* 6(1): 61–69.

French, M., and Zarkin, G. (1992). Effects of drug abuse treatment on legal and illegal earnings. *Contemporary Policy Issues* 10(2): 98–110.

Fuller, E. (2005). *Smoking, Drinking and Drug Use among Young People in England 2004.* London: Health and Social Care Information Centre.

Gandossy, R. P., Williams, J. R., Cohen, J., and Harwood, H. J. (1980). *Drugs and Crime: A Survey and Analysis of the Literature.* Washington, DC: National Institute of Justice, Government Printing Office.

Goddard, E., and Green, H. (2005). *Smoking and Drinking among Adults, 2004*. London: Office of National Statistics.

Goldstein, P. J. (1985). The drugs/violence nexus: a tripartite conceptual framework. *Journal of Drug Issues* 39: 143–174.

Goode, E. (1997). *Between Politics and Reason*. New York: St. Martin's Press.

Gossop, M., Marsden, J., and Stewart, D. (2001). *NTORS after Five Years. Changes in Substance Use, Health and Criminal Behavior during the Five Years after Intake*. National Treatment Outcome Research Study. London: National Addiction Centre.

Gossop, M., Marsden, J., Stewart, D., and Kidd, T. (2003). The national treatment outcome research study (NTORS): 4–5 year follow-up results. *Addiction* 98: 291–303.

Gossop, M., Steward, T., Treacy, S., and Marsden, J. (2002). A prospective study of mortality among drug misusers during a 4-year period after seeking treatment. *Addiction* 97: 39–47.

Gottfredson, D., and Exum, M. (2002). The Baltimore City Drug Treatment Court: one-year results from a randomized study. *Journal of Research in Crime and Delinquency* 39(3): 337–356.

Gottfredson, D. C., Najaka, S. S., and Kearley, B. (2003). Effectiveness of drug treatment courts: evidence from a randomized trial. *Criminology & Public Policy* 2: 171–196.

Goulden, C., and Sondhi, A. (2001). *At the Margins: Drug Use by Vulnerable Young People: Results from the 1998/9 Youth Lifestyle Survey*. London: Home Office.

Grella, C. E., and Joshi, V. (1999). Gender differences in drug treatment careers among clients in the clients in the national Drug Abuse Treatment Outcome Study. *American Journal of Drug and Alcohol Abuse* 25: 385–406.

Griffiths, P., Gossop, M., Wickenden, S., Dunworth, J., Harris, K., and Lloyd, C. (1997). A transcultural pattern of drug use qat (khat) in the UK. *British Journal of Psychiatry* 170: 281–284.

Haapanen, R., and Britton, L. (2002). Drug testing for youthful offenders on parole: an experimental evaluation. *Criminology and Public Policy* 1 (2): 217–244.

Hammersley, R., Forsyth, A., Morrison, V., and Davies, J. B. (1989). The relationship between crime and opioid use. *British Journal of Addiction* 84: 1029–1043.

Hammersley, R., Forsyth, A., and Lavelle, T. (1990). The criminality of new drug users in Glasgow. *British Journal of Addiction* 85: 1583–1594.

Hammersley, R., and Morrison, V. (1987). Effects of polydrug use on the criminal activities of heroin-users. *British Journal of Addiction* 82: 899–906.

Hartnoll, R. L., Mitcheson, M. C., Battersby, A., Brown, G., Ellis, M., Fleming, P., and Hedley, N. (1980). Evaluation of heroin maintenance in a controlled trial. *Archives of General Psychiatry* 37 (8): 877–884.

Health Protection Agency. (2005). *Shooting Up: Infections among Injecting Drug Users in the United Kingdom 2004. An Update: October 2005.* London: Health Protection Agency.

Heidensohn, F., and Brown, J. (2000). *Gender and Policing.* London: Macmillan.

Henggeler, S. W., Borduin, C. M., Melton, G. B., Mann, B. J., Smith, L. A., Hall, J. A., et al. (1991). Effects of multisystemic therapy on drug use and abuse in serious juvenile offenders: a progress report from two outcome studies. *Family Dynamics of Addiction Quarterly* 1 (3): 40–51.

Hirsch, E. D., Kett, J. F., and Trefil, J. (2002). *The New Dictionary of Cultural Literacy.* 3rd ed. Boston: Houghton Mifflin.

Holloway, K., and Bennett, T. (2004). *The Results of the First Two Years of the NEW-ADAM Programme* (Home Office Online Report 19/04). London: Home Office. Retrieved 10 April 2007 from http://www.homeoffice.gov.uk/rds/pdfs04/rdsolr1904.pdf

Holloway, K., and Bennett, T. (in press). Gender differences in drug use and associated problem behaviors among arrestees in the UK. Paper accepted for publication by *Substance Use and Misuse.*

Holloway, K., Bennett, T., and Farrington, D. P. (2005). *The Effectiveness of Criminal Justice and Treatment Programmes in Reducing Drug-Related Crime: A Systematic Review* (Home Office On-line Research Report 26/05). London: Home Office.

Holloway, K., Bennett, T., and Lower, C. (2004). *Trends in Drug Use and Offending: The Results of the NEW-ADAM Programme 1999–2002* (Home Office Findings 219). London: Home Office.

Home Affairs Select Committee. (2001). *The Government's Drug Strategy: Is it Working? Third Report.* London: House of Commons.

Home Office. (2002). *Updated Drug Strategy 2002.* London: Home Office.

Home Office. (2006). *The Arrestee Survey.* Retrieved 16 June 2006 from http://www.homeoffice.gov.uk/rds/offendingarrest.html.

Hopkins, N. (2002). Met warns London on cusp of drugs war. *The Guardian,* Thursday 21 November. Retrieved 10 April 2007 from http://www.guardian.co.uk/uk_news/story/0,3604,844055,00.html.

Hough, M. (1996). *Drug Misuse and the Criminal Justice System: A Review of the Literature.* London: Home Office.

Hser, Y., Anglin, M. D., and Booth, M. W. (1987a). Sex differences in addict careers. 3. Addiction. *American Journal of Drug and Alcohol Abuse* 13: 231–251.

Hser, Y., Anglin, M. D., and McGlothlin, W. (1987b). Sex differences in addict careers. 1. Initiation of use. *American Journal of Drug and Alcohol Abuse* 13: 33–57.

Hser, Y., Huang, D., Teruya, C., and Anglin, M. D. (2003). Gender comparisons of drug abuse treatment outcomes and predictors. *Drug and Alcohol Dependence* 72: 255–264.

Hser, Y., Huang, D., Teruya, C., and Anglin, M. D. (2004). Gender differences in treatment outcomes over a three-year period: a path model analysis. *Journal of Drug Issues* 34(2): 419–438.

Hser, Y. I., Grella, C. E., Hubbard, R. L., Hsieh, S. C., Fletcher, B. W., Brown, B. S., and Anglin, M. D. (2001). An evaluation of drug treatments for adolescents in 4 US cities. *Archives of General Psychiatry* 58: 689–695.

Jacobs, B., Topalli, V., and Wright, R. (2003) Carjacking, streetlife, and offender motivation. *British Journal of Criminology* 43(4): 19–34.

Johnson, B. D., Natarajan, M., Dunlap, E., and Elmoghazy, E. (1994). Crack abusers and noncrack abusers – profiles of drug use, drug sales and nondrug criminality. *Journal of Drug Issues* 24(1–2): 117–141.

Johnson, B. D., Wish, E., Schmeidler, J., and Huizinga, D. H. (1986). The concentration of delinquent offending: serious drug involvement and high delinquency rates. In B. D. Johnson and E. Wish, editors. *Crime Rates among Drug Abusing Offenders.* New York: Interdisciplinary Research Center, Narcotic and Drug Research.

Johnson, M. E., Brems, C., Wells, R. S., Theno, S. A., and Fisher, D. G. (2003). Comorbidity and risk behaviors among drug users not in treatment. *Journal of Addictions and Offender Counselling* 23(2): 108–118.

Johnston, L. D., O'Malley, P. M., and Eveland, L. K. (1978). Drugs and delinquency: a search for causal connections. In: D. B. Kandel, editor. *Longitudinal Research on Drug Use.* Washington, DC: Hemisphere, pp. 137–156.

Kandel, D. (2000). Gender differences in the epidemiology of substance dependence in the United States. In: Frank, E., editor. *Gender and Its Effects on Psychopathology.* Washington, DC: American Psychiatric Press, pp. 231–252.

Kauffman, S. E., Silver, P., and Poulin, J. (1997). Gender differences in attitudes toward alcohol, tobacco, and other drugs. *Social Work* 42(3): 231–241.

Kim, J. Y. S., and Fendrich, M. (2002). Gender differences in juvenile arrestees', drug use, self-reported dependence and perceived need for treatment. *Psychiatric Services* 53(1): 70–75.

Klee, H. (1997). *Amphetamine Use: International Perspectives on Current Trends.* Amsterdam, The Netherlands: Harwood Academic.

Kleiman, M. A. R. (2004). Flying Blind on Drug Control Policy. *Issues in Science and Technology*. Retrieved 15 June 2006 from http://www.issues.org/20.4/p_kleiman.html.

Klein, M. (2001). Resolving the Eurogang paradox. In: M. W. Klein, H. J. Kerner, C. L. Maxson, and E. G. M. Weitekamp, editors. *The Eurogang Paradox: Street Gangs and Youth Groups in the U.S. and Europe*. London: Kluwer Academic, pp. 7–20.

Klein, M., Kerner, H. J., Maxson, C. L., and Weitekamp, E. G. M., editors. (2001). *The Eurogang Paradox: Street Gangs and Youth Groups in the U.S. and Europe*. London: Kluwer Academic.

Kokkevi, A., Liappas, J., Boukouvala, V., Alevizou, V., Anastassopoulou, E., and Stefanis, C. (1993). Criminality in a sample of drug abusers in Greece. *Drug and Alcohol Dependence* 31: 111–121.

Langan, N. P., and Pelissier, B. M. M. (2001). Gender differences among prisoners in drug treatment. *Journal of Substance Abuse* 13: 291–301.

Leri, F., Bruneau, J., and Stewart, J. (2003). Understanding polydrug use: review of heroin and cocaine co-use. *Addiction* 98(1): 7–22.

Liriano, S., and Ramsay, M. (2003). Prisoners' drug use before prison and the links with crime. In: M. Ramsay, editor. *Prisoners' Drug Use and Treatment: Seven Research Studies* (Home Office Research Study 267). London: Home Office, pp. 7–22.

Lo, C. (2004). Sociodemographic factors, drug abuse, and other crimes: how they vary among male and female arrestees. *Journal of Criminal Justice* 32: 399–409.

Longshore, D., Hsieh, S., and Anglin, D. (1993). Ethnic and gender differences in drug users' perceived need for treatment. *International Journal of the Addictions* 28(6): 539–558.

Lupton, R., Wilson, A., May, T., Warburton, H., and Turnbull, P. J. (2002). *A Rock and a Hard Place: Drug Markets in Deprived Neighbourhoods* (Home Office Research Study 240). London: Home Office.

Maccoun, R. (2004). Misguided drug policy. *Issues in Science and Technology*. Retrieved 15 June 2006 from http://www.issues.org/21.1/forum.html.

Makkai, T. (2001). Patterns of recent drug use among a sample of Australian detainees. *Addiction* 96: 1799–1808.

Makkai, T., and Feather, M. (1999). *Drug Use Monitoring in Australia (DUMA): Preliminary Results from the Southport Site, 1999* (Trends and Issues in Crime and Criminal Justice, No. 142). Canberra: Australian Institute of Criminology.

Makkai, T., Fitzgerald, J., and Doak, P. (2000). Drug use among police detainees. *Crime and Justice* 49. Sydney: NSW Bureau of Crime Statistics and Research.

Makkai, T., and Payne, J. (2003). *Drugs and Crime: A Study of Incarcerated Males Offenders* (Research and Public Policy Series No. 52). Canberra: Australian Institute of Criminology.

Mares, D. (2001). Gangstas or lager louts? Working class street gangs in Manchester. In: M. W. Klein, H. J. Kerner, C. L. Maxson, and E. G. M. Weitekamp, editors. *The Eurogang Paradox: Street Gangs and Youth Groups in the U.S. and Europe.* London: Kluwer Academic, pp. 153–164.

Marsden, J., Gossop, M., Stewart, D., and Farrell, M. (2000). Psychiatric symptoms among clients seeking treatment for drug dependence: intake data from the National Treatment Outcome Research Study. *British Journal of Psychiatry* 176, 285–289.

McCance-Katz, E. F., Carroll, K. M., and Rounsaville, B. J. (1999). Gender differences in treatment seeking cocaine abusers: Implications for treatment. *American Journal on Addictions* 8: 300–311.

McGregor, K., and Makkai, T. (2003). Self-reported drug use: how prevalent is under-reporting. *Trends and Issues in Crime and Criminal Justice, No. 260.* Canberra: Australian Institute of Criminology.

Measham, F. (2003). The gendering of drug use and the absence of gender. *Criminal Justice Matters* 53: 22–23.

Menard, S., Mihalic, S., and Huizinga, D. (2001). Drugs and crime revisited. *Justice Quarterly* 18(2): 269–299.

Metrebian, N., Shanahan, W., Stimson, G., Small, C., Lee, M., Mtutu, V., and Wells, B. (2001). Prescribing drug of choice to opiate dependent drug users: a comparison of clients receiving heroin with those receiving injectable methadone at a West London drug clinic. *Drug and Alcohol Review* 20: 267–276.

Milner, L., Mouzos, J., and Makkai, T. (2004). *Drug use Monitoring in Australia: 2003 Annual Report on Drug Use among Police Detainees* (Research and Public Policy Series No. 58). Canberra: Australian Institute of Criminology.

Moore, J. P., and Cook, I. L. (1999). *Highlights of the 1998 National Youth Gang Survey* (OJJDP Fact Sheet, No. 123). Washington, DC: Office of Juvenile Justice and Delinquency Prevention, US Department of Justice.

Morentin, B., Callado, L. F., and Meana, J. J. (1998). Differences in criminal activity between heroin abusers and subjects without psychiatric disorders: Analysis of 578 detainees in Bilbao, Spain. *Journal of Forensic Sciences* 43: 993–999.

Morrison, S., and O'Donnell, I. (1994). *Armed Robbery: A Study in London* (Occasional Paper No. 15). Oxford: Centre for Criminological Research, University of Oxford.

Mwenda, L., and Kumari, K. (2005). *Drug Offenders in England and Wales 2003* (Home Office Findings 256). London: Home Office.

Mwenda, L., Ahmad, M., and Kumari, K. (2005). *Seizures of drugs in England and Wales, 2003* (Home Office Findings 265). London: Home Office.

Natarajan, M., and Belanger, M. (1998). Varieties of drug trafficking organisations: a typology of cases prosecuted in New York City. *Journal of Drug Issues* 24(4): 1005–1026.

National Center for Social Research and National Foundation for Education Research. (2006). *Drug Use, Smoking and Drinking Among Young People in England in 2005*. London: Department of Health.

National Criminal Intelligence Service. (2002). *UK Threat Assessment 2002: The Threat from Serious and Organised Crime*. London: National Criminal Intelligence Service.

National Criminal Intelligence Service. (2005). *UK Threat Assessment: The Threat from Serious and Organised Crime 2004/5–2005/6*. London: National Criminal Intelligence Service.

National Institute of Justice. (1997). *1996 Drug Use Forecasting: Annual Report on Adult and Juvenile Arrestees*. Washington, DC: US Department of Justice.

National Institute of Justice. (2003). *2000 Arrestee Drug Abuse Monitoring: Annual Report*. Washington, DC: US Department of Justice.

National Institute of Justice. (2004). *Annual Report 2003*. Washington DC: Office of Justice Programs, US Department of Justice.

National Treatment Agency. (2006). Retrieved 13 June 2006 from http://www.nta.nhs.uk/programme/national/perf_info_octo5/Nos_in_treatment_200405.pdf.

Neale, J. (2004a). Gender and illicit drug use. *British Journal of Social Work* 34: 851–870.

Neale, J. (2004b). Measuring the health of Scottish drug users. *Health and Social Care in the Community* 12(3): 202–211.

Nemes, S., Wish, E., and Messina, N. (1999). Comparing the impact of standard and abbreviated treatment in a therapeutic community. *Journal of Substance Abuse Treatment* 17(4): 339–347.

Office of National Drug Control Policy. (2005). *Drug Facts: Club Drugs*. Retrieved 25 May 2006 from http://www.whitehousedrugpolicy. gov/drugfact/club/index.html.

Parker, H., Aldridge, J., and Eggington, R. (2001). *UK Drugs Unlimited: New Research and Policy Lessons on Illicit Drug Use*. Basingstoke: Palgrave.

Parker, H., Aldridge, J., and Measham, F. (1998). *Illegal Leisure: The Normalization of Adolescent Recreational Drug Use*. London: Routledge.

Parker, R. N., and Auerhahn, K. (1998). Alcohol, drugs and violence. *Annual Review of Sociology* 24: 291–311.

Parry, C., Pluddeman, A., Louw, A., and Legget, T. (2004). The 3-Metros study of drugs and crime in South Africa: findings and policy implications. *American Journal of Drug and Alcohol Abuse* 30(1): 167–185.

Pearson, G., and Hobbs, D. (2001). *Middle Market Drug Distribution* (Home Office Research Study 227). London: Home Office.

Pearson, G., and Hobbs, D. (2003). King pin? A case study of a middle market drug broker. *Howard Journal* 42(4): 335–347.

Pelissier, B. (2004). Gender differences in substance use treatment entry and retention among prisoners with substance use histories. *American Journal of Public Health* 94(8): 1418–1424.

Pennings, J. M., Leccese, A. P., and de Wolff, F. A. (2002). Effects of concurrent use of alcohol and cocaine. *Addiction* 97(7): 773–783.

Perneger, T. V., Giner, F., del Rio M., and Mino, A. (1998). Randomised trial of heroin maintenance programme for addicts who fail in conventional drug treatments. *British Medical Journal* 317: 13–18.

Peters, R. H., Strozier, A. L., Murrin, M. R., and Kearns, W. D. (1997). Treatment of substance-abusing jail inmates. *Journal of Substance Abust Treatment* 14(4): 339–349.

Peters, R. J., Yacoubian, G. S., Baumler, E. R., Ross, M. W., and Johnson, R. J. (2002). Heroin use among southern arrestees: regional findings from the arrestee drug abuse monitoring program. *Journal of Addictions and Offender Counselling* 22(2): 50–60.

Pollak, O. (1950). *The Criminality of Women.* New York: A. S. Barnes.

Powis, B., Griffiths, M., Gossop, M., and Strang, J. (1996). The differences between male and female drug users: community samples of heroin and cocaine users compared. *Substance Use and Misuse* 31(5): 529–543.

Pudney, S. (2002). *The Road to Ruin? Sequences of Initiation to Drugs and Offending By Young People in Britain* (Home Office Research Study 253). London: Home Office.

Ramsay, M., Baker, P., Goulden, C., Sharp, C., and Sondhi, A. (2001). *Drug Misuse Declared in 2000: Results from the British Crime Survey* (Home Office Research Study 224). London: Home Office.

Rassool, G. H., and Kilpatrick, B. (1998). Working with diverse populations. In: G. H. Rassool, editor. *Substance Use and Misuse: Nature, Context and Clinical Interventions.* London: Blackwell Science, 1998, pp. 236–248.

Reid, G., Crofts, N., and Beyer, L. (2001). Drug treatment services for ethnic communities in Victoria, Australia: an examination of cultural and institutional barriers. *Ethnicity and Health* 6(1): 13–26.

Richter, K. P., Ahluwalia, H. K., Mosier, M. C., Nazir, N., and Ahluwalia, J. S. (2002). A population-based study of cigarette smoking among illicit drug users in the United States. *Addiction* 97(7): 861–869.

Rix, B., Walker, D., and Ward, J. (1998). *The Criminal Use of Firearms* (Ad hoc Policing and Reducing Crime Unit Publications, No. AH255). London: Home Office.

Roe, S. (2005). Drug misuse declared: findings from the 2004/05 British Crime Survey: England and Wales. *Home Office Statistical Bulletin 16/05.* London: Home Office.

Rounds-Bryant, J. L., Motivans, M. A., and Pelissier, B. (2003). Comparison of background characteristics and behaviors of African American, Hispanic, and white substance abusers treated in federal prison: results from the TRIAD study. *Journal of Psychoactive Drugs,* 35(3): 333–341.

Sanchez, J. E., Johnson, B. D., and Israel, M. (1985). *Drugs and Crime among Riker's Island Women.* San Diego, CA: Annual Meeting of the American Society of Criminology.

Sanders, W. B. (1994). *Gangbangs and Drive-Bys: Grounded Culture and Juvenile Gang Violence.* New York: Aldine de Gruyter.

Sangster, D., Shiner, M., Patel, K., and Sheikh, N. (2002). Delivering drug services to black and minority ethnic communities. *DPAS Paper 16.* London: Home Office.

Schifano, F., Di Furia, L., Forza, G., Minicuci, N., and Bricolo, R. (1998). MDMA ('ecstasy') consumption in the context of polydrug abuse: a report on 150 patients. *Drug and Alcohol Dependence,* 52, 58–90.

Schulte, C., Mouzos, J., and Makkai, T. (2005). *Drug Use Monitoring in Australia 2004: Annual Report on Drug Use among Police Detainees* (Research and Public Policy Series No. 65). Canberra: Australian Institute of Criminology.

Scott, P. (1956). Gangs and delinquent groups in London. *British Journal of Delinquency* 7: 4–26.

Sharp, C., and Budd, T. (2005). *Minority Ethnic Groups and Crime: Findings from the Offending, Crime and Justice Survey 2003* (Home Office Online Report 33/05). London: Home Office.

Shaw, V. N., Hser, Y., Anglin, D. M., and Boyle, K. (1999). Sequences of powder cocaine and crack use among arrestees in Los Angeles County. *American Journal of Drug and Alcohol Abuse* 25(1): 47–66.

Shropshire, S., and McFarquhar, M. (2002). *Developing Multi-Agency Strategies to Address the Street Gang Culture and Reduce Gun Violence among Young People* (Briefing No. 4). Manchester: Steve Shropshire and Michael McFarquhar Consultancy Group.

Siddique, M. (1992). *Action Study on the Misuse of Drugs in Manningham, Bradford.* Bradford, UK: Bradford Drugs Prevention Team.

Simpson, D. D., & Sells, S. B. (1974). Patterns of multiple drug abuse. *International Journal of the Addictions* 9(2), 301–314.

Singleton, N., Bumpstead, R., O'Brien, M., Lee, A., and Meltzer, H. (2003). Psychiatric morbidity among adults living in private households, 2000. *International Review of Psychiatry* 15: 65–73.

Singleton, N., Meltzer, H., and Gatward, R. (1999). *Psychiatric Morbidity among Prisoners in England and Wales.* London: Office of National Statistics.

Smith, D. A., and Polsenberg, C. (1992). Specifying the relationship between arrestee drug test results and recidivism. *Journal of Criminal Law and Criminology* 83(2): 364–377.

Smith, J. (2003). *The Nature of Personal Robbery* (Home Office Research Study 254). London: Home Office.

Spear, B., and Mott, J. (2002). *Heroin Addiction, Care and Control: The British System.* London: DrugScope.

Speckart, G., and Anglin, M. D. (1985). Narcotics and crime: an analysis of existing evidence for a causal relationship. *Behavioral Sciences and the Law* 3: 259–283.

Stelfox, P. (1998). Policing lower levels of organised crime in England and Wales. *Howard Journal* 37(4): 393–406.

Stewart, D., Gossop, M., Marsden, J., Kidd, T., and Treacy, S. (2003). Similarities in outcomes for men and women after drug misuse treatment: results from the National Treatment Outcome Research Study (NTORS). *Drug and Alcohol Review* 22: 35.

Taylor, B. (2002). *I-ADAM in Eight Countries: Approaches and Challenges.* Washington, DC: National Institute of Justice.

Taylor, B., and Bennett, T. (1999). *Comparing Drug Use Rates of Detained Arrestees in the United States and England.* Washington, DC: US Department of Justice.

Taylor, B., Brownstein, H., Parry, C. D. H., Plüddemann, A., Makkai, T., Bennett, T., and Holloway, K. (2003). Monitoring the use of illicit drugs in four countries through the International Arrestee Drug Abuse Monitoring (I-ADAM) program. *Criminal Justice: An International Journal of Policy and Practice* 3(3): 269.

Taylor, C. L., Kilbane, P., Passmore, N., and Davies, R. (1986). Prospective study of alcohol-related admissions in an inner-city related hospital. *Lancet* 2: 265–268.

Thornberry, T. P. (1998). Membership in youth gangs and involvement in serious and violent offending. In: R. Loeber and D. P. Farrington, editors. *Serious and Violent Juvenile Offenders: Risk Factors and Successful Interventions.* London: Sage, pp. 147–166.

Thornberry, T. P., and Porter, P. K. (2001). Advantages of longitudinal research designs in studying gang behavior. In: M. W. Klein, H. J. Kerner, C. L. Maxson, and E. G. M. Weitekamp, editors. *The Eurogang Paradox:*

Street Gangs and Youth Groups in the U.S. and Europe. London: Kluwer Academic, pp. 59–78.

Turner, S., Greenwood, P., Fain, T., and Deschenes, E. (1999). National Drug Court Institute review: perceptions of drug court: how offenders view ease of program completion, strengths and weaknesses, and the impact on their lives. *National Drug Court Review* 2(1): 61–86.

Turner, S., Petersilia, J. and Deschenes, E. P. (1992). Evaluating intensive supervision probation/parole (ISP) for drug offenders. *Crime and Delinquency* 38(4): 539–556.

Turpeinen, P. (2001). Outcome of drug abuse in a 20-year follow-up study of drug-experimenting school children in Finland. *Nordic Journal of Psychiatry* 55(4): 263–270.

UK Anti-Drugs Coordinator. (1999). *First Annual Report and National Plan.* London: Cabinet Office.

United Nations Office on Drugs and Crime. (2005). *World Drug Report 2005.* United Nations Publications.

Visher, C. A. (1991). *A Comparison of Urinalysis Technologies for Drug Testing in Criminal Justice*(National Institute of Justice Research Report). Washington, DC: National Institute of Justice, US Department of Justice.

Walters, G. D. (1994). *Drugs and Crime in Lifestyle Perspective.* London: Sage.

Wanigaratne, S., Dar, K., Abdulrahim, D., and Strang, J. (2003). Ethnicity and drug use: exploring the nature of particular relationships among diverse populations in the United Kingdom. *Drugs: Education, Prevention and Policy* 10(1): 39–55.

Weaver, T., Charles, V., Madden, P., and Renton, A. (2002). Comorbidity of substance misuse and mental illness collaborative study (COSMIC). *Summary of Research Funded by the Department of Health.* London: National Treatment Agency.

Weisner, C., Ray, G. T., Mertens, J. R., Satre, D. D., and Moore, C. (2003). Short-term alcohol and drug treatment outcomes predict long-term outcome. *Drug and Alcohol Dependence* 71: 281–294.

Welte, J. W., Zhang, L. N. and Wieczorek, W. F. (2001). The effects of substance use on specific types of criminal offending in young men. *Journal of Research in Crime and Delinquency* 38: 416–438.

Wexler, H., De Leon, G., Thomas, G., Kressel, D., and Peters, J. (1999). The Amity Prison TC evaluation. *Criminal Justice and Behavior* 26(2): 147–167.

White, H. R. (1990). The drug-use-delinquency connection in adolescence. In: R. A. Weisheit editor, *Drugs, Crime and the Criminal Justice System.* Cincinnati OH: Anderson.

White, H. R., and Gorman, D. M. (2000). Dynamics of the drug-crime relationship. *Criminal Justice* 1: 151–218.

Wilkinson, D. A., Leigh, G. M., Cordingley, J., Martin, G. W., and Lei, H. (1987). Dimensions of multiple drug use and a typology of drug users. *British Journal of Addiction* 82: 259–273.

Wincup, E., Buckland, G., and Bayliss, R. (2003). *Youth Homelessness and Substance Use* (Home Office Research Study 258). London: Home Office.

Wish, E. D., and Gropper, B. A. (1990). Drug testing by the criminal justice system: Method, research and applications. In: Wilson, J. Q., and Tonry, M., eds. *Drugs and Crime*. Chicago: University of Chicago Press, pp. 321–339.

Woody, G. E., McLellan, T., Luborsky, L., and O'Brien, C. P. (1987). Twelve-month follow-up of psychotherapy for opiate dependence. *American Journal of Psychiatry* 144(5): 590–596.

Wright, R., and Decker, S. (1997). *Armed Robbers in Action: Stickups and Street Culture*. Boston: Northeastern University Press.

Young, V. D., and Harrison, R. (2001). Race/ethnic differences in the sequences of drugs used by women. *Journal of Drug Issues* 31(2): 293–324.

Zhang, Z. (undated). *Drug and Alcohol Use and Related Matters among Arrestees*. Chicago: National Opinion Research Center.

Zimring, F. E. (1998). *American Youth Violence*. New York: Oxford University Press.

Index